SECOND EDITION

The Business
of MEDIA

*To the hard-working citizen activists who
promote the public interest by creating independent
media and holding corporate media accountable*

SECOND EDITION

The Business
of MEDIA
Corporate Media and
the Public Interest

David Croteau ■ William Hoynes
Virginia Commonwealth University   *Vassar College*

PINE FORGE PRESS
An Imprint of Sage Publications, Inc.
Thousand Oaks • London • New Delhi

For information:

Pine Forge Press
A Sage Publications Company
2455 Teller Road
Thousand Oaks, California 91320
sales@pfp.sagepub.com

Sage Publications Ltd.
1 Oliver's Yard
55 City Road
London EC1Y 1SP
United Kingdom

Sage Publications India Pvt. Ltd.
B-42, Panchsheel Enclave
Post Box 4109
New Delhi 110 017 India

Printed in the United States of America.

This book is printed on acid-free paper.

Library of Congress Cataloging-in-Publication Data

Croteau, David.
The business of media : corporate media and the public interest / David Croteau, William Hoynes. M— 2nd ed.
     p. cm.
Includes bibliographical references and index.
ISBN 978-1-4129-1315-7 (pbk.)
    1. Mass media—Economic aspects. I. Hoynes, William. II. Title.
P96.E25.C76 2006
338.4'70223—dc22   2005006493

07   08   09   10   9   8   7   6   5   4   3   2

Acquiring Editor:	Margaret H. Seawell
Project Editor:	Claudia A. Hoffman
Copy Editor:	Catherine M. Chilton
Typesetter:	C&M Digitals (P) Ltd.
Indexer:	Kathy Paparchontis

Contents

List of Exhibits

Preface to the Second Edition

We are pleased to provide a second edition of *The Business of Media*. Honored with the 2002 Robert Picard Award for its "significant contribution to the field of media management and economics" by the Association for Education in Journalism and Mass Communication, the original edition of this book was popular with educators, students, and scholars interested in better understanding the nature of our media system. Its analysis is as relevant as ever, so we have not altered the basic structure of the book. Instead, we have provided extensive revisions in the form of updated data and examples and have incorporated some of the most recent media developments into our analysis.

The media industry continues to change as corporate mergers and the expansion of new digital technologies are transforming the media landscape. We are witnessing the rise of media conglomerates of unprecedented size and, at the same time, a dramatic increase in the sheer volume of media content. More than ever, citizens are immersed in a media-saturated world.

It is precisely because the media surround us that it is often difficult to get perspective on their development. We need to step away from the headlines about the latest mergers or newest technologies to put the industry in perspective. We need to examine, instead, the basic dynamics that underlie the changing media industry and the possible influence these changes are having on society. *The Business of Media* tries to do just that.

Elsewhere, we have written more broadly from a sociological perspective about the interaction between media and society. Here, we focus in more depth on the changing media industry. In particular, we are concerned with the tension between the media industry's insatiable quest for profits and a democratic society's need for a media system that serves the public interest. As we explore that tension, we review the history of the industry and its evolving technologies, examine how the structure and business strategies of the industry are changing, and consider the potential influence the new media industry is having on society. We also look at how policy and citizen action can help to create media that contribute to a more vibrant public sphere.

More specifically, *The Business of Media* pursues three main goals. First, in Part I of the book, we provide a framework and historical context for considering the media industry. Drawing from both social and economic theory, we sketch out two conceptual frameworks for analyzing and evaluating media: a market model and a public sphere model. These two models direct us to very different sets of questions about the media, but each is useful to consider. The principles of the market model are helpful in understanding the rationale for industry actions. Most popular commentary about the media industry begins from market model assumptions. The public sphere model, however, introduces social issues into the discussion by highlighting the public interest role of the mass media. This framework is especially useful in evaluating the influences of the media on society. Before moving on to the next part of the book, we provide a brief overview of the media business in the 20th century.

In Part II of the book, we describe the recent major media industry trends. We map out the structural organization of the industry and show how it has changed in recent years. We then suggest how these structural changes have enabled media conglomerates to pursue a new set of strategies in their attempt to enhance profits, contain costs, and reduce risk. The focus of Part II is on issues and concerns from a market model perspective, although we also consider how the public sphere model would interpret the key features of the newly restructured industry.

In Part III, we use the public sphere model to provide a critical analysis of the contemporary media business. In particular, we assess the impact of the recent changes in the industry on media content and on social and political life. We argue that, in its expansive pursuit of profits, the highly concentrated media industry often fails to serve the public interest. We conclude by exploring how policy and citizen activism can help produce media that are more responsive to the needs of citizens in a diverse democratic society.

This book differs in several ways from others that cover similar territory. First, we take seriously the basic features of market systems, but we discuss these ideas in a way that is accessible to readers with little background in economics. Second, we use competing theoretical frameworks—the market model and the public sphere model—to highlight different aspects of the media industry. Third, we are critical of our current media system from a public interest perspective, but our serious consideration of market dynamics allows us to avoid an overly simplistic critique.

Acknowledgments

In the process of writing this book, we have been fortunate to have the support and assistance of various colleagues, friends, and students. We would like to thank Steve Rutter and his staff at Pine Forge Press for their patience and help in developing the original edition of this book, and to Margaret Seawell and her staff for their assistance with this second edition. Thanks also to Eric Elder, Johanna Buchignani, Sarah From, Caroline Lee, Kate Lefko-Everett, and Shawna Seth for their wide-ranging research assistance. We would like to acknowledge Pine Forge's reviewers, Jane Duvall Downing, University of Missouri, Columbia; Christopher H. Sterling, George Washington University; and Clay Steinman, Macalester College, for their helpful comments and suggestions on an earlier draft of this book. Finally, David Croteau would like to thank Cecelia Kirkman, without whom life would be much less interesting; and William Hoynes would like to thank Deirdre Burns for her continuing support, and Ben and Nick Hoynes, who are a daily inspiration.

Introduction

The New Media Industry and an Old Dilemma

In important respects, the business of media is unique. Unlike other industries, the media deal in ideas, information, and culture. They inform and entertain us, influencing how we understand ourselves and our world, as well as how we spend our leisure time. Because they play such significant political and cultural roles, the media hold a unique position in democratic societies that value free and creative expression, independent thought, and diverse perspectives. Indeed, in recognition of this public interest role, the only business specifically protected by the U.S. Constitution is the "free press."

In other ways, the business of media is like all other businesses. Nearly all major media companies are commercial corporations, whose primary function is creating profits for owners or stockholders. The yardstick by which the business performance of media companies is measured by investors includes few notches that mark public interest concerns about creativity, independent thought, and diversity. Instead, the measurements gauge sales, advertising revenue, and profits.

Thus we face a great dilemma in assessing the changing business of media and its significance for democratic societies. Which of these yardsticks—profits or public interest—should we use in measuring media's performance? Can both missions be simultaneously accomplished, or are they mutually exclusive goals? Does achieving one mission necessarily ensure the other? These are the basic quandaries that frame our discussion of the media business.

It is a business that is certainly worthy of examination. The multibillion-dollar media industry has been changing very rapidly as media conglomerates grow in size and scope, expanding their reach across the globe. As a result, media are fully integrated into people's everyday lives, reaching virtually everyone in industrialized societies and arguably commanding more public attention than any other single institution.

New technologies are helping to transform the 21st-century media industry into something quite different from its predecessors. Although these changes suggest exciting possibilities, they also raise troubling questions about ownership and control of information, about concentration of power, about the responsiveness of media to an increasingly diverse society, about the future of journalism, and about the relationship between media and citizens. These questions, too, are at the heart of our discussion.

❖ 21ST-CENTURY MEDIA

The 21st century began with a bang. On January 10, 2000, America Online, Inc. (AOL) announced that it would buy Time Warner Inc., creating a media giant of unprecedented size.[1] The $166 billion deal (about $184.1 billion in constant 2004 dollars[2]) was the biggest corporate merger ever. It was four times as big as Viacom's $38 billion ($43.8 billion) acquisition of CBS in the fall of 1999, which at that time had been the largest media merger ever. (It is a safe bet that by the time you read this book, there will have been more major media mergers, perhaps even larger than the AOL–Time Warner deal.)

In 1989, a $14.1 billion merger ($21.7 billion) between Time Inc. and Warner Communications, Inc. had created the world's largest media and entertainment company, Time Warner. By the late 1990s, after acquiring Turner Communications in 1995, Time Warner's holdings included many well-known names in cable (CNN, HBO, TNT), magazines (*Time, People, Sports Illustrated*), movies (Warner Bros.), music (Warner Music Group), television (WB), and sports (Atlanta Braves, World Championship Wrestling). Both Time and Warner were founded in 1922, and each company had been a mainstay of the media industry through the remainder of the 20th century. Now the media giant of the late 20th century was being gobbled up by a leader in the 21st-century Internet world.

AOL was founded in 1985, so compared with Time Warner, it was a new kid on the block. Like the Internet itself, however, AOL had grown quickly to include 20 million subscribers. It became the world's largest Internet service provider by making the confusing jungle of the Internet simpler and less intimidating for technologically unsophisticated first-time users. In the 1990s, it expanded through Internet-related acquisitions (e.g., CompuServe, Netscape). By the turn of the century, its stock value had surged to such a degree that it had the capital to buy the much larger Time Warner. With just $4.8 billion in annual revenue, AOL was buying Time Warner, a company with annual revenues more than five times as large ($26.8 billion).

The AOL–Time Warner merger was supposed to be a fusion of 20th- and 21st-century media. Time Warner would have access to a powerful Internet platform for reaching customers online. And AOL could now offer well-known Time Warner brand name products to its subscribers, making its service even more attractive. For example, on the Internet, AOL planned to promote CNN. On television, CNN would promote AOL. The massive media conglomerate AOL Time Warner not only owned dozens and dozens of major media properties, it also was involved in an intricate maze of joint ventures with many of its competitors.

AOL Time Warner was the leading example of a media conglomerate built to leverage the synergy—the idea that the whole is greater than the sum of the parts—of its holdings across the full range of media sectors. However, shortly after the deal was finalized in 2001, it became clear that AOL Time Warner was not the match made in heaven that its proponents had envisioned. Both AOL and Time Warner had their own distinct practices and traditions, and meshing the two corporate cultures turned out to be far more difficult than expected. In addition, after the dot.com stock bubble burst in 2001, revealing AOL's overinflated value, AOL was hardly in a position to be the lead partner in this new media company. Even worse, AOL was coming under increased scrutiny by federal prosecutors for illegal accounting practices that artificially inflated its revenue statements. Perhaps most important, the appearance of low-cost alternatives to AOL dial-up service, along with the emergence of high-speed broadband Internet access, posed a double threat to AOL's core business. All of this meant that AOL Time Warner was never able to implement its synergistic dreams.

AOL Time Warner's stock price declined significantly in the years after the merger, and the company reported record losses in 2002. In 2003, the architect of the merger deal, AOL's Steve Case, stepped down as chairman of AOL Time Warner; later that year, the company dropped AOL from its corporate name, returning to its previous Time Warner. At the end of 2004, Time Warner reached a deal with the Justice Department and the Securities and Exchange Commission, agreeing to pay $510 million to settle the investigations into AOL bookkeeping irregularities. Along the way, Time Warner sold off several pieces of the conglomerate, including its sports teams, CD and DVD manufacturing division, and Warner Music Group. Some on Wall Street believe that the next division to be sold will be the erstwhile buyer, AOL. In just a few short years, the biggest corporate merger in history became perceived by most business analysts as an absolute disaster.[3]

❖ THE LESSONS OF FAILURE?

The failure of AOL Time Warner is now legendary. With a down advertising market from 2001 to 2003 and a weak economy in the post–September 11 period, merger mania in the media industry slowed considerably in the immediate wake of the AOL Time Warner debacle. Some observers argued that the lesson of the AOL Time Warner failure is that bigger is not better and synergy is not a winning strategy.[4]

If that is the lesson of AOL Time Warner, other companies do not seem to have paid much attention. Although investment analysts are now far more skeptical of large media mergers,[5] the major media companies continue to add pieces to their media conglomerates, seeking to build new versions of the synergies that AOL Time Warner promised. For example, Viacom bought BET in 2001, to complete its full slate of music video channels, and acquired the online sports media leader sportsline.com and German music broadcaster VIVA in 2004. The News Corporation linked its FOX media content with a major satellite distributor by buying industry leader DirecTV. Sony purchased Metro-Goldwyn-Mayer and its coveted library of more than 4,000 films.

Other media companies have been even more ambitious. Comcast, the largest cable television and broadband Internet access provider in the United States, tried to purchase the Walt Disney Company in 2004. Invoking the language of synergy, Comcast CEO Brian Roberts described the proposed merger as a "wonderful opportunity to create a company that combines distribution and content in a way that is far stronger and more valuable than either Disney or Comcast can be standing alone."[6] Although Comcast's takeover bid failed, the effort demonstrates that the major media companies are continuing their quest to build integrated media conglomerates.

In 2004, General Electric, which already owned NBC, completed its acquisition of Universal. The expanded company aimed to leverage new cross-media synergies by linking NBC's television and cable business with Universal's film and television production business and its USA Networks. Echoing the rhetoric surrounding the AOL Time Warner deal 4 years earlier, NBC Universal Chairman Bob Wright gushed about the growth opportunities of "a highly integrated company with outstanding positions across a range of media."[7] His comments suggest that, in the end, the failure of AOL Time Warner may have been merely a temporary respite from the continuing growth of media conglomerates pursuing synergy.

NBC Universal represents one example of the newest breed of media conglomerate. Bigger, diversified, integrated, global, and powerful, the emerging media giants are the embodiment of broader industry trends. If we focus only on the particulars of the latest giant deal, we risk missing the larger dynamics they represent. When we step back from the trees and assess the forest, however, we find continuing changes with deep implications.

- ❖ Aided by technological changes, the number of media outlets and media products is growing at a rapid rate.
- ❖ People are spending more time and money consuming media products.
- ❖ Media corporations are getting much larger, often by merging with competitors.
- ❖ Some media companies are now part of even bigger conglomerates that are involved in a wide range of nonmedia businesses.
- ❖ Aided by technological innovations, media corporations are diversifying the range of media products they produce, resulting in the decline in distinct media industries (e.g., publishing, television, radio, video games, etc.) and the emergence of a more integrated multimedia industry.
- ❖ Increasingly, new media ventures are joint efforts between two or more major media conglomerates.
- ❖ The number of media corporations that own and control the bulk of all media products is shrinking.

These developments, which we will explore throughout this book, largely can be explained by looking at the economics of the media industry. To understand their significance, however, we must broaden our perspective to include political and social questions associated with the public interest.

In some ways, these changes in the media parallel changes in other industries. The banking and pharmaceutical industries, for example, have seen similar processes of consolidation and concentration in recent years. The media industry changes also have historical precedents. More than one observer has made a comparison between our high-technology information age and that of the industrial "Gilded Age" of a century ago. Then, it was the concentration of ownership in oil, railroads, and steel that accounted for the fortunes of "robber barons" such as Rockefeller, Vanderbilt, and Carnegie. In that period, a declining agrarian economy and an emerging industrial one served as the foundation for new business empires. Collusion, price fixing, the concentration of power, and the sometimes ruthless treatment of employees by these massive industrial trusts eventually led to government regulation in the name of the public interest.

In recent decades, the declining industrial economy has been accompanied by an emerging information-based economy that includes a vast media sector. This has been the foundation for new business empires. While some monopolies in the telecommunication (AT&T) and computer (Microsoft) industries have faced the attention of regulators, in general, political forces have favored deregulation, allowing for mergers and conglomeration on a scale not seen since the original robber barons. In these respects, then, what is happening in the media industry is not unlike what has happened in other segments of the economy in the past.

However, when these changes occur in the media industry, they hold special significance for democratic societies. Having to pay more for steel because just a few companies dominate its production is a major economic problem. Having just a few companies dominate the production and mass distribution of ideas, culture, and information raises broader and far more significant concerns and dilemmas.

❖ MEDIA IN A DEMOCRATIC SOCIETY

The business of media in a totalitarian state is fairly simple. Power is concentrated in the hands of a few—namely, the government. The media are owned and controlled by those in political power. The government is likely to use the media to promote culture and information that is consistent with its goals and to exclude dissenting views. Regular citizens watching, reading, or listening to the media are subjected to a steady stream of material that more or less reflects the interests and opinions of the ruling party.

In democratic societies, a free press and independent media are entrusted with a different and more complicated role. First, rather than serving as a propaganda machine for those in power, media are expected to reflect the range of creative visions and ideas that constitute a society's vibrant culture. Especially in a multicultural society such as the United States, mass media are the screens on which diverse images can be projected for all to see. Through entertainment, arts, and public affairs programming, the media allow us to learn about the history, culture, and experiences of people different from ourselves, as well as reflecting our own interests and identity in their images and content. This does not have to take the form of a dour civics lesson. Entertainment of all sorts—even music videos, sports, or comedy—is part of how we understand each other and our world.

Second, the media have the special task of providing independent information to citizens. Ideally, they are watchdogs of our freedoms, informing citizens about current events and debates and alerting us to potential abuses of power. In this context, a free press is a means by which the public interest is served. It is not an end unto itself.

Believers in democracy argue that the robust discussion, debate, and expression of thought that a free press facilitates is more likely to lead to just and competent social and political decisions. The alternative is an authoritarian society, which few people would find appealing. That is why independent media and freedom of the press are so highly valued and why the media play such a unique role in serving the public interest.

As we have noted, however, the grand mission of a free press coexists with the industry's more pedestrian function: to make a profit. A simple example crystallizes this tension. Anyone turning on the evening news is confronted with two simultaneous realities. The first is evident from the beginning of the broadcast. Theme music rises, computer-generated graphics slide across the screen, and the camera pans the "newsroom" set, settling on the perfectly coifed celebrity anchor. Show time! This is news as entertainment and spectacle. Dramatic images of bloody victims, flaming wreckage, and somber-faced politicians fill the screen. These are interspersed with brightly colored, high-energy commercials selling everything from deodorant to automobiles.

Welcome to media for profit, where the fundamental principle is to attract an audience to sell to advertisers. Even though you may not have paid anything to watch this specific network news broadcast, you are part of the large economic process that underlies such programs. You are the target of advertisers who hope to sell you their products. They speak to you as a consumer. They invite you to solve individual problems and improve your personal life by buying something. The market model of media is based on the ability of a network to deliver audiences to these advertisers. The more people watching a program, the higher the price the networks can charge for ad time. Lost audiences mean lost profits. The success of a program is largely measured in rating points among desirable demographics: those people to whom the advertisers want to speak. What sells is good. In essence, this is the market model of media. With some variation, it applies to all types of media.

However, the evening news still contains the vestiges of another model of media: the public sphere model. This was the model invoked by your junior high school teachers when they encouraged you to read a newspaper or watch the news so you would be informed about current events. You see hints of the public sphere model in the occasional "in-depth" story or series on a recurring social problem or policy debate. Here, the fundamental principle is that to act as responsible citizens, people need information about the issues and events occurring in their world. This is news as education and public service. Journalists, commentators, and analysts speak to you as a citizen. They invite you to learn about the public issues that face society and perhaps improve your community by acting on this knowledge—in the voting booth, in your community, and beyond. This model of media is based not on ratings and profits but on the ability to serve the impossible-to-quantify "public interest." An informed citizenry is assumed to be better for democracy than an ignorant one. What helps people to better understand their condition, their communities, and their world is valuable—whether or not it turns a profit. It provides essential cultural resources for responsible citizens. In essence, this is the public sphere model of media.

However, what is in the public interest may not be in the corporate interest. The major corporations that own the media—and are often involved in many other lines of business—may not want certain embarrassing stories to be publicized very widely (or at all). They may not want to encourage critical examination of their business practices or the effects their products have on communities or the environment.

They may not want stories or programs that offend their advertisers or interfere with the advertising pitch. They may want to avoid stories on subjects they deem "unpopular." Their ownership of the media gives them the potential to influence how a story is—or is not—covered. If the story affects the media industry as a whole, there may be widespread interest in *not* covering it. Media are supposed to be a watchdog of government, but who serves as a watchdog of corporate media? This is only one of the dilemmas facing our current media system.

Other aspects of this dilemma may not be as dramatic as conflict of interest concerns, but they are more routine and pervasive. A program on "The World's Bloodiest Serial Killers" might do well in terms of ratings, but its value in terms of the public interest is dubious at best. Does such a program glorify violence, perhaps encouraging some less-stable people to act similarly? What is the cumulative effect for society of airing countless hours of bloody violence as "entertainment"? How do we weigh the profitability of such programs against their possible negative social impacts?

Finally, the most fundamental dilemma may be that in the media world, entertainment is generally far more profitable than information. Bottom-line pressure usually steers media content away from serious substance that challenges people, to light entertainment that is familiar and comforting. Although such programming may be profitable, it usually makes little contribution to a more vibrant civic culture.

All of these quandaries are really variations on one recurring theme: the tension between profits and the public interest. There is nothing new about this basic dilemma; colonial printers publishing early newspapers made money from the trade. However, the media that the authors of the First Amendment knew were radically different creatures from the ones we have today. Not only have new types of media been introduced, the nature of media owners and producers and the scale of their operations has changed dramatically as well. The media conglomerates of today are unprecedented in human history. How these companies operate has been rapidly changing with the rise of Internet technology, conglomeration, integration, and globalization.

❖ PLAN FOR THE BOOK

This book examines recent changes in the media industry in light of their potential impact on society. In particular, it shows how we can understand recent changes by looking at the business of media through the "market model." It also shows how these changes and their impacts can be considered by using a different yardstick, a "public sphere" model of media.

Ours is not a simplistic tale of good versus evil. It is an honest attempt to grapple with the real dilemmas that face us with 21st-century media. Our technological capabilities offer unprecedented opportunities for the creation and wide distribution of more information than has ever been available before in human history. However, it is our social values, political decisions, and citizen demands that ultimately determine how this burgeoning technology will be used. Ours is also not a pedantic exercise intent on balancing "on the one hand" with "on the other hand." We have grave concerns about the current direction of the media industry, and we argue that public interest goals should be taken more seriously than they now are. We make our case for this position and show how much of the current debate about the future of media is really a debate about what standards should be applied in evaluating media performance.

Part I of this book introduces the underlying theoretical and historical context for our study of the media business. In chapter 1, we take a closer look at the two competing frameworks that can be used to evaluate the business of media; what we call the *market model* and the *public sphere model* of media. We use these models throughout the book both to explore the market logic at work in the media industry and to make sense of the broader consequences of recent developments in the media industry. In chapter 2, we provide a brief history of the rise of the media industry in the last century and examine the evolution of media policy in the United States.

In Part II, we examine the current state of the media business, with a focus on the market-oriented logic behind the recent changes in the industry. In chapter 3, we look at the recent trends in media ownership and structure, focusing on growth, integration, globalization, and ownership concentration. Chapter 4 focuses on the strategies of the new media giants, examining the current business practices that have accompanied the recent structural changes in the industry. These strategies include the pursuit of synergy, branding, market segmentation and product specialization, diversification, and joint ventures.

In Part III, we employ the public sphere framework to more critically examine the social, political, and cultural significance of the emergence of the new media conglomerates. Chapter 5 looks at the ways that current business strategies of the media giants shape the content of our mass media, paying particular attention to homogenization and imitation, trivialization and sensationalism, commercialization, and censorship. In chapter 6, we examine the influence of the media business on politics and society. Here we focus on the omnipresence of advertising, the fragmentation of the public, and the political activities of the major media companies. Finally, in chapter 7, we take a critical look at the future of both the media industry and media policy and explore some ways our media might more effectively serve the public interest.

PART I

Profits and the Public Interest

Theoretical and Historical Context

1

Media, Markets,
and the Public Sphere

This book is an introduction to the business of media. In it, we do three things. First, we sketch out some of the major changes that have occurred in the media industry in recent years. Second, we examine *why* these changes have occurred. Finally, we provide an assessment of these changes. The first of these tasks requires only that we review the public record on the media industry. Although there is certainly room for debate about what aspects of the changing industry ought to be highlighted, most of the basic patterns we discuss are well known and widely recognized by industry insiders and observers. How can we explain these changes? Why are they occurring? How can we judge the significance of these changes? Are they generally positive or negative developments? Should we be concerned or pleased about the direction in which the media business is headed? Those sorts of questions and assessments require that we have a framework from which to examine the media.

Evaluating the changes in the media industry is complex, however, because there are competing and very different frameworks from which to analyze the media business. In part, this is why there is so much disagreement in evaluations of the media; people are using different standards to judge what they see. The two perspectives we employ in this book can be referred to as the *market model* of media and the *public sphere model* of media. The former, which is the dominant framework within the media industry, is a widely familiar economic perspective that assesses media using the universal currency of business success: profits. We call it the market model because, to varying degrees, assumptions about how "free markets" operate form the core of this perspective. As with other industries, the media are conceptualized as primarily competitors in this marketplace.

The public sphere perspective is a less familiar one, so we take much more space here describing its elements. From this perspective, the media are defined as central elements of a healthy public sphere—the "space" within which ideas, opinions, and views freely circulate. Here, rather than profits, it is the more elusive "public interest" that serves as the yardstick against which media performance is measured.

Both frameworks are useful in better understanding the media. The media, for the most part, are made up of commercial, profit-seeking businesses. Media companies issue stock, compete for larger market share, develop new products, watch costs, look for opportunities to expand, and engage in all the other activities that constitute regular business practice. In various ways, owners, investors, employees, and audiences all experience the consequences of these business decisions. In most cases, media activities can be explained using the basic concepts that make up the market model. The market model, then, is especially useful in understanding why media companies behave the way they do. It is the framework to which most business people refer in explaining their actions.

There are serious limitations to the market model of media, however—businesses cannot be judged by profitability alone. Society has an interest in how industries perform that goes far beyond profits. Labor laws, environmental protections, and antifraud measures, for example, are all ways in which society puts limits on business practices in the name of the public interest—even at the expense of profits. This holds true for the media industry as well. Even the largest and most powerful media conglomerates must operate within a dynamic framework of social and political constraints that, in the name of the public interest, shape how businesses work. In particular, it is widely recognized that a vibrant public sphere is essential to the operation of a healthy democracy. The media play a crucial role in helping to create such a vibrant public sphere.

Understanding and assessing the media business requires us to explore both the underlying economic dynamics of the media industry and the extraeconomic role that is played by media in a democratic society. This chapter introduces the basics of both the market and public sphere models and suggests the value of extending our analytic framework beyond the bottom line to include service to the public interest as a core component in our assessment of the contemporary media industry.

❖ THE MARKET MODEL

The market model suggests that society's needs can best be met through a relatively unregulated process of exchange based on the dynamics of supply and demand. This model treats the media like all other goods and services. It argues that as long as competitive conditions exist, businesses pursuing profits will meet people's needs. As a result, advocates of this model generally call for private, unregulated ownership of the media. It is consumers in the marketplace, not government regulators, who will ultimately force companies to behave in a way that best serves the public.

The Advantages of Markets

The market model promotes the use of unregulated markets for the delivery of goods and services. For these markets to function properly, there must be a sufficient number of suppliers of a good. No single supplier or small group of suppliers should be able to artificially influence market dynamics. That would undermine the whole premise of a competitive, market-based economy. Assuming that there is sufficient competition, markets offer a number of overlapping advantages.

Markets Promote Efficiency. Without the cumbersome bureaucracies associated with centralized planning, markets tend to promote efficiency. Because they are constantly trying to increase profits, companies must develop new ways to deliver goods and services at the lowest cost. This encourages efficiency on the part of producers and ensures low prices for consumers.

This efficiency is lost when standardized models are implemented or vast regulatory procedures are established. They are also lost if competition is inadequate, because there is no longer an incentive to reduce costs. For consumers, uncompetitive markets tend to produce artificially high prices. There is no incentive for producers to keep prices attractive, because consumers have nowhere else to go. As a result, suppliers are able to set prices independent of market forces, gouging captive customers and undermining the basic supply-demand balance that characterizes healthy markets.

Markets Promote Responsiveness. Markets operate on the principle of supply and demand. As a result, they are responsive to what people want. In the marketplace, price serves as the key indicator of supply and demand. When demand goes up, price goes up, until an increase in supply restores equilibrium. The increase in supply materializes because companies, seeing the profits to be made, either enter the market or expand their already existing production to meet the increase in demand. When demand goes down, price drops to allow for the sale of surplus supply. In both cases, producers are responding to consumer demand as a result of basic market dynamics.

Markets Promote Flexibility. Not only do companies in market-based economies respond to what consumers want or do not want, the absence of centralized planning and control allows them to quickly adapt to the new supply-demand balance. Thus companies operating in market-based economies must be flexible in how they are organized and in what they produce so that they can respond to new market conditions. Again, competition is essential here, because flexible response is necessary only if competitors exist to lure customers away from unresponsive producers.

Markets Promote Innovation. In market-based economies, many different producers experiment with new products and services. The incentive of big profits promotes innovation as companies try to develop new products that will capture a larger market share or secure an untapped market segment. This constant experimentation with new products, services, and production processes results in a very dynamic and innovative industry. A lack of competition tends to discourage innovation. For example, in the media industry, lack of competition can lead to an unwillingness to take risks in producing innovative new projects. Instead, imitation of past successes is likely to be the key business strategy employed.

Markets Can Deliver Media Like Any Other Product. All of the features of markets described here are applicable to the media business. Market model advocates argue that, like any other producer of products, if the media industry is left unregulated, it will respond to consumer demand, develop innovative new products, and remain flexible and efficient. If media products are treated like any other products, consumers will be able to enjoy the benefits of market dynamics.

Market Structures and Types of Competition

The benefits of markets, as noted, occur only when there is robust competition. How do we know for sure that sufficient competition exists? One way is to examine the market structure in any given industry.

Market structure refers to the economic characteristics of particular markets, including things such as the level of ownership concentration, the amount of product differentiation, the types of entry barriers facing new competitors, and the extent of vertical and horizontal integration. Two of the key factors in assessing market structure are the number of firms supplying a product and the level of differentiation between products being offered. Exhibit 1.1 shows in simplified form how these two dimensions can be mapped out into different market structures. Of course, this typology is meant only to suggest some key variables to consider. Real-world markets fall along a more complex continuum than we present here. Still, this framework can be helpful when discussing the relationship between media and markets. Multiple firms do not necessarily ensure diversity in products. One or a few firms do not necessarily mean homogenized products.

Exhibit 1.1   Types of Market Structures

Level of Product Diversity	*Number of Supplying Firms*	
	One or a Few	*Many*
Low	Homogenized monopoly	Homogenized competition
High	Diverse monopoly	Diverse competition

Homogenized monopolies are the least desirable from a market perspective because they are not competitive and give consumers limited or no choices in products. To keep our example simple, imagine the lone one-screen movie theater in an isolated community and you begin to see the problems with homogenized monopolies. Consumers have no product choice. A single movie is offered each week and they must either take it or leave it—and they have no accessible competing theater to which they can take their business.

Diverse monopolies offer some advantage because they at least give consumers a wider variety of choices, even though there are only one or a few companies owning those options. In this example, perhaps our single-screen theater becomes a multiplex, simultaneously offering half a dozen different movies. From a consumer perspective, this is certainly an improvement, because there are now more choices, but it still presents serious problems. For example, because ownership is concentrated, the theater's owner has no incentive to keep ticket or concession prices low. Without competition, the owner is free to push prices as high as the market will bear—and because there is no alternative, consumers are likely to pay artificially inflated prices.

Homogenized competition presents its own set of problems. Imagine a number of competing theaters all showing mainstream Hollywood action-adventure films and adolescent comedies. The broad appeal of such films may be sufficient to meet the business needs of the competing theaters. Many people may well be satisfied with the limited range of movie fare. But for others, the differences between Vin Diesel and The Rock or Adam Sandler and Mike Myers may be no difference at all. The products being offered may be plentiful and affordable, but—partly because they are aimed at the broad mainstream audience—they do not come close to representing the diversity of movie tastes among the public. Increased volume of media products does not ensure increased diversity in products. This problem was neatly encapsulated in a 1994 song by musician Bruce Springsteen when he lamented that cable television had "57 Channels (and Nothin' On)."

Finally, *diverse competition* is usually the market ideal. Here, numerous sellers offer a wide range of products from which consumers can choose. A significant number of independently owned theaters might compete with similar theaters and at the same time target audiences spread widely across the range of public tastes and interests. Each would offer something distinctive, but enough overlap with competitors would exist so that consumers would have clear alternatives.

Our theater examples are artificially simple. The real world offers more complexity than is suggested here. However, these examples illustrate basic dynamics that, as we will see, are easy to forget amid the cacophony of contemporary media environments. They also illustrate the point that the market model is capable of addressing issues of diversity—a central concern of the public interest model.

It should be noted that, with a few exceptions, pure competition does not exist in the real world. Pure competition exists only when many different companies offer exactly the same product. (Some commodity markets, such as wheat or soybeans, can be said to exhibit characteristics of pure competition.) At best, markets achieve what is called *monopolistic* competition. That is, many firms offer similar, but not identical, products. (The term can be confusing: each company has a "monopoly" over its particular product, but the products are so similar that they are in direct "competition" with each other.)

Because from a market model competition is widely viewed as the core of a healthy media industry, federal communications regulatory policy has centered on the amount of competition that exists in the industry and on the ability of potential competitors to enter the market. As we will later see, the Hollywood studio system was broken up in the 1940s because it interfered with competition. The original NBC broadcast monopoly was broken up for the same reason. In such cases, government intervention occurred precisely because of belief in the necessity of competition for the commercial media industry.

As we will see, recent changes in regulatory policy have spurred an increase in ownership concentration within the media business. As the large media companies continue to grow, some aspects of the media industry are becoming uncompetitive, undermining the potential benefits of markets. Some critics call for more government intervention to restore competition to the media industry. Others, however, point to burgeoning technological developments as evidence that the media business is becoming more competitive than ever, rejecting the need for more regulation.

❖ THE PUBLIC SPHERE MODEL

The public sphere model suggests that society's needs cannot be met entirely through the market system. Because the market is based on consumer purchasing power, it behaves quite differently from the democratic ideal of "one person, one vote." In addition, the public sphere model argues that there are some societal needs that simply cannot be met via the market's supply and demand dynamic. It also contends that because it is vital to a robust democracy, media content cannot be treated as merely another product. Therefore, profitability cannot be the sole indicator of a healthy media industry. Instead, other public interest criteria—such as diversity and substance—are used in the public sphere model to assess the performance of media. From this perspective, government plays a useful and necessary role in ensuring that the media meet the needs of citizens, not just consumers.

The Concept of the Public Sphere

According to the public sphere model, media are more than just profit-making components of large conglomerates. Instead, they are our primary information sources and storytellers. As such, the media have become the core of a crucial democratic site that social theorists refer to as the public sphere.

The concept of the public sphere is associated with the German sociologist Jürgen Habermas, whose classic study *The Structural Transformation of the Public Sphere* described the importance of a vibrant public sphere for democratic societies.[8] Building on Habermas's work, a growing body of literature has argued that the principal way that mass media can contribute to democratic processes is by helping to cultivate social spaces for ongoing public dialogue.[9]

This model posits an open media system that is widely accessible. It argues that information should circulate freely, without government intervention to restrict the flow of ideas. Ownership and control of media outlets should be broad and diversified, with many owners instead of a few large ones. Ideally, some media channels would be publicly accessible for citizens to use to communicate with each other. If a strong democracy requires citizen participation, that participation is made meaningful by continuing, wide-ranging public discourse, to which the media can contribute immeasurably.

Fundamentally, the public sphere model views people as *citizens* rather than *consumers*. Furthermore, it contends that media should "serve" these citizens, rather than "target" potential consumers. Murdock, for example, suggests three important ways that communication systems are central for the constitution of citizenship.

First, in order for people to exercise their full rights as citizens, they must have access to the information, advice, and analysis that will enable them to know what their personal rights are and allow them to pursue them effectively. Second, they must have access to the broadest possible range of information, interpretation, and debate on areas that involve public political choices, and they must be able to use communications facilities in order to register criticism and propose alternative courses of action. And third, they must be able to recognize themselves and their aspirations in the range of representations on offer within the central communications sectors and be able to contribute to developing and extending these representations.[10]

Thus, for participatory democracy to function, citizens must learn how to take part, and they must have access to the resources necessary for meaningful participation. From a public sphere perspective, the potential contribution of media to such a democracy is in the work of creating and sustaining a citizenry that is prepared for participation in public life. It is a task for which markets are ill suited.

The Limits of Markets

Business journalist Robert Kuttner once wrote a book subtitled *The Virtues and Limits of Markets.*[11] As we have seen, the market model suggests that by pursuing profits, media firms simultaneously meet the needs of the audience. Thus the virtues of market dynamics will satisfy the public interest. However, the public sphere model of media shows the potential conflict between profit making and serving the public interest and, more generally, the significant limitations of markets.

Markets Are Undemocratic. Markets work by a "one dollar, one vote" mechanism. Thus, despite rhetoric to the contrary, markets are inconsistent with democratic assumptions. In markets, profits are the measure of success and money is the measure of clout. The more money you have, the more influence you have in the marketplace. Success in the marketplace can be translated into more influence on that market (sometimes by changing the rules in your favor), thus perpetuating a cycle whereby the rich tend to get richer and the poor (those who have been unsuccessful in the market) get poorer. This is contradictory to the basic democratic ideal that individuals have inherent and equal worth that justifies their basic rights ("All men are created equal . . . and are born with certain inalienable rights"). The values of their bank accounts should not enter into the equation. In terms of media, we have historically valued free expression as the core of a broader commitment to democratic deliberation. In this public sphere, citizens are equals, even if they have extremely different consumer power. However, because markets operate on a fundamentally different set of rules, there is good reason to be skeptical of the ability of market-oriented media to satisfy crucial democratic needs.

Markets Reproduce Inequality. Because markets are based on money, they tend to reproduce the inequality that exists in society. Rather than being an even playing field where individuals compete, players enter the market with widely unequal resources. The playing field is tilted in favor of those who already have advantages. An individual who enjoys the privileges of inherited wealth, elite education, or privileged social contacts has distinct advantages in the market. When it comes to media, those parties with significant resources may own or disproportionately influence media content; those with only modest means have little or no influence on what is produced. Media, therefore, may tend to reflect the views and interests of those with wealth and power and neglect the views and interests of others.

Markets Are Amoral. Markets make no judgment about what is bought and sold. They do not distinguish between products that might be good for society versus products that might be harmful. The market is designed to supply whatever there is a demand for. The market does not prevent the production and sale of child pornography, crack cocaine, snuff films, or rocket-propelled grenades. It is society, through its government's regulatory agencies, that must make such judgments. For nearly 250 years, the United States had an efficient market system that dealt in the acquisition and sale of human beings. There was nothing inherent in market theory that guarded against slavery. It took massive government intervention to change those practices.

Markets Do Not Necessarily Meet Social Needs. There are some needs that are distinctly social and unlikely to be met by the privatized market. Early fire protection, for example, used to be a market-based service available only to those who could afford to pay. If you could not afford the services of the private fire departments, you were on your own in case of a fire. It quickly became apparent, however, that this private market-based solution was no solution at all. In urban areas, fires could spread rapidly, regardless of which homeowners could afford fire protection. Public fire departments were established to address this social problem.

There are a whole host of services that societies deem important to provide to their citizens—regardless of market forces. State-supported public education, for example, is an attempt to provide citizens with access to a fundamental resource, regardless of their ability to pay. (Even recent calls for more market-oriented school "choice" still depend on government funds for schools.) In the United States, the range of such services—for example, limited public education, the right of an accused to legal counsel, and emergency health care for the indigent—is relatively narrow. In Canadian and European societies, the range of publicly available services, such as national health care, child care, and extensive public higher education, is much broader. Often, these are services for society's most vulnerable and least powerful citizens. Poor people, children, the mentally ill, and the physically disabled are just some of the many people who often are not well served by market structures. In addition, workers, consumers, minorities, and other groups in society depend on the intervention of government to help create a more level economic playing field. In fact, society depends on an extensive infrastructure of nonprofit, nonmarket institutions to meet social needs and to aid and support those whose needs cannot be met in the marketplace.

In many societies, the services provided outside of the commercial marketplace include public broadcasting and other media operations. (The United States has only a limited version of such services.) The rationale for public media is the same as with public education or health care: It is an invaluable resource that should be available to citizens regardless of their ability to pay, and the market does an inadequate job of meeting this need.

Markets Do Not Necessarily Meet Democratic Needs. Market forces and democratic goals may diverge as much as they coincide. Even relatively competitive media industries can, and often do, provide products that ill serve a democratic citizenry. Because of their inexpensive production costs and relative popularity among consumers, market forces might lead to the production of an ever-growing stream of light entertainment, pornography, or "news" about titillating scandals.

Indeed, it might make very good business sense for virtually all major media companies to produce programs, films, books, and other materials that are geared toward grabbing and holding the attention of consumers by shocking or pandering to them. Media companies might also target their products—whether they be news shows or contemporary music—at very narrow demographic groups, with the assumption that different groups have distinct interests and tastes.

In these cases, even if the media market is quite competitive, there is a good chance that what would be classified as market "success" would produce a kind of political and cultural failure. In the first instance, the proliferation of light and titillating entertainment supplants substantive information, educational media, or challenging cultural presentations, all of which are likely to have more value to democratic processes than to corporate media companies. In the second instance, highly targeted media can reinforce existing prejudices, help to widen the gap between different people, or contribute to a fragmented society in which people interact primarily with those in the same demographic group. Again, success in reaching a target audience may stifle meaningful democratic deliberation among equal (but different) citizens.

Both examples illustrate how crude, market-oriented media systems do not allow for any distinction between people's roles as consumers, which are private and individual, and their roles as citizens, which are public and collective. This is why market-oriented media have a tendency to produce economic benefits and simultaneously create (or at least help to sustain) democratic deficits.

Of course, noting the shortcomings of markets is not an endorsement of a media system that is centrally organized and government run. State media systems may be even more harmful to democratic processes than market-driven systems, providing even less support for vibrant discourse and meaningful free expression. Instead, by exploring the limitations of market-driven media, the public sphere model highlights the civic importance of media. In doing so, it argues that media cannot be treated as just another consumer product.

❖ WHY MEDIA ARE DIFFERENT FROM OTHER INDUSTRIES

One of the core assumptions that underlies the support of a privately owned, commercial media system is the notion that the media industry is just like other industries and media products are the same as other consumer products. Mark Fowler, Federal Communications Commission (FCC) chair during the Reagan administration, made this argument most famously when he declared that "television is just another appliance. It's a toaster with pictures."[12] Supporters of Fowler's position ask: If we permit the laws of supply and demand to determine the price and availability of toasters, why should we do anything different with the media industries? From this perspective, it appears as if market dynamics will give consumers the media products they desire. Producers, responding to what is popular (or in demand), will supply media that audiences have demonstrated (with their attention, money, or both) that they want. In this scenario, excessive regulation only disrupts these market processes by interfering with industry efforts to satisfy audience wants.

This kind of market model of media is rooted in the assumption that, as Fowler put it, media are simple appliances. This is only half of the argument, however. The market model also assumes that citizens are, most fundamentally, *consumers,* who have a potential interest in purchasing the mass media consumer products that are available. On the face of it, these assumptions—that the media supply goods for consumers—may seem reasonable, even quite obvious. Certainly, an important feature of the media world is consumption. We may buy a CD, book, or magazine in the same shopping trip in which we buy a new item of clothing or household cleanser. In short, we do consume media, many of us to the tune of substantial sums of money.

However, there are three primary reasons the media industry is different from other industries, making the market model analysis inappropriate. First, the central role of advertising in some forms of media creates unique market relationships that must be taken into account when assessing the media. In some respects, the media market is *not* responsive to audiences. Second, and more important, media cannot be considered as merely a product to be used by consumers. Instead, as the public sphere model suggests, media are resources for citizens with important informational, educational, and integrative functions. Third, the unique role that media play in a democracy is reflected in the legal protections the media enjoy in the United States. In the following discussion, we consider each of these in more detail.

Advertising and the Media

One reason the media industry is different from other industries is its unique market situation. Most businesses sell products or services to buyers. The market model is based on this traditional buyer-seller relationship. Media businesses, however, operate in what is called a *dual product* market. They simultaneously sell two completely different types of "products" to two completely different sets of buyers. As Albarran succinctly puts it, "First, they produce the media products (newspapers, TV programs, etc.) that are marketed and sold to consumers. Second, they provide access to consumers (readers, viewers) that is sold to advertisers."[13]

The balance between consumer revenue and advertiser revenue varies by media type. Books, for example, are similar to other products in that the individual consumer provides nearly all the revenue for publishers. Broadcast television and radio, at the other extreme, are free to consumers and rely entirely on advertisers for revenue. Other forms of media have dual revenue streams but usually rely mostly on advertisers. For print media, subscriptions and newsstand sales account for only about one third of newspaper and magazine revenue; advertisers make up the bulk of revenue. As the Internet develops, most sites are following the broadcast model of providing free content that is financed by advertising.

Individual consumers are aware of the first of these two markets. We are used to paying for newspapers, cable television, CDs, magazines, and other items. Here, we are in the traditional consumer role of buying a product for ourselves. However, it is less obvious that in the second media market, *we* are the products being sold; advertisers are buying our attention. As a result, the value of audiences goes well beyond the direct revenues they provide to media companies. Instead, audiences are important because they can be sold to advertisers. In essence, then, media content is often a kind of bait, intended to lure the audiences that are the valuable commodities for sale. The result is a market in which media companies need audiences but receive most of their revenue from advertisers, who may be interested in only very specific segments of the public.

This unique dual-product market status has significant implications when we assess the claim that unregulated markets respond to and satisfy the needs of consumers. In reality, to varying degrees, the consumers that media companies are responding to are advertisers, not the people who read, watch, or listen to the media. So, for example, some television programs with relatively low ratings are renewed, and more popular shows are canceled. If television networks simply responded to what *viewers* watched, this would never happen. It does happen, however, because the networks are really responding to advertisers, not viewers. If a program with modest ratings reaches a demographic group that is especially attractive to advertisers, it may be renewed in favor of a program with higher overall ratings but with demographics that are less appealing to advertisers. Higher income viewers, for example, are more appealing than lower income viewers because they are more likely to be able to afford the advertisers' products. Advertisers also have a strong preference for younger audiences and are relatively uninterested in consumers over the age of 50. Unlike a democratic "one person, one vote" dynamic, markets are explicitly tilted in favor of those with more money who are likely to spend it and, increasingly in recent years, geared toward the preferences of young people, whom advertisers see as valuable and potentially brand-loyal consumers.

Thus, even if we accept the claim that markets are responsive to buyers, we see that in the media marketplace these "buyers" are often advertisers, not the general public. This certainly challenges the belief that the unregulated marketplace adequately responds to the public's needs.

Media as Citizen Resources

The media industry differs from other industries in a second important respect. Because the media produce cultural and political goods that have different purposes from many other goods, the public sphere model conceptualizes media as citizen resources, not simple consumer products. Media can, and sometimes do, help provide citizens with what they need to be active participants in social and political life. In contemporary society, the media are central to processes of deliberation, education, and social integration.

Media are the primary suppliers of information to citizens, both about current events and long-standing issues. They inform for both individual decision making and, equally important, public deliberation. The health of our political discourse depends to a large degree on the quality of the information that the media circulate. Whether it be news about war or televised presidential debates, citizens rely primarily on media for information they need to actively participate in public life.

Media do more than simply inform citizens; they are also, in varying ways, informal educators. Media, often in entertainment formats, can provide us with a window onto our history, the experiences of others, and the views of people with whom we may never come into contact. In more formal ways, media can be educational, bringing learning opportunities to children and adults, probing complex intellectual or spiritual questions, and giving us the background and context to understand the contemporary world. (Indeed, even those who are most critical of the media—those who cry for censorship of what they consider to be inappropriate or offensive content—assume a powerful educational role for the media but fear that media "teach" the "wrong" lessons.)

In addition to their informational and educational functions, the media have the potential to promote social integration by bringing people together across geographic or social boundaries. In doing so, they can help constitute a shared identity based on the common reference points or beliefs that bind citizens to the society they collectively inhabit. Especially in a large, highly differentiated country such as the United States, media can enrich public life by promoting the notion that public dialogue matters and by providing spaces where people can both see parts of their own experience and be exposed to ideas, experiences, and cultures that they do not encounter in their day-to-day lives.

Because the media are important contributors to these educative, deliberative, and integrative processes, conceptualizing media simply through the language of consumption is inadequate. Instead, by focusing on the ways in which media are linked to the question of citizenship, we can see that the market model is far too narrow, because it neglects the cultural and political significance of the media. By insisting on analysis of the "rational" individual—what individual consumers, in the aggregate, "choose"—the market model obscures the social meaning of media. In the end, the fundamentally democratic role of the media is undermined if we conceptualize our relationship to media in terms of mere consumption.

The Unique Legal Status of Media

Because democracy and the ideal of free expression have long been linked in the political culture of the United States, the media industry continues to occupy a distinctive place in the American imagination. As part of a larger commitment to free speech and free expression, Americans generally consider a "free press" to be an essential requirement of a democratic society. Belief in the value of free expression is more than a cultural tradition, however; it is codified in law.

The media industry is different from other industries because it enjoys special legal protection. The First Amendment to the Constitution states that "Congress shall make no law ... abridging the freedom of speech, or of the press." The First Amendment gives the press a special status, protected from government regulation, because of its important role in informing the citizenry. Of course, such protections do not give members of the press license to violate the law. If news organizations engage in unlawful activities (e.g., theft) in their reporting, they can be prosecuted. News outlets that knowingly publish false and harmful information can be sued for libel. In fact, some corporations now view libel suits as a potentially expensive threat they can deploy when they want to try to intimidate investigative reporters. Even so, criminal and libel laws do not permit the government to prevent publication—to engage in "prior restraint"—of any specific material, even if reporters may face legal action later.

In contrast to the print media, broadcasters have not traditionally enjoyed such broad First Amendment rights. Because they use the public airwaves and rely on a government licensing system to allocate space and direct traffic on the limited electromagnetic spectrum, the courts have permitted government regulation of television and radio. The rationale for such regulations is that they serve the public interest, which broadcast law has historically identified as a central obligation of broadcasters who are granted licenses. Even here, however, the courts have concluded that broadcasters have substantial First Amendment rights. Government cannot define the specific content of broadcasts, although laws can require the presence of certain types of programs (e.g., children's or public affairs programs) intended to serve the public interest. Even though politicians routinely criticize television executives for broadcasting excessive sex and violence, government officials do not introduce legislation that regulates television content, because such a law would almost certainly be invalidated by the courts as a violation of the First Amendment. As we will see, debates about regulation of media almost always acknowledge the cultural and legal significance of the First Amendment rights of the media.

❖ THE TRADITION OF CIVIC RESPONSIBILITY

Although the principal players in the media industry have always been profit oriented, it has long been recognized that profit seeking must be balanced by recognition of the civic role of news, public affairs, and, to a lesser extent, entertainment media. Until recently, this broad public purpose of media was widely, if not universally, accepted.

The civic responsibility of the media has been most firmly recognized in the print media. As the code of ethics for the Society of Professional Journalists notes,

> Public enlightenment is the forerunner of justice and the foundation of democracy. The duty of the journalist is to further those ends by seeking truth and providing a fair and comprehensive account of events and issues. Conscientious journalists from all media and specialties strive to serve the public with thoroughness and honesty.[14]

Similarly, the Statement of Principles of the American Society of Newspaper Editors says,

> The First Amendment, protecting freedom of expression from abridgment by any law, guarantees to the people through their press a constitutional right, and thereby places on newspaper people a particular responsibility. . . . The primary purpose of gathering and distributing news and opinion is to serve the general welfare by informing the people and enabling them to make judgments on the issues of the time. . . . The American press was made free not just to inform or just to serve as a forum for debate but also to bring an independent scrutiny to bear on the forces of power in the society, including the conduct of official power at all levels of government.[15]

Thus newspapers and many magazines have long touted the special responsibility of the press to inform and educate citizens.

Broadcasters, too, recognize their role in serving the public. The Radio-Television News Directors Association's Code of Ethics and Professional Conduct begins with the observation that "Professional electronic journalists should operate as trustees of the public, seek the truth, report it fairly and with integrity and independence, and stand accountable for their actions."[16] Because broadcasters transmit signals through the public airwaves, all forms of broadcasting have been viewed, at least in part, as a public service. In fact, regulations on radio and television stations in the United States obligate them to serve the "public interest, convenience, and necessity,"[17] although, as we will see, the specific meaning of this kind of public service has long been contested.

Other media forms, too, have been closely associated with the American ideals of free speech. Films and music, for example, have been widely recognized as providing a forum for the expression of a wide range of stories, concerns, and emotions. In this sense, they also can be understood as providing a type of public service.

Profit seeking and public service are not either-or propositions. Instead, the civic responsibilities of media have historically been met within the framework of commercial business. This has always included incidents and trends that have put the pursuit of profits above the public interest; still, there is a strong history of attempting to balance the two. However, as the media industry grew and consolidated in the 1980s and 1990s, that delicate balance shifted even further in favor of pursuing greater profits over concern for public service. Even though it has been marginalized in recent years by a growing concern for profits within the media industry, the public service role of the media is still recognized and invoked, especially by the professional associations that represent the journalists who work for the major media.

❖ THE PUBLIC INTEREST

If the media industry is different, in important respects, from other industries, the underlying conceptual reason is that media outlets have a distinctive relationship with the public. Rather than simply supplying consumer goods in a free market context, media in a democratic society are expected to serve the public interest. It is no small task, however, to define what *public interest* means or how our mass media can serve in this capacity. In fact, critics often find it easier to identify what is *not* in the public interest—too much violence in television or news that is too focused on crime, for example—than to explain what serving the public interest entails.

Market enthusiasts, on the other hand, can point to a straightforward definition of the public interest by inverting the term: The public interest becomes what the public is interested in. From this perspective, those media that are popular, by definition, serve the public interest. However, by defining the public interest as what is sufficiently popular (and profitable), the strict market model effectively dismisses the broader cultural and political significance of media. Narcotics and prostitution have proven to be enduringly popular among some segments of the public, but simply because the public is interested in such things, can we really say they are in the public interest?

If we take seriously the idea that media are more than simply a vast and profitable industry, that they are important components of a democratic society, we need to pay attention to what it means for media to serve the public interest. To be sure, there are no easy answers. Seventy years of broadcast regulation has demonstrated the dynamic nature of defining the public interest. Instead of identifying a timeless and rigid set of guidelines, which would not be likely to withstand changing cultural norms or the emergence of new technologies, what we need is a framework with which to define the parameters of what it means for media to serve the public interest.

Promoting Diversity, Avoiding Homogeneity

Media serve the public interest to the extent that they portray the diversity of experiences and ideas in a given society. Only through exposure to a wide range of perspectives can citizens begin to truly understand their society and make informed decisions. Mainstream ideas and the views of those in power have a variety of avenues through which they can be expressed, including that of the major media. The media, however, must serve the public interest by regularly including ideas that are outside the boundaries of the established consensus. In this way, media become a place where old ideas can be scrutinized and where new ideas can emerge and be debated. With a focus on diversity that welcomes disagreement and dissent, media can make a significant contribution to democratic public life.

In the context of a large and complex media system, diversity has several meanings. At the most general level, a healthy public sphere is nourished by a media system that provides a diverse menu of media fare. Citizens should have a wide range of options in both content and format. Television systems, for example, should provide different kinds of programming and provide viewers with choices among substantively different alternatives. Book publishers and music labels should offer a wide range of types of books and music, giving citizens choices that include the traditional and the innovative, the currently popular and the less known.

On a more specific level, the public interest is enhanced by a media system that presents a diversity of views and stories, giving citizens a window on their world that is multicultural and offers many different perspectives. Diversity in this sense refers not only to differences in race, class, and gender but also to substantive political or ideological differences. It does little to enhance diversity to have more women and minorities as political commentators if, for example, all they do is repeat well-worn assumptions that had previously come from white men. Citizens should have access, among the diverse media fare, both to people and views that they find similar and to people and views that are very different from their own. In addition, a vibrant public sphere is nurtured not only by media products that are considered "serious" but also by media that give citizens pure diversion and the opportunity for enjoyment. A diverse media system offers media that are serious, challenging, and issue oriented; media that are fun and entertaining; and much that is both informative and entertaining at the same time.

Until recently, advocates of a public interest approach focused almost exclusively on the importance of news media for public life. That was because the information provided in the news was so obviously a central requirement for an active citizenry. However, it is a mistake to see news as the only media form that contributes to democracy. Other types of media play important roles as well. Internet Web sites, talk radio programs, and television talk shows all facilitate public dialogue about current issues. Books can contribute to and spur public discussion. Even films and music can participate in and stimulate public debate about significant ideas and issues.

Media do not have to be explicitly "informational" to engage with public issues. We encounter public life through the stories we hear, tell, and experience. Today, it is our media, both new and old, that are our preeminent storytellers. As a result, forms of media that we classify as entertainment can play an important role in public life through the stories that they circulate.

The flip side of diversity is homogeneity. As we will see later, market forces tend to promote homogeneous media products, as firms attempt to reach broad mainstream audiences. The "formula" system behind many Hollywood movies and the standardized formats adopted by most local news broadcasts are just two examples of homogenized media. However, this homogenization strategy tends to squelch media that are offbeat or idiosyncratic because they do not have a broad appeal. In effect, it helps undermine diversity. Serving the public interest requires a media system that is innovative and diverse in both substance and style. From the profit-oriented market model perspective, this kind of approach is risky. From a public interest–oriented public sphere perspective, this kind of approach is essential.

Substance and Innovation Without Elitism

The media also serve the public interest to the extent that they provide citizens with substantive information and innovative entertainment. A diverse array of formulaic "fluff"—or many different versions of "reality television"—is no diversity at all. The public sphere model acknowledges that what people *want* may not always be the same as what they *need*. Media need to serve as spaces within which citizens may be informed, engaged, challenged, and entertained. In the course of providing such substance and innovation, media must avoid propagating elitism.

Media must be willing to devote the space, time, and resources to informing the public about substantive issues, providing a wide range of perspectives. They must find new and engaging ways to communicate this information. In doing so, they must directly speak to the apathy and cynicism of many Americans. For example, in national elections, roughly half of all eligible voters stay away from the polls. The nonparticipation rate is even higher for state and local elections. Still, most media stick to well-worn horse race–style election coverage, tracking daily assessments of who is winning, inadvertently contributing to the alienation many people feel from political life. Media that truly served the public interest would use such events to substantively examine the challenges facing our democracy. Who are these nonvoters? Why have they stayed away from the polls? What do these nonvoters think about the political process? Why do they so often see the choice of candidates as no choice at all? Why do other democracies have much higher voter turnout? Can we learn something from these other democracies? Seriously and regularly addressing such questions would be a step toward including the views of many who are now left out of an election process—as entertainment aimed primarily at "likely voters." It would also begin to spark more debate and discussion about how to revitalize our democracy and make it more inclusive. That would be a key element of substantive election coverage.

In entertainment media, innovation and risk taking—including promoting fresh perspectives, developing new formats, and welcoming controversy—are part of what it means to serve the public interest. Because such efforts can be financially risky, market-driven media are loath to regularly take such an approach. In addition, mainstream media advocates point to the millions of people who pack movie theaters, buy CDs, and watch television shows as evidence that they are already giving the people what they want. In fact, market enthusiasts have effectively painted public interest advocates as elitists who think they know the public's interests better than the public does.

Public sphere advocates need to take such charges seriously, in part because some critiques of commercial media *can* be elitist. The potential danger in the market model is that only what is widely popular may be considered valuable—important contributions that are out of the mainstream may be left out. The potential danger in the public sphere model is that only what is approved by the elite may be considered valuable—important contributions that are broadly popular may be left out. For example, according to Ien Ang, public service broadcasting in Britain was long considered to be a benevolent, but paternalistic, effort to promote and preserve the "best" of British culture.[18] There is certainly value in nurturing aspects of culture that are not widely popular, but such efforts must avoid paternalism by focusing on inclusive diversity rather than on the promotion of more rarefied definitions of "quality" media.

We must also remember that the public sphere approach to media is only elitist if we assume that popular desire is born and not made. We know, however, that popular tastes are shaped—for example, by a media industry that sometimes spends more on advertising and promoting a film than on making it. In fact, a whole range of decisions are made by the powerful media industry elite that greatly influence the range of media to which we are regularly exposed. Before the public ever gets to choose, record companies pick which of their bands will and will not receive support with major promotional campaigns. Book publishers decide, prior to publication, which books are likely to be bestsellers and which have narrower appeal. Television network executives can, in essence, decide the fate of a program by whether it is placed in a popular time slot or relegated to the scheduling equivalent of Siberia. In its own way, then, the commercial media industry—and the advertisers who support it—impose their own preferences on the public, although the rhetoric of the market often cloaks these routine decisions. Isn't this, too, a form of elitism?

By focusing on the importance of the public interest, public sphere advocates are underscoring the value of extraeconomic goals such as diversity, substance, and innovation. Citizens need both information and entertainment, but on both counts, they need to have the opportunity to see their own experiences reflected and to be challenged by others. In short, when we talk about the public interest, we are identifying the media system as one of the key arenas in which citizens are constituted, are informed, and can deliberate.

❖   CONFLICTING LOGICS

The two approaches we have been exploring—the market and the public sphere models—provide different lenses for seeing and evaluating recent developments in the media industry. The market model frames a great deal of public discourse about the media industry and is the only language with any currency in the media business itself, but whenever critics or citizens complain about the performance of mass media, public sphere concerns are likely to be present.

Exhibit 1.2 summarizes some of the principal differences between these two approaches, demonstrating that the market and public sphere frameworks provide distinct perspectives on fundamental media questions.

One of the most telling differences between these two approaches is their divergent ways of envisioning the audience. The market model views the audience as a market of consumers both of media products and of the goods and services presented in the accompanying advertising. *Diversity*, from this perspective, is primarily a strategy for targeting particular demographic market segments. In the public sphere model, the audience is not conceived as a market, nor are individual members of the audience seen simply as consumers. Instead, the audience is perceived as a public, who, according to Ien Ang, should be "reformed, educated, informed as well as entertained—in short, 'served'—presumably to enable them to better perform their democratic rights and duties."[19]

The market model view of the audience is certainly the predominant, perhaps the only serious, perspective within the media industry.

Exhibit 1.2 Summary of Media Models

	Market Model	Public Sphere Model
How are media conceptualized?	Private companies selling products	Public resources serving the public
What is the primary purpose of the media?	Generate profits for owners and stockholders	Promote active citizenship via information, education, and social integration
How are audiences addressed?	As consumers	As citizens
What are the media encouraging people to do?	Enjoy themselves, view ads, and buy products	Learn about their world and be active citizens
What is in the public interest?	Whatever is popular	Diverse, substantive, and innovative content, even if not always popular
What is the role of diversity and innovation?	Innovation can be a threat to profitable standardized formulas. Diversity can be a strategy for reaching new niche markets.	Innovation is central to engaging citizens. Diversity is central to media's mission of representing the range of the public's views and tastes.
How is regulation perceived?	Mostly seen as interfering with market processes	Useful tool in protecting the public interest
To whom are media ultimately accountable?	Owners and shareholders	The public and government representatives
How is success measured?	Profits	Serving the public interest

For example, the so-called educational news program *Channel One,* which provides a 12-minute program (including 2 minutes of ads) to more than eight million school children each day, uses the language of the public sphere model in telling school administrators that it is interested in promoting active citizenship. In its promotional material directed at potential advertisers, however, *Channel One* boasts about its unique ability to provide a "direct pipeline" to a highly coveted teen market. In the market model, audiences are valued solely for their potential purchasing power, because what matters most is whether people purchase media products (books, CDs, movie tickets, etc.) and make themselves available to the advertisers who pay for access to our attention (through television, radio, magazines, etc.). As a result, those who lack significant purchasing power, especially the poor, are of little interest to the media industry.

Even in noncommercial media explicitly identified as a nonprofit public service, it can be difficult to escape the market mentality. In recent years, public television in the United States has responded to the growth of cable and satellite television by identifying more aggressive promotion as a key to future success. Although there are crucial differences between public and commercial television, public television still operates squarely within a market framework. The audience, although smaller than its commercial counterparts, is pitched to potential sponsors as an attractive market because it is more upscale than the network audience and has great buying power. Public broadcasters have identified the PBS brand as a potentially valuable commodity and have developed promotional strategies and additional revenue streams based on extending the PBS brand beyond television to records, books, online sites, and so on. This includes developing brand name merchandise, particularly for children, derived from PBS programs.

The media's role in facilitating democracy and encouraging citizenship has always been in tension with its status as a profit-making industry. Mediating between these two has been the government, whose regulations (or lack thereof) have fundamentally shaped the environment within which the media operate. The next chapter reviews this regulatory environment and explores how media policy has changed with the explosion of mass media.

2

The Rise and (De)Regulation of the Media Industry

The media and entertainment industry is among the fastest growing sectors of the American economy, producing an expanding variety of products that are ubiquitous in our everyday lives. The history of media's growth and the interplay between the business of media and the regulation of media are the subjects of this chapter. We can give only a brief sketch of this complex history, but it provides some context for our later discussion of more recent changes. We begin with a case study as one example of the growth of media companies, the evolution of the media industry, and the central role regulators have played at key moments in media history.

❖ THE CHANGING BUSINESS OF MEDIA AND REGULATION: THE CASE OF ABC AND DISNEY[20]

Since the early 1980s, the business barons from Hollywood and Wall Street have gathered annually for an exclusive media and technology conference in Idaho's Sun Valley, hosted by investment banker Herbert A. Allen, Jr. The heads of large media conglomerates and communications companies, and major investors such as billionaires Ted Turner, Bill Gates, and Warren Buffett, meet and discuss business in what *Newsweek* magazine described as an "annual mogulfest" that is always "packed wallet to wallet." A *Washington Post* reporter quipped that at these events, "The sports of choice are golf, tennis and rearranging the pieces of the entertainment industry."

At Allen's 1995 retreat, Disney CEO Michael Eisner bumped into billionaire investor Warren Buffet—who owned 13% of Capital Cities/ABC. Out of the blue, Eisner asked if Disney might be able to buy Cap Cities. "I just spit it out," Eisner later recalled. Buffet was interested, and he invited Eisner to a picnic with Cap Cities/ABC chief Tom Murphy to discuss the issue. With that, the stage was set for what, up to that point, was the biggest media acquisition in history. The key players in this effort had previously discussed possible deals, but the chance meeting at that elite retreat triggered a week and a half of highly secret negotiations that quickly resulted in an agreement. The announcement of the megadeal stunned the business and media world and sent both Cap Cities/ABC and Disney stock soaring. In one day, Warren Buffet's investments increased in value by nearly half a *billion* dollars.

No one was more surprised by the whole deal than the host of ABC's *Good Morning America*, Charles Gibson. Twenty-five minutes after going on the air, Gibson learned through his earpiece from his producer that Disney had bought the network. Within the hour, Gibson was interviewing Eisner and Murphy about the $19 billion deal ($23.8 billion in constant 2004 dollars; subsequent references to mergers and acquisition values note the constant 2004 dollar value in brackets). When the enthusiastic Murphy asked Gibson if he were not proud about joining the Disney family, the visibly uncomfortable host tried a joke. "I never thought I'd work for a guy named Mickey," he said, referring to Disney's cartoon icon. Murphy did not laugh. The awkwardness continued later, when, in a closed-circuit news conference shown to ABC employees, ABC's evening news anchor, Peter Jennings, asked Eisner and Murphy whether "the sheer concentration of power, too much being held by too few hands" was good for the public.

Many concerns about Disney's takeover took the form of Mickey Mouse jokes. Editorial cartoons appeared showing ABC news anchor Peter Jennings and *Nightline* host Ted Koppel wearing Mickey Mouse ears. An illustration of Mickey Mouse in a three-piece business suit smoking a big cigar accompanied a national newsmagazine's story about the deal. Invoking the famous tag line from TV's old *Mickey Mouse Club,* ABC journalist Jeff Greenfield joked that maybe the network's slogan would become "AB—See ya real soon."

Jokes aside, the Disney–Capital Cities/ABC deal was an example of the rapidly changing nature of media ownership in the late 20th century. This deal was also an example of the tendency of federal regulators since the mid-1980s to allow consolidation in the media industry to advance relatively unchecked. Finally, despite regulator approval, this deal raised serious concerns about media consolidation, as suggested by Gibson's awkward exchange and Jennings' question.

When Cap Cities chief Tom Murphy was asked, in the wake of the Disney deal, about his proudest achievement, he readily acknowledged, "Money is how I've always kept score." That is what worries so many people. If money and profits are the only scorecards by which we measure the media industry—the market model approach that we outlined in chapter one—then the public interest concerns at the heart of the public sphere approach are left out in the cold. For example, there is often concern about the level of commitment that profit-oriented executives of entertainment conglomerates have to news divisions that historically have had a more public-interest orientation.

Although much of the media's most dramatic growth and change took place in the late 20th century, industry change and the questions it raises about the relationship between media and society go back much further. Buried in the history of the companies involved in the Disney deal is the story of a rapidly growing industry and the shifting terrain upon which the profits versus public interest debates have taken place. At various times, changing technologies, evolving political preferences, and varying social norms have contributed to one side or the other increasing its influence.

The Rise and Assimilation of ABC[21]

The genealogy of ABC can be traced back to the Radio Corporation of America (RCA) (see Exhibit 2.1). RCA had been created in 1919 as a joint venture by Westinghouse, General Electric, AT&T, and United Fruit. Because it owned the patents on key radio technology, RCA had a virtual monopoly on that medium. RCA launched the National Broadcasting Company (NBC), which had two separate networks,

Exhibit 2.1   Key Moments in ABC's Corporate History

1919	Radio Corporation of America (RCA) created as joint venture by Westinghouse, General Electric, AT&T, and United Fruit. RCA later launches two radio networks, known as "Red" and "Blue."
1941	FCC rules that RCA must sell one of its networks; RCA sues to block FCC order, but court rules RCA's broadcast monopoly violates antitrust laws.
1943	Blue network is sold and renamed the American Broadcasting Company (ABC).
1948	Supreme Court rules against Hollywood studio monopoly.
1953	In compliance with the court's ruling, Paramount sells its theater chain, which then merges with ABC network.
1954	ABC launches joint ventures with Walt Disney to build Disneyland and create television program of the same name.
1966	International Telephone and Telegraph (ITT) attempt to take over ABC is abandoned after concerns over conflict of interest.
1985	Capital Cities buys ABC for $3.5 billion, leading to major cuts in ABC's news division.
1995	Disney buys Capital Cities/ABC for $19 billion.
2001	Disney purchases Fox Family Worldwide from News Corp. and relaunches the station as ABC Family.

known by the names "Red" and "Blue." However, in 1941, the courts found that RCA's broadcast monopoly violated antitrust laws. To promote competition in the newly emerging television medium, the FCC ordered NBC to sell one of its networks. In 1943, conservative businessman Edward Noble (inventor of Life Savers candy) bought the Blue network for $8 million [$88.3 million] and renamed it the American

Broadcasting Company (ABC). Out of an antimonopoly action, then, ABC was born.

Meanwhile, the Supreme Court ruled in 1948 that the ownership of movie studios, distribution networks, and theaters by a single company also constituted an illegal monopoly. We discuss this case further later on. To comply with the ruling, Paramount sold its theater chain. In 1953, this newly independent theater chain merged with the then-struggling ABC network. The ABC-Paramount merger raised new concerns. Two FCC commissioners voted against approving the merger because they believed the new company would again be a "monopolistic multimedia economic power." But the merger was approved.

A year later, ABC launched a joint venture with Walt Disney. ABC guaranteed $4.5 million ($32 million) of Disney's loans and invested in a one third ownership of a new Anaheim, California theme park, to be called Disneyland. In exchange, Disney provided the network with a new, 1-hour weekly TV program of the same title and gave ABC access to its 600-title library of animated feature films. The agreement was unusual at the time because movie studios resisted showing their material on television for fear that it would undermine the movie business. Disney, however, used the national television network platform to present a hodgepodge of animal documentaries, edited versions of Disney movies, and frequent "behind-the-scenes" features that blatantly promoted the Disneyland theme park and various studio projects. ABC also gave Disney a minute at the end of each Disney program to promote its latest film.

Concern about concentrated media power was raised again in 1966 when International Telephone and Telegraph (ITT)—a major conglomerate with a vast portfolio of international holdings—attempted to take over ABC. This time, the major concern was that the news division could be used to support the financial interests of ITT's many business efforts, an obvious conflict of interest. By a slim four to three vote, the FCC approved the merger. The majority of FCC commissioners argued that ITT's ownership of ABC would pose no more threat to journalistic integrity than RCA's ownership of NBC. However, Commissioner Nicholas Johnson responded that "to say that because RCA owned NBC, ITT must be allowed to acquire ABC, is to say that things are so bad there is no point in doing anything to stop them from getting worse." Invoking the interest of ABC's journalistic independence, the Justice Department asked the U.S. Court of Appeals to block the impending merger. Daunted by the likelihood of protracted litigation, ITT withdrew from the deal.

By the mid-1980s, cable television was emerging as a major competitor to broadcast television, and the political climate had changed significantly. Part of the Reagan administration's agenda was to *dereg*ulate businesses, and the media were no exception. Newly relaxed ownership rules and a sympathetic political environment resulted in all three TV networks changing hands with little concern from regulators. In 1985, it was announced that Capital Cities would buy ABC in a $3.5 billion ($6.2 billion) deal. The purchase was possible only because of the recent easing of regulations that allowed a network to own 12 television stations instead of the previous limit of seven. After the buyout, corporate pressure quickly forced the ABC news division to cut costs and become profitable, like the entertainment divisions. By 1987, about 300 news staffers had lost their jobs—one fifth of the entire news division. After ownership changed at NBC and CBS, a similar orientation toward enhancing profits also occurred at those news divisions.

The deregulatory environment still ruled in 1995 when Disney—another company with a web of holdings—bought Cap Cities/ABC for a startling $19 billion ($23.8 billion) in what was then the largest buyout in U.S. media history and the second largest in all of U.S. business history. Investor Warren Buffet publicly boasted that the deal was a "merger of the No. 1 content company with the No. 1 distribution company." In another era, this would have been the very definition of a monopoly. This time, antimonopoly concern from regulators was nowhere to be found.

Instead, Congress was, at the time, making plans to again *ease* the restrictions on the number of media outlets a single company could own. Although most politicians did not appear to be concerned about the mergers, consumer advocates were. Gene Kimmelman, codirector of the Consumers Union, noted, "The marketplace is receiving a green light from Congress to consolidate in a manner that is dangerous to the development of multimedia competition." Regulators, however, did not share this concern.

Since its acquisition of Capital Cities/ABC, Disney has continued to expand; most recently, Disney purchased Fox Family Worldwide and launched the new ABC Family cable channel. Disney is one of the leading global media giants, with revenues of more than $30 billion in 2004. In addition to its vast empire of Disney and ABC brands, its holdings in entertainment, sports, and news include some of the best known names in the world, including Touchstone Pictures, A&E, ESPN, NHL's Mighty Ducks of Anaheim, Hyperion Books, and the news programs *World News Tonight* and *Nightline*.

As the history of ABC and Disney shows, growth, mergers, joint ventures, and debates about ownership issues are nothing new in the media business. As this history also shows, however, concerns about the impact of profit seeking on the public interest are also long-standing. To better understand both, it is useful to look more closely at the growth of the media industry, its shifting response to new technologies, and the evolving efforts to regulate it.

❖ THE GROWTH OF MEDIA

There are various ways to gauge the growth of the media industry over the past century. One simple way is to catalogue the emergence of new forms of media technology during that time: movies, radio, television, computers, videocassette recorders, communication satellites, video games, and all forms of digital media are 20th-century media. As new media technologies developed, media products proliferated, adding to a growing menu of media options.

Another important sign of the growth of the media industry is the remarkable expansion in the range of the places where we consume media. The printed word, in the form of newspapers or books, has long been portable. Reading is possible just about anywhere that there is adequate lighting and whenever the eyes are not being used for other activities. Early forms of other media usually required the consumer to go to a special place to use the particular medium. People went to the theater to watch a film. They sat in their living rooms to listen to gramophones or to the early, large radio consoles. Later, they did the same with television. By the late 1980s, the bulky home computer was providing early glimpses of the Internet and other digitally based media.

But in the development of each medium, portability was eventually introduced, allowing for the expansion of media into many other social spaces. The radio left the living room to become commonplace in other parts of the house and in automobiles. Eight-track and cassette tape players, too, became common equipment in cars, eventually to be displaced by CD players. Portable media equipment, such as the transistor radio and the Walkman tape player, meant that people could listen to music just about anywhere—while riding the bus or subway, working out at the gym, or walking in the park. Soon, MP3 players, such as Apple's iPod, permitted listeners to carry their entire music collection—with thousands of songs—on a hand-held device that could be used with headphones or plugged into speakers. Televisions became much smaller, entering bedrooms, kitchens, and other areas of the house. TV screens also went public, appearing routinely in airports, bars, banks, classrooms, and other locations; tiny portable screens began appearing on camping expeditions, beach trips, and other outings. Television screens and DVD players became optional equipment in minivans and some automobiles. With videotape and digital video-disks, movies could go anywhere that television screens were available. The office personal computer has given many workers routine access to the Internet, but home and office PCs are being supplemented with laptop computers and a host of smaller, more portable computer devices that can access the Internet and perform other computer functions, all without wires. The cell phone, with the capacity to take and transmit pictures, send text messages, and browse the Internet on a pocket-sized device, is indicative of how the media world continues to expand. In effect, the opportunities for media consumption have expanded dramatically and become fluid, entering all social spaces and becoming an intimate part of our daily lives.

With this expansion has come growth in the circulation of various forms of media in the United States. Daily newspaper circulation grew from 41 million in 1940 to more than 62 million in 1990, before declining to 55 million by 2003 in the face of new forms of electronic competition.[22] The number of books published rose from 91,514 during all of the 1940s to 175,000 in 2003 alone.[23] The number of cable television subscribers increased from 650,000 in 1960 to 74 million by 2004.[24] The sales of recorded music grew from $2.4 billion in 1975 ($8.5 billion) to more than $14 billion ($15.5 billion) in 2000, before declining to $10.7 billion in 2003 ($11.1 billion).[25] Sales of prerecorded home entertainment—on videocassettes and DVDs—to U.S. dealers rose from 3 million units in 1980 to more than 1.3 billion in 2003.[26] With the exception of the newspaper industry—where consolidation has led to declining circulation for daily newspapers, although Sunday newspaper circulation has remained stable and ad revenues have increased—the distribution, revenues, and audience size of other sectors of the media industry expanded dramatically in the last half century.

Newer segments of the media industry grew at an extraordinary pace in recent years. The cellular telephone industry, increasingly integrated into the audio and video industry, increased in number of subscribers from 5 million in 1990 to 159 million in 2003. The number of employees in the cellular telephone industry also grew dramatically, from 21 million to more than 205 million between 1990 and 2003.[27] The percentage of households with Internet access grew from 26% in 1998 to 55% in 2003.[28] And the video game industry, which emerged with the 1985 launch of Nintendo's NES console in 1985, exploded in the late 1990s, growing from fewer than 25 million game-playing households in 1998 to 55 million video game–playing households in 2004. In 2001, the video game industry, with annual revenues in excess of $10 billion per year, surpassed the film industry's domestic box office receipts, and video gaming continues to grow at a rapid pace, with industry analysts projecting revenue growth to $16 billion by 2008.[29]

Finally, there are plenty of economic data that demonstrate the growth of the media industry over the past half century. Perhaps the most dramatic growth has been in the size of the advertising industry. Between 1950 and 2003, the total amount spent on advertising in the United States—in constant 2004 dollars—increased from $44.7 billion to more than $258.6 billion.[30] Advertising revenue increased substantially in all of the four largest ad-supported media—newspapers, radio, television, and magazines (see Exhibit 2.2)—in the period between 1980 and

Exhibit 2.2   Advertising Revenue, 1950-2003, in Constant 2004 Dollars

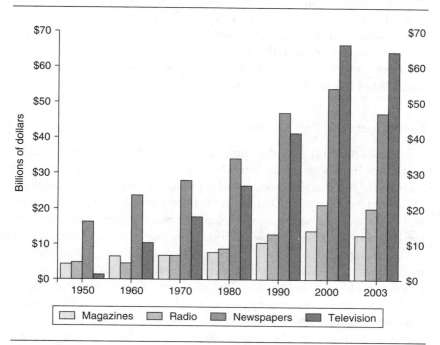

Source: U.S. Bureau of the Census (1981, 1990, 2004-2005).

2003. At the same time, a new medium emerged, the Internet, which grew from zero advertising in 1990 to more than $7.3 billion in 2003.[31] Internet advertising grew significantly in 2004, with industry analysts projecting that Internet ad revenue will reach $13.8 billion by 2006.[32]

All of this growth in the media has had major social and political implications, in addition to economic significance. The omnipresence of media is a very recent phenomenon that has literally changed how we live and how we learn about the world beyond our immediate experience. The very fact that "round-the-clock" media seem so unremarkable is an important sign of how much the media industry has influenced us. At the same time, however, social and political factors have affected the economic development of the media industry. The sociology of media highlights this two-way interaction between media and society.[33]

❖ THE EVOLUTION OF MEDIA

The interplay of media and society has been shaped significantly by the emergence of new technologies. As the media industry grew through the 20th century, it also evolved to incorporate and adapt to new forms of media. Thus, although many of the underlying questions about the relationship between for-profit media and a vibrant public sphere cut across historical periods, the business strategies of media corporations have been rooted in a specific historical context and technological climate. What follows is a brief overview of this evolution.

Newspapers and Press Barons

Critics of today's media conglomerates often appear nostalgic for some past time when short-term, bottom-line pressures were not such a powerful force in the media world. In fact, an implicit underpinning of contemporary press criticism seems to be the image of a news media less focused on attracting an audience and more geared toward informing the public. Critics of newer forms of electronic media, from television onward, often identify the era when print was the dominant medium as the model of a public service media system.[34]

It would be a mistake, however, to assume that profit pressures on media content are a new or even recent development. Such pressures have shaped mass media at least since the development of a popular commercial press in the 19th century. Instead of drawing a clear dividing line between the "serious" news of a past, print-oriented era and the "soft" news of the present, image-oriented era, we need to see how business strategies within the media industry have evolved as media conglomerates grew and new technologies emerged. During our examination of this evolution, we must also pay attention to the historically unique and medium-specific ways that profit orientation has influenced media companies.

The newspaper industry has long been shaped by business dynamics that stress audience size and advertiser satisfaction. In fact, we would have to go back a long way, to the partisan press of the early 19th century, to find news that was not shaped by such business concerns. During the era of the partisan press, when newspapers were run primarily by political parties, the news was linked to broader political goals rather than to economic ones. News content was aimed at achieving these political goals. Still, as media historian Gerald Baldasty has shown, the press moved toward a commercial model in the second half of the 19th century as the emphasis shifted away from political information and persuasion and toward profit making. The result of commercialization, according to Baldasty, was the beginning of news that needed to entertain readers—the precursor of the often-lamented tendency of today's mass media to attract a large audience by aiming programming toward the lowest common denominator.[35] With a profit orientation, it mattered less what the media content was, as long as it translated into profits.

As the news became a commercial entity in the late 19th century, newspapers began to develop new strategies to attract readers. No longer did newspaper owners assume that they were printing political information for the party faithful. Instead, the new commercial press sought to sell papers to a broad public and turn that large circulation into revenue by selling space in the newspaper to advertisers wanting to reach a mass audience. To reach this mass audience, newspapers broadened the types of stories they covered and began to move away from a strict focus on politics to include regular coverage of such areas as sports, entertainment, and fashion. Such coverage not only enhanced the appeal of the newspaper to new groups of potential readers, it also helped to attract new advertisers trying to promote products in related areas. Even today, when newspapers add new sections—on technology or home improvement, for example—it is a good bet that the driving force behind the expansion is the opportunity to bring in new advertisers.

As the commercial news industry grew in the late 19th century, the newspaper business became increasingly competitive. When William Randolph Hearst bought the *New York Journal* in 1895, New York became the focus of a long-standing competition for readers between Hearst's newspaper and Joseph Pulitzer's *New York World*. Pulitzer, who took over the small-circulation *World* in 1883, increased circulation tenfold in his first year by filling the paper with a combination of sensational human interest stories, juicy headlines, and illustrations, along with hard-edged stories and editorials that focused on social injustices. This "new journalism" was widely copied at the time and proved to be a formula that significantly boosted circulation. When Hearst arrived on the scene, the circulation wars heated up, as both the *World* and the *Journal* made efforts to outflank each other. The result was a turn toward an even more sensational version of the news, full of inflammatory headlines and garish pictures, with stories that focused on sex and scandal.

This style, dubbed "yellow journalism" (the precursor of today's tabloid news) was most visible during the months leading up to the Spanish American War in 1898. Led by Hearst's reporters, many newspapers were full of sensational stories of atrocities committed by the Spanish in Cuba. Hearst, a proponent of American military involvement, encouraged intervention with dramatic stories of injustice in Cuba. The stories made for good newspaper copy, but they were often of questionable veracity. In a now famous incident, after hearing that his reporter and illustrator planned to leave Cuba because the situation was so quiet, Hearst cabled his staff in Havana with the message: "Please remain. You furnish the pictures and I'll furnish the war."[36]

By 1908, Hearst owned nine newspapers (including three in New York and two in Chicago) and a major wire service, giving him a burgeoning newspaper empire that would grow into the multimedia Hearst Corporation. At Hearst's papers, sensational stories and political influence went hand in hand. In addition to his reporting about the conflict in Cuba, Hearst used his papers and their sensational style to criticize political corruption and attack his political enemies.

Hearst papers regularly vilified President William McKinley and railed against the large corporate "trusts." Perhaps most of all, Hearst's papers supported his many campaigns for public office, including a successful run for Congress and unsuccessful bids to become mayor of New York City, governor of New York State, and president of the United States. Throughout all these campaigns, Hearst used his newspapers to attack his opponents, promote his own name and stature, and cover issues in ways favorable to his campaign. Ultimately, Hearst was not nearly as successful a political candidate as he was a businessman. Still, Hearst remained a high-profile figure with political influence, largely because his newspaper empire gave him a national platform that was rare for his day.[37]

For Hearst, media ownership was an avenue into politics. Even when he did not hold office, he wielded influence through his crusading and sensational newspapers. Hearst's complex role as journalist, businessman, and politician shows both the business dynamics that push news toward entertainment and the political questions raised by the growth of media conglomerates.

Radio and the Rise of Corporate Media

In the early years of the 20th century, a struggle for control of radio and over the definition of its proper use brought corporate interests, the U.S. military, and amateur operators into conflict. Corporate interests, including the American Marconi Company, owned by the man who had demonstrated the use of his "wireless" at the 1899 America's Cup in New York City, sought private control of the airwaves, to use them for profit. The U.S. Navy sought government control of the airwaves, to use them for official purposes, especially during wartime. Amateur radio enthusiasts, known as "radio boys" in the years before 1920, saw the airwaves as a form of public property, to be used by citizens to communicate with each other.

Before 1920, corporate "wireless" operators saw radio as a form of point-to-point communication. At the same time, amateurs were beginning to listen to radio for pleasure and were experimenting with broadcasting music and information. Radio changed dramatically in 1920 when a Pittsburgh department store, hoping to increase sales of their radio equipment, ran a local newspaper advertisement for a musical program broadcast by amateur Frank Conrad. Shortly thereafter, Westinghouse, one of the major manufacturers of radio sets, began financing Conrad's station as a means of selling its radios. Radio manufacturers and department stores quickly jumped into the business of broadcasting by setting up stations to stimulate sales of radio sets. In 1922, with radio listening becoming a popular activity, telephone company AT&T established WEAF in New York and began selling airtime in what was called "toll broadcasting," the precursor to sponsored programming and broadcast advertising. The broadcast model, with an emerging mass audience and programming financed by the sale of airtime, was now in place.[38]

Even as the broadcast model emerged, however, the organization of the new broadcast industry was still up for grabs.[39] Who would have access to the airwaves and under what conditions? What role would the government play in regulating the medium? In the wake of World War I, the U.S. government was concerned that foreign business interests led by Marconi would dominate the radio business. In response, it incorporated the Radio Corporation of America with the help of AT&T, Westinghouse, and General Electric. As the debate over how to organize the emergent radio industry evolved in the 1920s, the corporate players and their allies in government argued that a profit-based, commercial radio industry was best suited to serve the national interest.

They made their case by contrasting their preferred model of a corporate-organized broadcasting system with either an industry dominated by "foreign interests" or radio run by the government. A radio industry led by American corporations would not be a threat to the nation, they argued, nor would it permit excessive government control of information.

In the early 1920s, then–U.S. secretary of commerce Herbert Hoover organized a series of conferences to explore the future of radio with various parties interested in the emerging industry. These conferences affirmed the notion that a corporate-led, commercial radio industry would best represent the general interest of the American public. The alternatives included reserving radio spectra for nonprofit use by amateurs and community groups. However, this was rejected as a system that would be oriented toward "special interests."

The result of these conferences was the Radio Act of 1927, which created the Federal Radio Commission (the precursor to the FCC), which had the principal task of granting federal licenses allowing stations to broadcast over the airwaves. This new licensing system, which gave licenses to for-profit broadcasters, established what became our commercial broadcasting system.

With technology evolving rapidly, however, this system was not cemented in 1927. Over the next several years, debate ensued about how and why nonprofits, such as educational groups, would be excluded in this new broadcasting industry. The underlying question in this debate was, If radio is such a powerful medium, shouldn't it be used for something other than programming to a mass audience and selling commercial products? The debate continued into the early 1930s, as broadcast reformers tried to carve out space for noncommercial uses of the airwaves, challenging the increasingly powerful radio industry. As late as 1935, Senator Robert Wagner introduced legislation that would have made all previous radio licenses null and void and set aside 25% of all the top AM frequencies for educational institutions. This would have reopened the question of whether broadcasting in the United States should be organized on commercial lines. Wagner's bill was doomed, however, because of lobbying from the National Association of Broadcasters, the primary organization representing the interests of commercial broadcasters. By 1935, the contours of the commercial broadcasting industry were firmly established. It was only in the late 1990s that community access to radio was again seriously debated. However, this new discussion was limited to licensing low-power radio stations to community groups to help fill the voids left by commercial radio. The National Association of Broadcasters again lobbied to prevent the licensing of low power stations, but limited licensing of 10- and 100-watt stations began in 2000.

By supporting new radio programs to stimulate sales of their hardware, then turning to advertising so that they could generate revenue from broadcasting (not just manufacturing), corporate broadcasters in the 1920s ultimately defined the underlying strategy of the industry that would predominate for nearly a half century. However, this commercial model of broadcasting did not just appear out of thin air, nor was it inevitable. The commercial model is no more "natural" than the very different model of state-organized broadcast systems—based on Britain's BBC—that emerged throughout most of Europe. In those countries, government, not corporations, played the central role in developing radio. Even in the United States, it took more than 20 years for the advertising-supported, for-profit radio industry to develop. This period included intense debate about the social implications and political ramifications of the newly emerging technology. It also saw a struggle between different sectors of society as the new ground rules were debated. The process of defining radio was social, not just economic; a process that established rules for the functioning of the emerging radio markets. In the case of the United States, commercial interests clearly were the victors over the concerns of other citizens.

The Television Era

Television arrived on the scene in the late 1940s and became a household staple faster than any previous home appliance. By 1960, almost 90% of American households had television sets, making television a central part of American life. Following the commercial model that had been shaped 25 years earlier by radio, the television industry—dominated by the same companies as radio—relied on the same program and revenue strategies that radio used so successfully in earlier decades.

The limited channel capacity and the significant investment capital required to produce television programming meant that the radio networks were in the best position—financially, technically, professionally, and politically—to exploit the new medium. As a result, until the late 1970s, television was dominated by three major networks (ABC, NBC, and CBS) with roots in the radio industry. As with radio, these television networks produced programs for a mass audience and sold the attention of these audiences to advertisers at a premium.

Throughout the 1960s and 1970s, the television networks regularly attracted larger audiences than any other form of media, with tens of millions of households tuned in to network programming each night. To meet profit expectations, network executives tried to schedule programs that would attract large audiences. They generally selected shows that were "safe"—that would not offend any significant portion of the potential audience. Because all three major networks were competing for shares of the mass mainstream audience, they followed similar business strategies that led them to develop very similar programs. In many respects, television of this period was a homogenized monopoly, with just three networks offering viewers little product diversity. The sameness of so much network television was no accident; it was the result of the underlying commercial logic of an industry focused on mass audiences.

Network television's success at garnering such large audiences made it the preferred destination for most national advertisers. After all, where else could advertisers reach such a sizable audience with visually attractive sales pitches? With advertisers providing virtually all of the revenue for the networks, television fast became more of an entertainment and marketing medium than a public service medium. Although critics regularly invoked the language of the Communications Act of 1934, which required broadcast stations to serve "the public interest, convenience, and necessity," the networks had little interest in developing programs that were oriented toward public service. News could bring prestige to the networks, but it was not seen as profitable. Similarly, there was little interest in quality children's programming. Perhaps most important, virtually all programming was bland and inoffensive so as not to drive away audiences or advertisers.

FCC Chair Newton Minow's famous 1961 speech to the National Association of Broadcasters made this point quite clearly. Minow criticized broadcasters for offering audiences a "vast wasteland" of programming and argued that commercial broadcasters were squandering the "public's airwaves."[40] Network television was a good forum for advertisers, entertaining diversion for viewers, and a source of large profits for the networks and affiliate stations. From a market model perspective, it was a success. But as Minow's comments pointed out, the commercial television industry did little to contribute to a vibrant public sphere.

Coexisting With Television

There can be little doubt that network television was the dominant medium of the second half of the 20th century. Even as the networks lost audience share in the 1980s and 1990s, network television continued to attract the largest media audiences and therefore continued to be an attractive medium for advertisers. When television rapidly became the dominant form of mass media in the United States, executives in other media industries were forced to develop new strategies to survive.

The challenge for the radio, film, newspaper, and magazine industries was to figure out how to coexist with television, which was eroding the size and attentiveness of their audiences. If television was a "movie theater in the home" or a "radio with pictures"—two of the early characterizations of the medium—then why would people go to the movies or turn on the radio? With television's seductive visual presence and no cover price, leaders in the print media worried that television would lure audiences away from reading.

Television did not destroy its rivals. Instead, it supplanted them, becoming the center of a multifaceted media industry. The older forms of media survived but had to change in the new climate. Market dynamics shaped this transition, as pretelevision media looked for strategies to increase revenues and cut costs. Older media found ways to respond to their increasing marginalization and were able to prosper economically. These developments were indicative of both the voracious appetite of Americans for mass media and of the complementary nature of the different media. These provided lessons that would propel a new wave of conglomeration in the 1980s and 1990s and shape the development of digital media in the early 21st century. Just as important, however, the survival of older forms of media demonstrates the limits of the mass audience approach of network television, which left large segments of the population available to be targeted by both new media products and advertisers.

Radio Survives

Radio survived the shift toward television by focusing on the youth market and, with the help of technological developments, becoming a local instead of national medium. Radio could not effectively compete directly with television for a national mass audience. Television sets rapidly took the place of radios in the family living room and popular radio programs and personalities quickly moved to television. In response, the radio industry changed formats in an effort to coexist with television. Radio stations moved away from the old staples of network serials and variety shows. In fact, fewer local stations were airing *any* network programs. Instead of traditional family entertainment fare, local radio stations focused more programming on music. New technologies, including advances in sound recording and the licensing of the FM portion of the spectrum in the 1950s, gave broadcast music a much clearer sound. At the same time, new and smaller radio sets were also becoming easier to manufacture and more affordable for the public.

As the radio moved out of the living room, households were likely to purchase smaller sets for their kitchens or bedrooms, and car radios became standard. As a result, radio survived the introduction of television by developing new formats that encouraged listeners to turn the radio on "in the background" while they did other things, something that was more difficult to do with a visual medium such as television. With the medium's new role, radio programmers looked for low-cost fare that did not require the undivided attention of the audience. Thus they replaced the celebrity host with the local deejay and substituted recorded music for costly original productions.

Perhaps most important, with television looking toward a mass audience defined largely in family terms, radio began to focus on the youth audience. Up to this time, many mass media firms had done little to target specific segments of the audience.

Indeed, the sheer size of the audience was the key to financial success. Radio, however, moved—at first tentatively in the 1950s and more boldly in the 1960s and beyond—to view teenage music listeners as their bread and butter. Historian James Baughman argues that it was television's success with the adult audience that forced local radio stations to seek out a new audience. It led local radio to attend to audience "subgroups."[41]

Even as radio moved from the center to the periphery of American life, the strategic decisions of radio station managers and the advertisers who supported them opened a new chapter in the media business. Because more media were competing for audience attention and advertising revenue, audiences that previously had been defined as too small to be important were now reconsidered. Youth had not been worth targeting when a broader mass audience was available. But with little chance of profiting with such a mass audience strategy because of television's appeal, radio focused on young people as a distinct audience segment and began programming rock 'n' roll music aimed at the youth market.

In retrospect, this was just the beginning, and the radio executives who moved toward this targeted approach were probably motivated by necessity, not by a vision of a new media world. By the 1980s and 1990s, however, with new audience measurement techniques available and the mass audience fragmenting much more, target marketing and segment programming would become the norm. The origins of this trend should be seen clearly. Efforts to appeal to audience subgroups did not arise from a public-spirited commitment to serving all sectors of the audience. It was market logic at work. The youth market was not fully tapped, either as a media audience or as an advertising target, and radio's focus on youth was an effort to exploit that untapped market. In the 1980s, cable's MTV would follow similar logic. In short, radio's early move toward youth audiences was the result of a business strategy in a medium that was trying to survive in the face of television's dominance.

Print Media Adapt

Print media also faced new challenges in the television era. As television grew more popular and moved to the center of American culture, the newspaper and magazine industries faced a twin threat.

Readers were spending more time with their eyes on the screen instead of the page, and national advertisers, convinced that audiences were headed toward television, were moving their campaigns to network television.

The rise of television did not spell the end of the print media. Even after the introduction of television, newspapers retained their role as the major providers of local news, but with growing competition for advertisers and a population that was moving to the suburbs, the urban newspaper business did begin to change. The steady decline of the two-paper town began in the 1950s, as a growing number of urban papers closed and suburban papers emerged. Facing threats to circulation, many newspapers cultivated a middle or upper middle class readership and began developing new advertising-friendly sections, trends that would only increase in the 1980s and 1990s. Gannett's launching of *USA Today* in 1982—a paper with bite-sized news stories and plenty of colorful photos and graphics sold in a vending box that resembled a television set—was indicative of the ways in which newspapers began to imitate the style and format of television.

The threat to magazines, many of which competed directly with television for national advertisers, was even more severe. Much like the radio industry, the magazine industry retooled and adapted to the new media environment. Economic necessities were the key factors shaping the evolution of magazines. In the 1950s, industry leaders began to transform their products to survive in an era when they would be a secondary medium in the shadow of television.

The magazine industry followed a strategy similar to radio; general interest national magazines became specialized magazines with demographically targeted audiences. One indication of change in the magazine industry was the financial failure of several high circulation national magazines. Between 1969 and 1972, three of the most widely read magazines in the country—the *Saturday Evening Post, Life,* and *Look*—all folded. Each of these weekly magazines had more than 6 million readers, but they all had maintained such high circulation figures by charging very low subscription rates, counting on advertising revenues to stay afloat. As national advertisers shifted their attention—and their dollars—toward television, the national magazines that offered general interest fare to a mass audience (just what television was offering) quickly lost ground with advertisers.

Advertisers, in fact, deserted these national magazines before readers did. Despite continuing popularity among readers, the economics of the magazine industry led to the shutdown of these widely read publications. This is a classic example of the unique dynamics involved in the "dual-product" market within which media firms operate. In this case, even though magazines were able to attract a large readership, it was abandonment by advertisers that led to the demise of these publications. The market was responding to the "customer" who really mattered: advertisers.

With television dominating the national media scene, particularly in the eyes of advertisers, the magazine industry turned toward specialized publications for niche markets. Such targeted publications— for young women or sports fans or nature lovers—could succeed in financial terms with smaller circulations because they attracted specialized advertising that was directed at the target audience. Advertisers interested in reaching demographically specific audience segments (by age, gender, region, etc.) or readers with a passion for a specific set of activities (sports, cooking, etc.) were perfect matches for the new specialized magazines. These new magazines, which began to populate the newsstands beginning in the 1960s, provided a high-profile alternative for advertisers who did not want, or could not afford, the national marketing campaigns that were the domain of network television.

Another way in which the magazine industry responded to the ascendancy of television was by focusing attention on television itself. The success of *TV Guide,* launched in 1953, showed that magazines about television were popular with both audiences and advertisers. Over time, television and the more general world of celebrities and entertainment would become a staple of magazine content. In this way, the magazine industry helped to promote the television and movie industries and, simultaneously, attract readers because of their interest in television and movies. This prefigured the growing trend of "synergy" that would later drive the media industry toward horizontal integration, a subject we explore in later chapters.

Movies Evolve

For the movie industry, the rise of television presented an immediate and rather dramatic challenge. With television providing a version of the theater in the home, movie audiences had less incentive to go out for visual entertainment. Indeed, as television became a fixture in the American home in the 1950s, the movie industry struggled with severe economic problems. The number of theatergoers declined, theaters in less-populated areas closed, and the movie business began to lose its place in the cultural center.

Despite such economic woes, the movie industry, just like the other pretelevision media, survived the crisis brought on by the change in the media landscape. To do so, the movie industry developed new approaches to the business of movie making. Driven by efforts to keep costs down and maximize revenues, two of these strategies helped to set the stage for the growth of the multimedia conglomerates of the 1990s.

Fewer and "Bigger" Movies. To cut costs, the major movie studios started to produce fewer movies. Faced with a decline in audience size and with even loyal moviegoers attending movies less frequently, decreasing the number of new releases was an effort to bring the supply of movies in line with demand. Although the 1950s were a time of significant industry contraction, with a major cut in the number of employees in the movie business, the idea was not just to scale back the industry. Instead, as the strategy evolved, it was directed toward producing films that would be "bigger" and more glamorous than the programs available on the small television screen. Of course, such big films could be very expensive to produce and promote, but if they hit a chord with the public, these movies could return very large revenues. Thus, the cultural phenomenon of the "blockbuster" was born.

Blockbuster films are expensive, high-profile movies that, when successful, can return enough profit to cover the losses from dozens of other, less popular films. The late 1990s saw a renewed interest in "smaller," relatively cheap films that defied studio formulas but attracted substantial audiences. Still, blockbusters remain the center of the business strategy of the major movie companies.

The production and marketing of blockbuster films has come a long way since the 1960s. The roots of the blockbuster can be seen in the way that the movie industry adapted to the rise of its new cousin and competitor, television. The effort to define going to the movies as a festive and important cultural activity worth leaving home for, coupled with the strategy of trying to strategically focus the public's attention on a smaller number of motion pictures, helped produce a distinctive brand of movie making that emphasized an early version of the blockbuster.

Creating for Television. Instead of simply competing in what was a losing battle, Hollywood developed strategies for working with television. Because the networks sought to fill their airtime with visually oriented entertainment, the industry that had been producing such fare for the big screen was an excellent partner. After initially refusing to provide programs for television for fear that this would further erode theater audience, the film companies shifted gears when it became clear that television had become the dominant medium. By the late 1950s, Hollywood studios were the leading producers of prime-time network television programming, demonstrating the compatibility between these two rival industries.

Thus the movie industry became a supplier of programming for the dominant medium of the time, giving Hollywood a revenue stream that would complement its traditional box office receipts. Then, when the VCR became a household staple in the 1980s and the DVD player entered homes in the 1990s, video and DVD sales and rentals provided the movie business with a third major revenue stream. Perhaps most important, this supplier-broadcaster relationship between film and television was an early sign of the economic fit between television networks and movie companies. With broadcasters seeking to assert control over program production and movie studios looking for outlets to distribute and promote their products, from a market model perspective, the integration of the two industries made increasing economic sense.

Beyond the Broadcast Model

New forms of digital media emerged in the 1990s that began to move much of the industry beyond the "broadcast model" of media that the radio and television industries had pioneered. Rather than a limited number of media products supported entirely by advertisers targeted to a mass mainstream audience, the new media landscape featured many more media outlets producing content for smaller niche audiences available via various fee structures.

Two distinct marketing strategies emerged to give consumers access to vast libraries of media content. One approach is to sell media content in bite-sized units. For example, in a return to the days of marketing "singles," consumers can use the Internet to once again buy individual songs rather than a complete album. Similarly, cable television expanded its offering of "on demand" services, allowing viewers to purchase access to specific films or other programming, to be viewed at a time chosen by the viewer. Even newspapers began selling access to individual stories from their online archives for a small fee.

In contrast to this "bite-size" approach, the sale of subscription services is the other marketing strategy that has emerged as an alternative to the traditional broadcast model. In the most common example of this, the vast majority of U.S. households subscribe to either cable or satellite television systems and pay a monthly fee for access to dozens or hundreds of channels. The subscription model has moved to other forms of media as well. For example, the digital video recorders popularized by TiVo allow users to make better use of all those television channels—for a monthly subscription fee. Music enthusiasts can subscribe for a monthly fee to digital music services, such as Rhapsody, that provide unlimited listening access to thousands of songs via the Internet, or they can subscribe to satellite radio offering commercial-free music and programming. Movie lovers can pay a flat monthly fee to choose from vast online catalogs of DVDs that are delivered via the mail. Students and professors can pay a monthly fee to subscribe to an online library that includes access to tens of thousands of full-text academic books and articles.

The route to the Internet, too, includes a monthly subscription fee for online access. Some Internet Service Providers tried, but failed, in their effort to apply the broadcast model to the Internet. Providers such as NetZero—named for its initial plan of providing free Internet access—intended to sell advertisers access to their online users but had to revert to a fee-based system. Once online, web surfers find that a growing number of brand name Web sites have "premium" content available to subscribers only. Monthly or by-the-minute fees are also standard fare for cell phones, as they incorporate more media features—becoming digital cameras and photo distribution media, as well as tools for web surfing, text messaging, game playing, and television watching. What all these examples share is a shift from media content that is exclusively supported by advertisers, as with the broadcast model, to content that is accessed by consumers for a fee.

One result of the growth of fee-based digital media is the growing importance of the wires—or "pipeline"—that connects consumers to this panoply of media content. With the broadcast model, content was king. The key variable in that model was which programs would attract the largest and most desirable audience to sell to advertisers. Fee-based digital media have highlighted the significance of the physical infrastructure—phone lines, cable connections, and satellites—that facilitate access to the vast array of available media content. As the major media companies jockey for position in the digital media environment, questions about ownership of phone lines, cable companies, cell tower networks, and satellite systems are likely to be at the center of both corporate media strategy and media policy.

Setting the Stage for the Contemporary Media Industry

As early as the 1980s, many of the basic contours of the contemporary media industry were in place. The mass audience was fragmenting and more media were focusing on specific target audiences. The spread of cable television and a heightened emphasis by advertisers on the importance of demographics only enhanced this process of specialized media content and segmented media markets. In addition, with the audience continuing to fragment, the emphasis on the big hit—blockbusters, bestsellers, platinum records—only increased. With so many media competing for audience attention, and one major success potentially meaning the difference between profit and loss on the annual ledger sheet, hits and their accompanying stars became the driving forces in the media industry.[42]

Finally, with an increasing focus on the complementary nature of the different media, especially the benefits of promotional efforts across different media, the seeds of a new type of conglomeration were ready to grow. Earlier media conglomeration had seen efforts to build companies that controlled production and distribution within a single medium. By the 1980s, the stage was set for the new conglomerates that owned and operated production, manufacturing, and distribution across the range of different media industries. These developments were only reinforced by the later rise of digital media and fee-based services.

❖ MEDIA POLICY AND THE PUBLIC INTEREST

As the media industry has grown and changed during the past century, the definition of the kind of media industry that best serves the public interest has also evolved. Media policy, largely implemented by federal regulators, is a key factor that shapes the business strategies within the media industry. The effort to define the public interest and to craft and enforce rules that protect it play an important role in shaping the direction of the media system we have. As we have seen, the regulatory climate of the day led to the breakup of some early conglomerates; RCA was forced to sell one of its networks, which became ABC. Conversely, the *de*regulatory climate of the 1980s and 1990s helped spur the growth of new and bigger conglomerates. The public outcry over a new round of deregulation in the early 2000s suggests that questions about the obligations of media to the public are back on the table again.

In Whose Interest?

Media policy, the body of laws and regulations that influence the shape of the media world, is often misunderstood. In fact, with the First Amendment's guarantee of freedom of the press providing the foundation for government media relations in the United States, discussions of media policy often begin and end with an argument that government should maintain a "hands off" attitude when it comes to the mass media.

However, the situation is far more complex than the question of whether the government should intervene. As we saw earlier in this chapter, the commercial model of broadcasting—the advertising-sponsored, corporate-owned television and radio systems—emerged from government policies that defined the public interest in a particular way and awarded broadcast licenses to profit-seeking owners. The government, in effect, created and regulated an industry in such a way as to protect the interest of commercial broadcasters. Alternative models that were proposed, like the public service approach developed in Britain or a nonprofit model supported by educational groups, would have required a different set of media policies, protecting the interests of a different group of interested parties. In either case, government intervention would have been necessary.

Our commercial media system, therefore, relies on many different forms of government intervention to exist. For example, government policy that makes advertising costs tax deductible is a crucial part of what makes advertising-oriented media—newspapers, magazines, television, radio—financially viable. Special postal rates facilitate subscription-based media. Copyright law serves the interests of just about all media by making it illegal to repackage and sell, for example, books or videos without permission of the copyright holder. In short, the media industry relies on a complex set of laws and regulations that help to define both the playing field and the rules of the game. Rather than *whether* the government should intervene, the real issue is *how* the government should intervene.

Antitrust Law

Among the various policy tools that the government has employed in its regulation of industry is the Sherman Antitrust Act. The Sherman Act, originally the basis for breaking up industrial monopolies such as Standard Oil in the early 20th century, is intended to protect the public from the power and control of the major owners in highly concentrated industries. When a small number of owners control a particular industry, they can exercise inordinate power in determining distribution, prices, and the development of new products or related industries. In short, the Sherman Act makes monopoly ownership unlawful if it harms the public, gives monopoly owners an unfair advantage in other industries, or restrains new competition.

The specific meanings and uses of antitrust law have been debated throughout the 20th century and beyond. Policy makers and legal scholars face complex questions about the definition of *monopoly*, what is harmful to the public, and what makes for an unfair advantage. Antitrust is best understood on a case-by-case basis, because each effort to use antitrust law must include a specific argument as to why a particular industry structure is illegal. In addition, antitrust actions require political will, because the targets are generally powerful and successful corporations. As a result, it can be difficult to make generalizations about the legal status of corporate monopolies. The highly concentrated media industry has at times been defined as acceptable and at other times has been the subject of legal challenges.

Perhaps the best known antitrust action in the media industry was the 1940s breakup of the motion picture monopoly. At the time, a round of media mergers had left the movie industry dominated by five major companies that produced, distributed, and exhibited films across the nation—Fox, RKO (Radio-Keith-Orpheum), Warner Brothers, Loew's, and Paramount. These five companies produced most of the popular films of the time and owned large theater chains, mainly in the most populated metropolitan areas. As a result, the U.S. Justice Department argued that this ownership structure gave the five majors inordinate control over the industry. In particular, the Justice Department argued that the control of both production (movies) and exhibition (theaters), allowed the majors to inflate prices for films, made it virtually impossible for independent producers to gain access to movie theaters, and gave the majors the power to force independently owned theaters to show smaller, less popular films along with the hits. Neither small studios nor independent theaters could effectively compete with the major Hollywood studios, which had vertically integrated structures that gave them enormous competitive advantages.

In 1948, the U.S. Supreme Court ruled that the major movie companies were indeed exercising illegal control over the industry and that the ownership of movie studios, distribution networks, and theaters by a single company constituted an illegal monopoly. The court agreed with the Justice Department argument that the integrated ownership arrangement greatly reduced competition, threatening the First Amendment rights of citizens to have access to diverse ideas. The court ordered the majors to sell their theater chains and outlawed various trade practices that the studios had used to thwart independent producers. As a result of the ruling, the five majors divested themselves of various elements of their entertainment empires. This successful antitrust action had a dramatic impact on the motion picture industry, prying open a space in the film business for smaller producers and foreign films and giving movie theaters more independence.

The antitrust action that broke up what was called the Hollywood Studio System had a lasting impact on the media business, leading to long-standing concern among regulators and policy makers about vertical integration within the media industry. For example, in the 1970s and 1980s, in an effort to prevent a monopoly of television production and exhibition, the television networks were forbidden from owning the programs they broadcast. By the 1990s, however, in a climate of deregulation, movie studios were back in the business of owning distribution channels (both movie theaters and television networks), and the television networks were permitted to produce and own their programming.

In the late 1990s, the antitrust suit against Microsoft Corporation—the dominant computer software company, now increasingly involved in media ventures—raised new questions about monopoly within the rapidly changing media industry. The Justice Department argued that Microsoft had illegally used its monopoly of computer operating systems (Windows) to strong-arm others in the industry in ways that limited innovation and harmed consumers and to gain an unfair advantage in the development of Internet-oriented technologies. In particular, the government argued that the "bundling" of Microsoft's program Internet Explorer, which is used to browse the World Wide Web, with its Windows operating system illegally restrained the development of Web-browsing software and other Internet-oriented applications. The decision in April 2000 by Judge Thomas Penfield Jackson indicated that Microsoft had, indeed, violated antitrust law, and the Justice Department called for a breakup of the media and software giant. The decision was later overturned on appeal, on the grounds that Judge Jackson's comments to journalists during the trial gave an appearance of a bias against Microsoft. Although Jackson's "findings of fact" about Microsoft's business practices were largely unchallenged by the Court of Appeals, in 2001, the new Bush Administration elected not to pursue the breakup of Microsoft and agreed to settle the case.

Microsoft survived this long-running court battle, but its past business practices continued to haunt the software giant. In a series of suits, several competitors alleged various forms of antitrust violations, all of which led to out of court settlements. Microsoft paid AOL Time Warner $750 million to settle its suit over illegal actions taken against the Netscape browser, which competed with Microsoft's own Explorer browser. Microsoft paid Sun Microsystems $1.6 billion to settle a suit over various anticompetitive practices. It paid Novell $536 million to settle another similar suit. In 2003, RealNetworks sued, accusing Microsoft of illegally monopolizing the growing field of digital music and video with its Media Player program. In 2004, the European Commission agreed and fined Microsoft a record $497 million for antitrust violations.

The initial ruling in the Microsoft case, coupled with its ongoing legal problems, are likely to make this a kind of landmark of antitrust law for the information age.

Serving the Public Interest

Beyond antitrust actions to break up monopolies, media policy has been shaped by twists and turns in the definition of how best to serve the public interest. Since the initial Communications Act of 1934, which created the Federal Communications Commission, companies awarded broadcast licenses have been required to serve "the public interest, convenience and necessity." The meaning of *the public interest* and strategies for protecting it have been the subject of much debate. Beneath the competing rhetoric, "serving the public interest" has largely been associated with a vibrant media system that is open to various points of view and forms of expression.

Policy makers have, in large measure, based the rationale for media policy on the need for *competition* and *diversity* within the media industry. However, even these terms are often the subject of intense debate: How much competition? Among whom? What kind of diversity? How best to promote diversity? Also, it is not always clear that both competition and diversity can be promoted by the same policies. In fact, in highly concentrated industries, such as television or motion pictures, competition for the mass audience has historically led to imitation instead of innovation.

One series of policies has been defensive in nature. These policies try to prevent any single owner from controlling too large a slice of the media pie. For example, long-standing regulations have limited the number and reach of television and radio stations that any one company can own. Also, one owner cannot generally own a television station and a daily newspaper in the same city. This attempt to prevent monopoly can be justified from either a market or a public sphere perspective. From a market perspective, the lack of competition associated with monopolies undermines the various benefits provided by markets. From a public sphere perspective, monopolies are not likely to lead to diverse and independent media content. These defensive policies were historically driven by the goal of preventing media companies from controlling information and imagery too much or holding too much local market power. In sum, media policies governing ownership structures have been based on the assumption that a competitive media environment, resulting in many voices, best serves the public interest.

Other policies have tried to promote diversity more proactively. Rather than relying on competition, at times policy makers have implemented regulations with diversity as a principal goal. For example, the Fairness Doctrine, in effect from 1949 to 1987, required television stations to include "different opposing positions on public issues of interest and importance."[43] The Newspaper Preservation Act of 1970 permitted joint ownership or operation of daily newspapers in the same market in an effort to stop the decline of multinewspaper towns. In 1996, the FCC adopted new rules requiring television networks to broadcast at least 3 hours per week of educational children's programming.

Media companies have historically opposed all such regulations, arguing that such policies are intrusive, costly, and ultimately harmful to a public that is served by for-profit businesses operating in line with audience desires. As we will see, this view has become increasingly prevalent, even among policy makers, at a time when deregulation of the media and most other industries has been on the rise.

Deregulation and the Market

In the 1980s, policy makers in the Reagan Administration argued that most regulation of the media industry was, in fact, not in the public interest. Led by Reagan's FCC Chair Mark Fowler, whose metaphor of television as toaster-with-pictures captured the idea that the media industry was no different from any other industry, media policy in the 1980s emphasized the market model as a means for serving the public interest. From this perspective, the public interest could only be defined as what interested the public, as indicated by the media that were most popular.

This deregulatory approach is based on the market assumption that supply and demand is the only appropriate way of evaluating the public interest. Those media that serve some public interest are profitable and therefore survive; those media that do not serve the public interest eventually fail because they do not satisfy a significantly large enough constituency. From this perspective, there is very little need for a proactive media policy, because the market is essentially self-regulating. The public interest is served by unregulated, profit-seeking media aiming to satisfy public desires.

This kind of market approach to media policy pays little or no attention to policy goals that may not be economic in nature. There is little room for social goals such as diverse expression, a media environment that is informational and not purely entertainment oriented, or media for largely underserved publics. In the 1980s and 1990s, a wide range of media regulations were either loosened or lifted altogether. The Fairness Doctrine was abolished in 1987; the 1970 FCC regulations concerning financial interest and syndication ("fin-syn" rules) that prevented television networks from owning their own programming were lifted in 1993; policies limiting ownership of radio and television stations were relaxed in the 1980s and 1990s. More generally, federal regulators adopted a more relaxed attitude toward enforcing existing regulations. Broadcast station license renewals became a formality, as regulators opted not to regularly evaluate whether licensees served the public interest. Also, although the Children's Television Act was enacted in 1990, the Federal Communications Commission did little to enforce it, allowing stations to claim that old cartoons such as *The Jetsons* and *The Flintstones* were educational programming. It was only after educators and media advocacy groups mobilized a public campaign that new FCC rules requiring 3 hours each week of educational programming were instituted in 1996.[44]

Perhaps more important, the market model equates cultural worth with economic success—that which is profitable is valuable, and cultural goals that are not profitable are ultimately not worth achieving. When the market model drives media policy, the core agenda for policy makers revolves around how to "free" media companies from regulations so that they can pursue, most vigorously, their profit-maximizing strategies. Ultimately, in the deregulated media industry, it is business strategy, with its focus on attracting audiences and exploiting new markets, that furnishes the language of media policy.

By the mid-1990s, new digital technologies were rapidly evolving, the media industry was expanding, the major media conglomerates were continuing to grow, and more than a decade of market-oriented media policy had helped to move the dominant definition of *public interest* toward an interpretation that required a deregulatory stance. Major media and telecommunication companies, however, remained dissatisfied with a media policy that, despite recent deregulation, was still organized around the 1934 Communications Act. To move the media business into the digital age, exploiting the new technologies and developing innovative products, the major media companies argued for a wholesale rewriting of the laws and regulations that guide U.S. media policy.

With media industry lobbyists working hard on Capitol Hill and media companies providing large campaign contributions to both political parties, the stage was set for the most far-reaching media legislation in 50 years, the Telecommunications Act of 1996.[45] This act spurred major changes in the media industry and escalated the rhetorical conflation of the public interest with economic success. In 2003, the Federal Communications Commission, led by FCC Chair Michael Powell, moved to deregulate the media industry even further. Despite considerable public opposition, the FCC adopted new policies that would significantly weaken media ownership rules. However, a 2004 court ruling blocked implementation of these new ownership rules and renewed public and Congressional debate about media ownership policy.

In the next two chapters, we explore recent changes in media industry structure and strategies. These changes set the stage for the creation of the Telecommunications Act and, in turn, more changes were hastened by its passage.

PART II

Industry Structure and Corporate Strategy

Explaining the Rise of Media Conglomerates

3

The New
Media Giants

Changing Industry Structure

The industry publication *Advertising Age* compiles an annual list of the 100 largest U.S. media corporations, based on their media-related revenue. The ranking includes only media supported by advertising and thus leaves out important sectors, such as movie studios, but it still gives a useful overview of a significant part of the media industry. In 1984, the magazine identified the American Broadcasting Corporation (ABC) as the largest U.S. media company, with $2.8 billion ($5.2 billion) in U.S. revenues. Twenty years later, in the 2004 edition, Time Warner topped the list with $29.3 billion in U.S. revenues—about 6 times as much as the 1984 leader, after adjusting for inflation, and roughly the equivalent of 1984's top eight companies combined. The revenue that made ABC number one in 1984 would not even have qualified it for the top 10 in 2004; it would have been 14th. In addition, in the years since 1984, the *Ad Age* list has changed in an important way. It now includes data for total worldwide revenue. As the 2004 list showed, Time Warner, America's largest media company, generated another $10.3 billion *outside* the United States, for total annual revenue of $39.6 billion—nearly 8 times ABC's revenues from 20 years earlier.[46]

As such numbers reveal, the scale of the media industry has changed. Media companies have gotten much bigger, often by swallowing up other media firms to form ever larger conglomerates. As new media technologies have gained prominence—cable, Internet, satellite—these too have been swept up in the consolidation process. A quarter century of such mergers has transformed the organizational structure and ownership pattern of the media industry, leaving behind a few media giants.

❖ MAKING SENSE OF MERGERS

As we saw in the previous chapter, at various points in history, anti-monopoly concerns have resulted in the dismantling of media conglomerates. In more recent years, facilitated by an increasingly lax regulatory environment, major media companies have been buying and merging with other companies to create ever larger media conglomerates, all of which are now global in their activities. In the process, the dilemmas associated with the market and public sphere models of media have been dramatically highlighted.

From a market perspective, industry mergers can be understood as the rational actions of media corporations attempting to maximize sales, create efficiencies in production, and position themselves strategically to face potential competitors. Despite the growth in media conglomerates, many observers believe the profusion of media outlets made possible by recent technological developments—especially cable, the Internet, and satellite—makes the threat of monopolistic misbehavior by these media giants highly unlikely. How can we talk about monopolies, they ask, when we have moved from a system of three television networks to one that has hundreds of channels? How can a handful of companies monopolize the decentralized Internet? The media industry as a whole has grown, they also note, and the larger media companies simply reflect the expansion of this field.

The public sphere perspective directs us to a different set of concerns. Growth in the number of media outlets, for example, does not necessarily ensure content that serves the public interest. Centralized corporate ownership of vast media holdings raises the possibility of stifling diverse expression and raises important questions about the powerful role of media in a democratic society. Even with new media outlets, it is still a handful of media giants who dominate what we see, hear, and read. The expansion of new media technologies has only strengthened, not undermined, the power and influence of new media conglomerates.

To assess the utility of these competing interpretations, we must first familiarize ourselves with the recent changes in the industry. This chapter describes these structural changes. Drawing primarily from the market approach to media, the next chapter examines the common industry practices that have emerged as a result of these structural changes. In chapters 5 and 6, we draw primarily from the public sphere approach to assess the impact of these industry changes on media content and on broader social and political life.

❖ STRUCTURAL TRENDS IN THE MEDIA INDUSTRY

The basic structural trends in the media industry have been characterized in recent years by four broad developments.

1. *Growth.* Mergers and buyouts have made media corporations bigger than ever.

2. *Integration.* The new media giants have integrated either horizontally, by moving into multiple forms of media such as film, publishing, radio, and so on; or vertically, by owning different stages of production and distribution; or both.

3. *Globalization.* To varying degrees, the major media conglomerates have become global entities, marketing their wares worldwide.

4. *Concentration of Ownership.* As major players acquire more media holdings, the ownership of mainstream media has become increasingly concentrated.

Some of these phenomena are overlapping or interrelated developments. However, to describe the specifics of these developments, we examine each separately.

Growth

The last 25 years have seen expansive media growth. Not only is the number of media outlets available via cable, satellite, and the Internet greater than ever, but, as we have seen, the media companies themselves have been growing at an unprecedented pace. In large part, this growth has been fueled by mergers. In 1983, for example, the largest media merger to date had been when the Gannett newspaper chain bought Combined Communications Corporation—owner of billboards, newspapers, and broadcast stations—for $340 million ($652 million). In 2000, AOL acquired Time Warner in a $166 billion deal ($184.1 billion), which was *282 times* as much as the Gannett-CCC deal. No doubt, some other merger will produce an even bigger deal.

Such enormous growth in conglomeration was largely fueled by a belief in the various benefits to be had from being big. Larger size meant more available capital to finance increasingly expensive media projects. Size was also associated with efficiencies of scale. Most important, integrated media conglomerates could exploit the "synergy" created by many outlets in multiple media. *Synergy* refers to the dynamic in which components of a company work together to produce benefits that would be impossible for a single, separately operated unit of the company. In the corporate dreams of media giants, synergy occurs when, for example, a magazine writes about an author, whose book is converted into a movie (the CD soundtrack of which is played on radio stations), which becomes the basis for a television series, which has its own Web site and computer games. Packaging a single idea across all these various media allows corporations to generate multiple revenue streams from a single concept. To do this, however, media companies have to expand to unprecedented size.

While discussions about reducing media regulation dominated public discourse, the scale of media growth increased. Big media players—with sometimes stunning frequency—merged with or bought out other big media players (see Exhibit 3.1). Eventually, however, the scale and pace of these mergers produced growing public concern, which led to intense debates about the need to regulate media growth. Investor concern was also aroused regarding the benefits to shareholders of the increasing size of the media conglomerates.

To better understand this wave of mergers and acquisitions, it is informative to take a closer look at one example, the Viacom-CBS deal mentioned earlier.

(Text continues on page 85)

Exhibit 3.1   Select Media Mergers and Acquisitions of $1 Billion
(Current) or More (1985-2004)

Year	The Deal	Value (in billions of U.S. dollars)	
		Current	Constant 2004
1985			
	News Corp. buys Metromedia (six TV stations) as launching pad for new Fox network	$1.6	$2.8
	Turner Broadcasting buys MGM/United Artists	1.5	2.7
	General Electric buys RCA (owners of NBC network)	6.4	11.4
	Capital Cities buys ABC television network	3.5	6.2
1986			
	National Amusements (movie theaters) buys Viacom	3.4	5.9
1987			
	Sony buys CBS Records	2	3.4
1989			
	Time Inc. merges with Warner Communications	14.1	21.7
	Sony acquires control of Columbia Pictures and TriStar Studios	4.8	7.4
1990			
	Matsushita Electric Industrial Co. buys MCA (Universal Studios, Geffen Records, Motown)	6.6	9.6
1993			
	US West buys a quarter share of Time Warner	2.5	3.3

(Continued)

Exhibit 3.1 (Continued)

Year	The Deal	Value (in billions of U.S. dollars)	
		Current	Constant 2004
1993	Viacom buys Paramount Communications (Universal Studios, Geffen Records, New York Knicks, publishing)	8.3	11
	Viacom buys Blockbuster	4.9	6.5
	Telecommunications, Inc. (TCI) repurchases Liberty Media, which it had spun off earlier (in prelude to failed Bell Atlantic takeover)	3.5	4.6
1994			
	Cox Cable buys Times Mirror Cable	2.3	3
	US West buys Wometco and Georgia Cable TV	1.2	1.6
1995	(Telecommunications Act introduced in Congress)		
	Gannett buys Multimedia Inc.	2.3	2.9
	Time Warner buys Houston Industries	2.5	3.1
	Time Warner buys Cablevision Industries	2.7	3.4
	Seagram's (beverages) buys 80% of MCA from Matsushita, renames it Universal Studios	5.7	7.1
	MCI buys 10% share of NewsCorp	2	2.5
	Westinghouse Corporation buys CBS (3 years later, Westinghouse changes the company name to CBS Corporation)	5.4	6.8
	Walt Disney Co. buys Capital Cities/ABC	19	23.8
	Time Warner buys Turner Communications	8.5	10.7
	TCI buys Viacom's cable TV system	2.3	2.9

Year	The Deal	Value (in billions of U.S. dollars)	
		Current	Constant 2004
1996	(Telecommunications Act passed)		
	Westinghouse (CBS) buys Infinity Broadcasting (radio stations)	4.9	6
	News Corp. buys New World Communications Group, Inc.	3.6	4.4
	US West buys controlling interest in Continental Cablevision	10.8	13.2
	A. H. Belo Corporation buys Providence Journal Company	1.5	1.8
	Tribune Company buys Renaissance Communications (TV stations)	1.1	1.3
1997			
	Microsoft buys an 11.5% stake in Comcast Corp	1.1	1.3
	Reed Elsevier and Wolters Kluwer merge (print, electronic publishing, databases; Lexis/Nexis)	7.8	9.3
	Newscorp buys International Family Entertainment	1.9	2.3
	TCI buys one third of Cablevision Systems	1.1	1.3
	Westinghouse (CBS) buys American Radio Systems	2.6	3.1
	Westinghouse (CBS) acquires Gaylord (Country Music TV and The Nashville Network)	1.6	1.9
1998			
	AT&T buys TCI	53.6	62.8
	Bertelsmann buys Random House/ Alfred Knopf/Crown Publishing	1.3	1.5

(Continued)

Exhibit 3.1 (Continued)

Year	The Deal	Value (in billions of U.S. dollars)	
		Current	Constant 2004
1998	America Online (AOL) buys Netscape (Internet browser)	4.2	4.9
	Seagram buys Polygram (music)	15.1	17.7
1999			
	DirectTV (Hughes Electronics) buys PrimeStar	1.8	2.1
	Charter Communications buys Bresnan Communications (cable)	3.1	3.6
	AT&T buys MediaOne	54	61.9
	@Home Corp. buys Excite (Internet company)	6.7	7.7
	Columbia House (owned by Time Warner and Sony) merges with online retailer CDNow	2	2.3
	CBS buys King World (syndicated television programs)	2.5	2.9
	Yahoo! buys GeoCities, Inc. (Internet company)	4.7	5.4
	Yahoo! buys broadcast.com	5.7	6.5
	VNU (Dutch publisher) acquires Nielsen Media Research	2.7	3.1
	CBS (Infinity Broadcasting) buys Outdoor Systems (billboards)	6.5	7.5
	Viacom merges with CBS	38	43.6
	Cox Communications buys cable assets of Gannett Co.	2.7	3.1
	Cox Communications buys TCA Cable TV, Inc.	3.3	3.8
	Cox Communications buys Media General, Inc.	1.4	1.6

Year	The Deal	Value (in billions of U.S. dollars)	
		Current	Constant 2004
1999	Clear Channel Communications buys AMFM, Inc. (260 radio stations, billboards)	23	26.4
2000			
	AOL acquires Time Warner	166	184.1
	Tribune Company buys Times Mirror Company	6.5	7.2
	Telefonica of Spain acquires Lycos (Internet portal)	12.5	13.9
	Gannett acquires Central Newspapers (six dailies)	2.6	2.9
	Vivendi buys Seagram (Universal, Polygram)	34	37.7
	NewsCorp (Fox) buys ten TV stations from Chris-Craft Industries	5.4	6
	Univision buys 13 TV stations from USA Networks	1.1	1.2
	Viacom buys Black Entertainment Television (BET)	3	3.3
	Clear Channel buys SFX Entertainment (concert promotion, sports talent agency)	4.4	4.9
2001			
	Disney buys Fox Family Worldwide (cable channel)	5.3	5.7
	AOL Time Warner buys IPC Media (British magazines)	1.7	1.8
	Vivendi buys USA Networks	10.3	11.1
	General Electric (NBC) buys Telemundo Communications Group	2.7	2.9
	Vivendi buys Houghton Mifflin (publisher)	2.2	2.4
	Comcast buys AT&T Broadband (cable)	52	56.1

(Continued)

Exhibit 3.1 (Continued)

Year	The Deal	Value (in billions of U.S. dollars)	
		Current	Constant 2004
2002			
	Univision buys Hispanic Broadcasting	3.5	3.7
	General Electric (NBC) buys Bravo cable network	1.3	1.4
2003			
	News Corp. buys controlling interest in Hughes Electronics (DirecTV)	6.6	6.9
	Investor group led by Edgar Bronfman (formerly of Seagram's) buys Warner Music Group	2.6	2.7
	General Electric (NBC) buys Vivendi Universal Entertainment	5.2	5.4
	Liberty Media buys out Comcast's share of QVC	8	8.3
	Sony and Bertelsmann merge their music units into Sony BMG	5	5.2
2004			
	Kohlberg Kravis Roberts buy majority interest in PanAmSat (owned by DirecTV)	4.3	4.3
	Sony-led investor group buys MGM Studios	4.8	4.8

Source: Media accounts.

Note: Most dates refer to the announcement of the deal. Many deals were not finalized until the following year. Constant dollar adjustments are based on the Bureau of Labor Statistics' Consumer Price Index and should be considered approximate.

The Viacom-CBS Merger

In September of 1999, Viacom announced its merger with CBS.[47] The huge deal combined CBS's television network, its 15 TV stations, more than 160 radio stations, and several Internet sites with Viacom's well-known cable channels (e.g., MTV, Nickelodeon, Showtime, TNN), 19 television stations, movie and television production (Paramount Pictures, UPN), publishing (Simon & Schuster), theme parks, and more. At the time, the $38 billion ($43.6 billion) merger was bigger than any previous deal between two media companies, resulting in a huge media conglomerate (see Exhibit 3.2).

CBS was created in 1928 and has long been a major broadcaster with a strong radio and television presence. Through much of its history, it was popularly associated with its news programming, especially with Edward R. Murrow and Walter Cronkite, who were among the preeminent journalists of their day.

CBS dominated network broadcasting through much of the 1960s. In 1963, CBS owned nine of the top ten prime-time shows and all ten of the top ten daytime shows. In its heyday, it was known as the "Tiffany Network" because of its high-quality programming. In the mid-1980s, the network went into decline after being taken over by Loew's, which instituted cuts in the CBS news division as one way to increase profits. Ten years after the Loew's takeover, CBS was sold again, this time to the Westinghouse Corporation, an electrical hardware manufacturer that changed its name to CBS Corporation.

Viacom is a much younger company. In 1970, the FCC introduced new regulations requiring networks to purchase their programs from independent producers. The rules meant that networks could not own their new programs and could not sell the rights to air reruns of their old programs—a process known as "syndication." The goal, according to the FCC, was "to limit network control over television programming and thereby encourage the development of a diversity of programs through diverse sources of program services."[48] This became known as the "financial interest and syndication" rules, or "fin-syn" for short. Viacom was created in 1971 as a spin-off of CBS to comply with these new FCC regulations. To sell the syndication rights to its old programs, such as *I Love Lucy* and *The Andy Griffith Show,* CBS was required to create a new corporate entity, separate from the network. Thus Viacom was born.

In 1986, National Amusements, a movie theater chain headed by Sumner Redstone, purchased Viacom for $3.4 billion ($5.9 billion), keeping the name for the new company. Viacom grew quickly,

(Text continues on page 88)

Exhibit 3.2   Simplified List of Viacom Holdings (2004)

Television broadcast networks and stations

- ❖ CBS Television Network
- ❖ United Paramount Network (UPN)
- ❖ Viacom Television Stations Group (16 CBS affiliate stations, 18 UPN affiliate stations, 5 other stations)

Cable television

- ❖ Music Television (MTV), MTV2
- ❖ VH1
- ❖ Country Music Television (CMT)
- ❖ Nickelodeon
- ❖ Nick at Night
- ❖ Black Entertainment Television (BET)
- ❖ Comedy Central
- ❖ NOGGIN
- ❖ Spike TV
- ❖ TV Land
- ❖ Logo
- ❖ Showtime, Showtime en Espanol, Showtime Extreme
- ❖ Sundance Channel (joint venture with Robert Redford and Universal Studios)
- ❖ The Movie Channel (TMC)
- ❖ FLIX

Radio

- ❖ Infinity Broadcasting—175+ radio stations
- ❖ Westwood One (equity interest)—radio network syndicated program and producer, including Metro Networks/Shadow Broadcast Services, the largest supplier of traffic, news, sports, and weather programming to the broadcasting industry

Film and television production, distribution, and exhibition

- ❖ Paramount Pictures
- ❖ Paramount Television Group (including Paramount Network Television, Viacom Productions, Spelling Television, Big Ticket Television, Paramount Domestic Television, and Paramount International Television)

- ❖ Paramount Home Entertainment
- ❖ MTV Films
- ❖ MTV Productions
- ❖ Nickelodeon Studios
- ❖ Nickelodeon Movies
- ❖ Wilshire Court Productions
- ❖ Spelling Entertainment Group
- ❖ Spelling Films
- ❖ Republic Entertainment
- ❖ Worldvision Enterprises
- ❖ Hamilton Projects
- ❖ United International Pictures (joint venture with Universal)
- ❖ CBS Production
- ❖ Eye Productions
- ❖ King World Productions
- ❖ BET Pictures
- ❖ Famous Players (Canada)
- ❖ United Cinemas International (joint venture with Universal)—more than 90 theaters in Asia, Europe, and South America

Publishing

- ❖ Anne Schwartz Books
- ❖ Archway Paperbacks and Minstrel Books
- ❖ Lisa Drew Books
- ❖ MTV Books
- ❖ Nickelodeon Books
- ❖ Star Trek
- ❖ Washington Square Press
- ❖ BET Books
- ❖ Simon & Schuster Adult Publishing Group (including Atria Books, Kaplan, Pocket Books, Scribner, Simon & Schuster, Free Press, Touchstone, Fireside Group)
- ❖ Simon & Schuster Children's Publishing (including Aladdin Paperbacks, Atheneum Books for Young Readers, Little Simon, Margaret K. McElderry Books, Simon & Schuster Books for Young Readers, Simon Pulse, Simon Spotlight)

(Continued)

Exhibit 3.2 (Continued)

Music

- ❖ Famous Music (copyright holders of more than 100,000 songs)

Internet

- ❖ CBS.com
- ❖ CBSNews.com
- ❖ CBSSportsLine.com (equity interest)
- ❖ CBSMarketWatch.com (equity interest)
- ❖ CBSHealthWatch.com (equity interest)
- ❖ iWon.com
- ❖ MovieTickets.com
- ❖ MTV.com
- ❖ VH1.com
- ❖ Nickelodeon.com
- ❖ BET.com
- ❖ SpikeTV.com

Retail, theme parks, outdoor advertising, other

- ❖ Paramount Theme Parks: Carowinds (Charlotte, NC), Great America (Santa Clara, CA), Kings Dominion (Richmond, VA), Kings Island (Cincinnati, OH), Canada's Wonderland (Toronto), Star Trek: The Experience (Las Vegas)
- ❖ Viacom Outdoor
- ❖ Viacom Consumer Products (licensing for Viacom products)

Source: Viacom Web sites, Hoover company profiles, and media accounts.

purchasing other media enterprises. Most notably, in 1993, it bought Paramount for $8.3 billion ($11 billion) and Blockbuster Video for $4.9 billion ($6.5 billion). From a stepchild of CBS, Viacom had become a media giant in its own right. In 1999 the circle was completed, as Viacom returned to purchase its former parent, CBS, for $38 billion ($43.6 billion), creating a new Viacom that was estimated to be worth more than $70 billion ($80.3 billion).

Why was a much smaller media company broken up in 1971 because of fear of monopoly and a much larger company allowed to keep growing by acquisitions in 1999? The explanatory equation is something like this: Technology + politics = deregulation. It was the combination of changing communications technology, coupled with a conservative shift in national politics, that led to major deregulation of the media industry. This deregulation, in turn, allowed media corporations to expand rapidly, almost exponentially.

Changing Technology

New technology is one key element facilitating industry changes. When CBS was forced to spin off Viacom in 1971, television viewers usually were limited to relatively few options, namely, the national broadcast networks (ABC, CBS, and NBC), public television, and perhaps one or two local independent stations. By the end of the century, there were six national broadcast networks of varying sizes (including FOX, WB, UPN), along with countless numbers of channels available via cable or satellite. In 2002, for the first time, the number of television channels receivable by the average U.S. household reached more than 100, according to Nielsen Media Research.[49] In this world of proliferating media outlets, media corporations argued that many ownership regulations were no longer needed.

If television offered abundant choices, critics of regulation contended, then the Internet was virtually limitless in its offerings. In its early days, especially, the Internet was seen even by many critics of mainstream media as an antidote to big media. Because of the apparently low cost of entry and virtually no-cost distribution, it was thought to be a way to level the playing field between large media conglomerates and smaller independent producers. This, too, was a part of the argument against regulation of big media.

Still, although technology has undoubtedly changed the face of media, these developments can come at a high price. For example, cable and satellite television technologies have made hundreds of channels available to consumers. However, these new options—unlike traditional broadcast television—are expensive alternatives that some Americans cannot afford. By 2005, a "basic" cable package cost consumers about $40 a month, and premium channel options could easily double or even triple that bill. As a result, nearly a third of American households had only basic cable, and another third had access to at least some premium options, for a total household penetration of about 62%—a figure that has fallen in recent years as satellite television subscriptions have expanded to reach about 20% of U.S. households. That leaves nearly one in five households dependent entirely on broadcast television.[50]

Perhaps more important, more channels have not necessarily meant more diversity. Instead, many of the cable options simply air either reruns of broadcast programs or a certain type of previously existing programming (sports, music videos, etc.) 24 hours a day. *More* content does not necessarily mean *different* content.

The Internet, too, has shown signs of becoming dominated by major media giants. For a short period of time, many major media companies were not heavily involved in Internet ventures. As a result, there was a brief window of opportunity for new companies to get established. However, as this first stage of the industry passed, a second consolidation stage took place.

Two major types of players were driving this consolidation stage. First, as successful new Internet companies saw the value of their stock rise, they often tried to solidify that value by buying something tangible with the money—often other media firms. That way, when stock prices on overvalued Internet companies fell—as they inevitably did— these companies still had valuable, although more traditional, media assets. Second, after small ventures began showing how the Internet might be used for commerce, major media players stepped in and either bought smaller companies or forced them to merge to remain in business. Thus established companies used their resources to buy their way into the expanding Internet market.

These large-scale companies make it difficult for new companies to compete independently. By 2000, the once relatively low startup cost of running a significant World Wide Web site—originally touted as a central reason for the Internet's revolutionary character—routinely exceeded $1 million.[51] As a result, media companies with major capital to invest now dominate the most popular sites on the World Wide Web.[52]

The Politics of Deregulation

If technology provided the tracks upon which deregulation was able to ride, then conservative, probusiness politics was the engine that propelled it along. The relaxation of key regulations was absolutely essential for the rapid expansion of media conglomerates.

Earlier antimonopoly regulation sometimes prevented the growth of major media conglomerates—or even required their dismantling. As we saw in chapter 2, the Justice Department's breakup of the

Hollywood studios was one example of reaction to a single media company owning the means of producing, distributing, and exhibiting media products. The fin-syn regulations, too, were implemented to prevent control of production and distribution from resting in the hands of a single company. More recently, however, overall growth in media outlets and a more conservative, probusiness political environment has contributed to the significant relaxation of ownership regulations that eventually produced widespread public concern and legal challenges.

The 1980s was a period of deregulation that affected many different industries, including the media. Regulatory agencies—in this case, the FCC—became staffed by appointees who shared many of the basic probusiness and antiregulatory sentiments of the Reagan administration. This shift gave a green light to the first round of media mergers in the mid-1980s. In 1988, Time Inc.'s annual report to stockholders stated flatly that "by the mid-1990s, the media entertainment industry will consist of a handful of vertically integrated worldwide giants. Time Inc. will be one of them."[53]

Simultaneously, with the growth of larger media companies, the number of media outlets expanded, especially in the areas of cable and satellite television. These new technologies were a key reason that, in 1993, a U.S. District Court ruled that broadcast networks should no longer be subject to many of the fin-syn regulations. Previously, television networks acquired programming from outside producers, who continued to own the programs. However, after the elimination of fin-syn rules, networks were free to air their own programming.

With deregulation, networks pressured independent producers to give up ownership rights, and they increasingly relied on programming produced by their corporate parent. For example, in the summer of 1999, Disney formalized its vertical integration in television by merging its television production studios with its ABC network operations. The shift was aimed at controlling costs by encouraging the in-house development and production of programs by Disney/ABC for broadcast on the ABC network.[54] Other networks pursued similar changes, and the result was the dramatic consolidation of program ownership in the television industry. In 1990, the four major networks owned just 12.5% of the new series they broadcast. By 2002, that figure surged to nearly 80%.[55] Such integration would have been impossible without changes in the fin-syn regulations.

The 1996 Telecommunications Act

The antiregulatory sentiment in government that reigned under the Republican Reagan and Bush administrations continued into Democrat Bill Clinton's administration. Nowhere was this clearer than in the passage of the wide-ranging 1996 Telecommunications Act. The act had been heavily promoted by the media and telecommunications industries, leading even the *New York Times* to editorialize, "Forty million dollars' worth of lobbying bought telecommunications companies a piece of Senate legislation they could relish. But consumers have less to celebrate." The *Times* went on to argue that the bill's "antiregulatory zeal goes too far, endangering the very competition the bill is supposed to create."[56]

However, antiregulation ruled the day, and among the many provisions of the act were those that relaxed the rules governing the number of media outlets a single company may own (see Exhibit 3.3). Although the Telecommunications Act was promoted using a market approach, which emphasized more competition, the changes actually helped to fuel a new wave of media mergers and acquisitions. This trend was most dramatic in radio, where, by 2000, 75 different companies that had been operating independently in 1995 were consolidated into just three, led by Clear Channel Communication which owned over 1200 stations.[57]

As a sort of permanent codification of antiregulatory sentiment, the 1996 Telecommunications Act required that the FCC examine and justify its ownership regulations every 2 years. As a result, the push to deregulate the media continued incessantly. In the summer of 1999, the FCC eased restrictions on the number of local radio and television stations a single company could own. The FCC eliminated regulations restricting companies to one local TV station in a market. Instead, companies were allowed to own two stations as long as at least eight other competitors were in the same market and one of the company's two stations was not among the market's top four. Other conditions, too, such as a failing station, could now be used to justify multiple station ownership. In a reflection of the convergence of media forms, another regulatory change allowed for a single company to own two TV stations and six radio stations in a market as long as there were at least 20 competitors among all media—cable, newspapers, and other broadcast stations.[58]

Consumer advocates bemoaned the changes, arguing that they once again would lead to more media outlets in fewer hands. Media

Exhibit 3.3   Select Ownership Rules Changes in the 1996
Telecommunications Act

Previous Rules	New Rule Changes
National television A single entity ❖ can own up to 12 stations nationwide *or* ❖ can own stations reaching up to 25% of U.S. TV households	❖ No limit on number of stations ❖ Station reach increased to 35% of U.S. TV households
Local television A single entity can own only one station in a market.	❖ Act called for review. ❖ In 1999, FCC announced it would allow multiple station ownership in a single market under certain circumstances.
National radio A single entity can own up to 20 FM and 20 AM stations.	No limit on station ownership
Local radio A single entity ❖ Cannot own, operate, or control more than 2 AM and 2 FM stations in a market ❖ Audience share of co-owned stations may not exceed 25%	Ownership adjusted by market size ❖ In markets with 45+ stations, a single entity cannot own more than 8 stations total and no more than 5 in the same service (AM or FM) ❖ In markets with 30-44 stations, 7 total, 5 same service ❖ 15-29 stations, 6 total, 4 in the same service ❖ 14 or fewer stations, 5 total, 3 same service (but no more than 50% of the stations in the market) ❖ Limits may be waived if the FCC rules it will increase the total number of stations in operation

executives, on the other hand, had something to cheer about. Lowell "Bud" Paxon, owner of PAX TV, greeted the changes by saying, "I can't wait to have a glass of champagne and toast the FCC!" Barry Diller, chairman and CEO of USA Networks, observed, "This is a real significant step. . . . This is going to change things."[59]

He was right. Less than a month after these FCC regulatory changes, Viacom and CBS announced their plans to merge—a deal that would have been impossible before the relaxation of FCC regulations. Thus, as the 20th century came to a close, a loose regulatory environment allowed Viacom and CBS to create a new media giant that, at the time

- ❖ Was the nation's largest owner of TV stations
- ❖ Was the nation's largest owner of radio stations
- ❖ Controlled the nation's largest cable network group
- ❖ Controlled the nation's largest billboard company
- ❖ Was the world's largest seller of advertising

In an earlier era, such concentrated market power would probably have been met by regulatory roadblocks. In a new age of deregulation, the deal was approved.

More FCC Deregulation and a Citizens' Revolt

The deregulatory fervor of the 1980s and 1990s continued into the new century. When Michael Powell became chair of the FCC during the administration of George W. Bush, he virtually ridiculed the idea of protecting the public interest. "The night after I was sworn in, I waited for a visit from the angel of the public interest," Powell said in a speech. "I waited all night but she did not come. And, in fact, five months into this job, I still have had no divine awakening."[60]

With such a patently probusiness and antiregulatory chairman at the helm, the FCC continued to roll back regulations on media ownership. For example, even with the 1999 weakening of ownership rules, the newly expanded Viacom violated existing regulations after its takeover of CBS. For one thing, it both owned the CBS network and had a 50% stake in the UPN network, and FCC regulations forbade a network owner from having an ownership interest in another network. For another, Viacom's television stations could reach nearly 40% of American households, but the FCC cap was 35%.[61] The FCC was accommodating, however. In 2003, they changed the rules so that a single company could not own any two of the *top four* networks, effectively exempting Viacom's ownership of the smaller UPN network. They also raised the national audience cap to 45%.

These deregulation efforts were part of a broader set of changes the FCC proposed in 2003, which included

❖ Lifting a ban on "cross-ownership," thus allowing a single company to own both a TV station and a daily newspaper in the same market, as long as the market had at least three stations

❖ Easing restrictions on TV station ownership to allow one company to own two stations in midsized markets and three stations in the largest markets

❖ Adjusting radio ownership rules so that a single company could own up to eight stations in the largest markets with at least 45 stations, seven stations in markets with 30 to 44 stations, six stations in markets with 15 to 29 stations, and three stations in markets with 14 or fewer stations.[62]

However, after nearly two decades of deregulation, resulting in increasingly large media conglomerates, this time proposed deregulation met with widespread opposition from citizens. During their public comment period, the FCC was flooded with hundreds of thousands of e-mails and letters, nearly all opposing the proposed changes. The outpouring constituted the greatest number of comments received on any issue in the FCC's history and was so great that it overwhelmed both the agency's voice comment phone line system and its Internet server.[63] The FCC eventually held just a single public hearing on the issue in conservative Richmond, VA, but even this drew vocal opponents to the changes.[64] Some dissenting FCC commissioners took it upon themselves to hold more hearings in different parts of the country, even if their chairman refused to attend. Prominent politicians, including Republican John McCain, expressed outrage at the proposed changes. But as with the 1996 Telecommunications Act, the mainstream news media gave scant coverage to the proposed changes or the opposition to it.[65]

The FCC efforts at further deregulation created a firestorm of organized public opposition from diverse organizations ranging from the conservative Parents Television Council, the National Rifle Association, and the Catholic Conference of Bishops to the liberal Media Access Project, Writers and Screen Actors Guilds, and Code

Pink—the latter of whom, evoking Chairman Powell's earlier speech, demonstrated wearing angel costumes to remind him of the FCC's responsibility to protect the public interest. Although he may not have had a divine awakening, in the face of widespread opposition to his deregulation efforts, Chairman Powell certainly learned that many people still believed in protecting the public interest.

Despite the uproar, the Bush Administration held firm, and the FCC passed the rule changes in a split vote along party lines. The opposition did not stop, however. In September 2003, using a rarely invoked procedure, the U.S. Senate passed a "resolution of disapproval" repealing all the FCC rule changes—but could not overcome a threatened presidential veto. Instead, in a compromise move, Congress rolled back the national audience cap from 45% to 39%—just enough to accommodate Viacom and NewsCorp, whose FOX network also reached 39% of households.

In the summer of 2004, a federal appeals court ruled in favor of the Prometheus Radio Project (a Philadelphia-based, low-power radio collective), in a suit led by the Media Access Project (a nonprofit, public interest telecommunications law firm), against the FCC rule changes. The court invalidated many of the reasons cited by the FCC for its actions and ordered the FCC to reconsider all of its 2003 rule changes, effectively stopping their immediate implementation.

Thus the growth in media conglomerates has been fueled, in part, by the changing regulatory environment. In the years when public interest concerns about monopolies were preeminent, media companies were constrained in their ability to grow unchecked. However, with the rise of more media outlets via new technology, the conservative shift toward business deregulation starting in the Reagan administration, and the media industry's lobbying clout, media corporations have been relatively unencumbered in their ability to grow. Ironically, however, this very growth has triggered a public backlash that has dampened the enthusiasm for unbridled deregulation and set the stage for future regulatory battles.

Integration

Media empires are nothing new. As we saw in chapter 2, William Randolph Hearst built a powerful newspaper empire that wielded considerable political clout. However, the scale of the contemporary conglomerates is unprecedented. The pinnacle of the Hearst empire during Hearst's lifetime would be just a small part of today's megamedia corporations. In fact, the Hearst empire lives on in the form of a multimedia conglomerate many times the size of anything that existed when Hearst was alive. The Hearst Corporation Web site touts the company as "one of the largest diversified communications companies. Its major interests include magazine, newspaper and business publishing, cable networks, television and radio broadcasting, internet businesses, TV production and distribution, newspaper features distribution, and real estate."[66] Having long outgrown the newspaper empire of its founder, the company's holdings by 2004—in addition to more than 20 daily or weekly newspapers—included 28 television stations; 2 radio stations; partial ownership of major cable channels such as ESPN, A&E, and Lifetime; 18 magazines with 100 international editions; 20 business-to-business services; and minority ownership of numerous other well-known media properties, such as Netscape Communications, Broadcast.com, iVillage, and XM Satellite Radio.

Beyond sheer scale, one of the key differences in today's media companies is the wide variety of media they comprise. Hearst owned newspapers. Today's media giants are likely to be involved in almost all aspects of the media: publishing, television, film, music, the Internet, and more.

The next piece of the puzzle for ambitious media companies is likely to be video games, which provide various opportunities for product development and cross promotion, as well as a new venue for advertising. Video games based on major motion pictures are now released the same day films open, and media conglomerates are now developing top-selling video games into movies. Hit television shows, such as *CSI* and *ER*, are developing video game versions of their programs.[67] In addition, video game soundtracks have become a prime site for promoting new music and there is growing competition among record labels to get their acts into the top-selling video games.[68] With video game audiences growing rapidly, advertisements embedded in games and appearing on game-related Web sites are fast-becoming attractive supplements (and sometimes alternatives) to traditional broadcast advertising. Time Warner's 2004 acquisition of video game publisher Monolith may have been the first step in the move by the media conglomerates to integrate video games into their multimedia portfolios.

A conglomerate by definition consists of many diverse companies. Using our earlier example of Viacom in Exhibit 3.2, we can better understand the relationships among individual companies by considering the idea of horizontal and vertical integration.

Horizontal Integration

A media corporation that is horizontally integrated owns many different types of media products. Viacom is clearly a horizontally integrated conglomerate because it owns, among other things, properties in broadcast and cable television, film, radio, and the Internet—all different types of media.

Companies integrate horizontally for two general reasons. First, as we will see in more detail in the next chapter, some companies believe that they can use their diverse holdings to better market and promote their media products. Owning properties across media allows one type of media (e.g., CBS Sports) to promote and work with another type of media (e.g., CBSSportsLine.com). Viacom's ownership of the *Star Trek* franchise, to use another example, has allowed it to develop and promote a variety of products that cut across media, including several television series, films, books, video games, and even a theme park. The result of such efforts, corporate executives hope, is a company that exploits its synergy potential by becoming greater than the sum of its parts.

This sort of integration can be seen every time Hollywood releases a major summer blockbuster. The movie is usually accompanied by a soundtrack CD and music video, related publishing ventures (books, calendars, etc.), an Internet site (often with audio or video clips of the film), and television specials exploring the "making of" the movie, not to mention the countless movie T-shirts, paraphernalia, and fast-food chain promotional tie-ins. In the hands of an integrated media conglomerate, what was once a film release now becomes an integrated media campaign of enormous proportions.

The second development encouraging integration involves technological change. It used to be that each medium was a distinct entity. Text-based products were distributed on paper (magazines, books, newspapers). Music and other audio products were available on vinyl records or magnetic tapes (reel-to-reel, cassette, 8-tracks). Video products were either shown as films in a theater or were available on videocassettes for home use. The radio and television broadcast media used analog signals to make audio and video widely available without actually physically distributing their media products. Each medium, therefore, had its own distinct format, and media companies tended to focus on their one specific media specialty.

All that has changed with the coming of the digital age. Digital data—the 1s and 0s that make up binary code—are the backbone of contemporary media products. With the transformation of text, audio, and visual media into digital data, the technological platforms that underlie different media forms have converged, blurring the lines between once-distinct media.

One visible example of convergence is the compact disk. This single digital data storage device can be used for text, audio, video, or all three simultaneously. Its introduction—along with other types of digital data storage devices—has changed the nature of media. The personal computer is another symbol of change. It can be used to create and read text documents; show static and animated graphics; listen to audio CDs or digital music files; play CD computer games that combine audio, video, and text; watch digital videos; access and print photos taken with a digital camera; and surf the Internet, among other things. All this is possible because of the common digital foundation now available for various media.

The significance of digital data extends way beyond CDs and computers. Now the digital platform encompasses all forms of media. Television and radio broadcast signals are being digitized and analog signals phased out. Newspapers exist in digital form on the Internet, and their paper versions are often printed in plants that download the paper's content in digital form from satellites. This allows for simultaneous publication in many cities of national papers such as *USA Today*. Filmless digital movie theaters are beginning to appear, where movies, digitally downloaded via the Internet, are shown on a sophisticated computerized projector.

The convergence of media products has meant that media businesses have also converged. The common digital foundation of contemporary media has made it easier for companies to create products in different media. For example, it was a relatively small step for newspapers—with content already produced on computers in digital form—to develop online World Wide Web sites and upload newspaper articles to them. Thus newspaper publishers have become Internet companies. In fact, many media have embraced the Internet as a close digital cousin of what they already do. The music industry, to use another example, has responded to the proliferation of bootlegged digital music files (early Napster, Kazaa, etc.) by developing its own systems to deliver music via the Web to consumers (iTunes, Rhapsody, etc.)—for a fee, of course. The industry's response to bootlegged movies is not as fully developed but will likely follow suit.

Furthermore, convergence has eroded the walls between what used to be three distinct industries: media, telecommunications, and computers. Major cable TV companies have entered the phone service business and offer cable-based broadband Internet access. "Baby Bells" and long-distance phone companies have gotten involved in video delivery and Internet access. Computer software firms are teaming up with cable companies to create various "smart boxes" that facilitate delivery of cable-based media and communications services. Internet service providers have entered the telephone business, offering net-based phone service. Integration, therefore, involves even companies outside of the traditional media industry, making it more difficult than ever to mark clear boundaries.

Vertical Integration

Although horizontal integration involves owning and offering different types of media products, vertical integration involves owning assets involved in the production, distribution, exhibition, and sale of a single type of media product. In the media industry, vertical integration has been more limited than horizontal integration, but it has been playing an increasingly significant role. For some time, there was a widespread belief that "content is king." That is, the rise of the Internet and cable television, in particular, had led to an explosion in outlets available to deliver media products. Consequently, owning the media content that was to be distributed via these channels was widely believed to be more valuable than owning the distribution channels themselves.

However, some developments have brought this belief into question. As we saw in the previous chapter, the supplanting of the advertiser-based "broadcast model" by fee-based efforts has contributed to increased interest in more vertical integration. In addition, with the elimination of most fin-syn rules, interest in vertical integration resurfaced, enabling broadcast networks to once again produce and exhibit their own programs. In the content versus conduit debate, as one *New York Times* profile put it, "Now, many big media companies are concluding that it is more powerful to own both."[69] Or, as media pioneer Ted Turner colorfully explained, "Today, the only way for media companies to survive is to own everything up and down the media chain. . . . Big media today wants to own the faucet, pipeline, water, and the reservoir. The rain clouds come next."[70]

Viacom's vertical integration can be seen, for example, in the fact that it owns film production and distribution companies (e.g., Paramount Pictures) and theater chains to show first-run films (e.g., Famous Players and United Cinemas International theater chains). Viacom also owns premium cable channels (e.g., Showtime, The Movie Channel), basic cable channels (e.g., Comedy Central, Spike TV), and broadcast networks (CBS and UPN), all to air a film after its rental life is over. Thus, when Viacom produces a movie, it is assured of multiple venues for exhibition.

When we understand the basic idea of integration, we can see why many industry observers saw the Viacom-CBS deal as logical. First, CBS was the owner of one of the premier exhibition spaces: the CBS network, one of the "Big Four" television networks. However, it did not have major program production facilities, nor was it positioned to take advantage of the elimination of most "fin-syn" regulations. Viacom, however, was very strong in production but owned only a 50% stake in a small broadcast network, UPN. It did not, therefore, have a premier venue for broadcasting. Bringing Viacom and CBS together created a new company with much better vertical integration.

The merger also dramatically enhanced the company's horizontal integration. In many ways, the strengths of one company complemented the weakness of the other. CBS's primary strengths in television broadcasting, radio, outdoor advertising, and the Internet were all areas of weakness for Viacom. In turn, Viacom's strengths in film, cable television, and publishing filled gaps in the CBS holdings.

Mergers and acquisitions, therefore, are often carried out to bolster a company's holdings in an attempt to become more strongly integrated—horizontally, vertically, or both. The numerous mergers that have left an industry dominated by large companies have also produced an industry in which the major players are highly integrated.

At first glance, the average person may be unaware of these trends that have reshaped the media industry. It is usually difficult to discern that apparently diverse media products are, in fact, all owned by a single company. Take television, for example. If you surf the television universe, you might come across a local CBS affiliate, MTV, Comedy Central, Nickelodeon, BET, Showtime, a UPN affiliate, VH-1, The

Movie Channel, Spike TV, and Country Music Television. It is virtually impossible for the casual viewer to realize that all of these are actually owned—wholly or in part—by Viacom. It is even less likely that average viewers connect the owner of all these stations with the owner of their local theme park, movie theater, and radio stations. Again, one company could own them all: Viacom. However, Viacom is not unique in this regard. The same phenomenon is true of other collections of disparate media outlets that are owned by the other media giants.

Globalization

Growth in the size and integration of companies has been accompanied by another development: the globalization of media conglomerates. More and more, major media players are targeting the global marketplace to sell their products.

There are three basic reasons for this strategy. First, domestic markets are saturated with media products, so many media companies see international markets as the key to future growth. Media corporations want to be well positioned to tap these developing markets.

Second, media giants are often in a position to effectively compete with—and even dominate—the local media in other countries. These corporations can draw on their enormous capital resources to produce expensive media products, such as Hollywood blockbuster movies, which are beyond the capability of local media. Media giants can also adapt already successful products for new markets, again reaping the rewards of expanding markets in these areas.

Third, by distributing existing media products to foreign markets, media companies are able to tap a lucrative source of revenue at virtually no additional cost. For example, a movie shown in just one country costs the same to make as a movie distributed globally. Once the tens of millions of dollars involved in producing a major motion picture are spent, successful foreign distribution of the resulting film can spell the difference between profit and loss. As a result, current decision making as to whether a script becomes a major film routinely includes considerations of its potential for success in foreign markets. Action and adventure films translate well, for example, because they have limited dialogue, simple plots, and rely heavily on special effects and action sequences. Sexy stars, explosions, and violence travel easily to other cultures. Comedies, however, are often risky, because humor does not always translate well across cultural boundaries.

We can see examples of globalization strategies in the case of Viacom. In our listing of Viacom's holdings (Exhibit 3.2), we greatly simplified the chart for clarity. However, hidden behind some of those assets is what amount to mini–global empires. For example, MTV is a popular Viacom cable channel, reaching about 80 million U.S. households.[71] It originated as a venue for record companies to show music videos to advertise their artists' latest releases. Over time, MTV added an evolving stable of programs (e.g., *The Real World, Road Rules, Beavis and Butthead, TRL, The Osbournes*) and events (e.g., *MTV Video Music Awards, MTV's Spring Break*) that were aimed at the lucrative teen and young adult market.

MTV has described itself in publicity material as having an environment that is "unpredictable and irreverent, reflecting the cutting edge spirit of rock n' roll that is the heart of its programming." In reality, MTV is a well-developed commercial formula that Viacom has exported globally by making small adjustments to account for local tastes. In fact, MTV is really a global collection of MTVs (see Exhibit 3.4). Together, these MTV channels are available in nearly 400 million households in 166 countries and territories. That, Viacom says, makes MTV the most widely distributed network in the world. More than three quarters of the households that receive MTV are *outside* of the United States.

Viacom's global ventures do not end with MTV. Virtually every aspect of its media business has a global component. Examples include the following specifics:

❖ Major motion pictures are routinely distributed internationally, and many earn more money for Viacom internationally than they do in the United States.

❖ Famous Players Theatres Canada operates more than 660 screens in more than 100 locations. United Cinemas International—a joint venture with Universal—operates more than 100 theaters in Asia, Europe, and South America.

❖ Paramount International Television distributes more than 2600 series and movies internationally.

❖ Publisher Simon & Schuster has international operations in both the United Kingdom and Australia and sells books in dozens of countries.

❖ Nickelodeon distributes its children's programming in more than 100 countries and, much like MTV, operates its own cable

(*Text continues on page 107*)

Exhibit 3.4 The Global Reach of MTV (2004)

Program Service	Territory	Language
Asia		
❖ MTV China (regional feed)	Certain provinces in China	Chinese
❖ MTV India (regional feed)	India, Sri Lanka, Bangladesh, Nepal, Pakistan	English, Hindi
❖ MTV Mandarin (regional feed)	Brunei, certain provinces in China, South Korea, Philippines, Singapore, and Taiwan	Mandarin
❖ MTV Southeast Asia (regional feed)	Brunei, Thailand, Singapore, Philippines, Indonesia, Malaysia, Vietnam, Hong Kong, South Korea, Papua New Guinea	English
❖ MTV Indonesia*	Indonesia	Bahasa Indonesian
❖ MTV Japan*	Japan	Japanese
❖ MTV Korea*	South Korea	Korean
❖ MTV Philippines*	Philippines	English and Tagalog
❖ MTV Thailand*	Thailand	Thai and English
Australia		
❖ MTV Australia*	Australia	English
Europe		
❖ MTV U.K. and Ireland (regional)	United Kingdom, Ireland	English

(Continued)

Program Service	Territory	Language
❖ MTV Netherlands (regional)	Netherlands	Dutch
❖ MTV Spain (regional feed)	Spain	Spanish
❖ MTV France (regional feed)	France	French
❖ MTV Central (regional feed)	Austria, Germany, Switzerland	German
❖ MTV Portugal (regional feed)	Portugal	Portuguese
❖ MTV Nordic (regional feed)	Sweden, Denmark, Norway, Finland	English
❖ MTV European (regional feed)	Belgium; France; Greece; Israel; Romania; and 30 other territories, including some in the former Soviet Union, the Middle East, Egypt, Faroe Islands, Israel, Liechtenstein, Malta, and Moldova	English
❖ MTV Italia*	Italy	Italian
❖ MTV Poland*	Poland	Polish
❖ MTV Romania*	Romania	Romanian
❖ MTV Russia*	Russia	Russia

Exhibit 3.4 (Continued)

Program Service	Territory	Language
Latin America		
❖ MTV Latin America (3 regional feeds)	Argentina, Bolivia, Brazil, Chile, Ecuador, Peru, Colombia, Costa Rica, Dominican Republic, El Salvador, Guatemala, Honduras, Mexico, Nicaragua, Panama, Paraguay, Puerto Rica, Uruguay, Venezuela	Spanish
❖ MTV Brasil*	Brazil	Portuguese
North America		
❖ MTV Canada	Canada	English

Source: Viacom's annual Securities and Exchange Commission report, Form 10-K, March 15, 2004.

* Joint venture or licensing agreement.

channels across the globe. These include Nickelodeon Latin America, Nickelodeon in the Nordic region, Nickelodeon Turkey, Nickelodeon U.K., Nickelodeon Australia, and the Nickelodeon Global Network. Nickelodeon even has theme parks in Australia and other locations.

❖ Viacom's production companies license and coproduce programs based on U.S. hits to be sold in international markets. These include *Entertainment Tonight/China,* a 50-minute Mandarin-language series produced in cooperation with the Chinese government, and other national versions of the *Entertainment Tonight* series that appear in the United Kingdom, Germany, and other countries.

International revenues are making up an increasingly large percentage of the income of such companies as Viacom, Disney, Time Warner, and News Corp. As a result, all major media conglomerates are now global players, representing a major shift in industry structure.

Concentration of Ownership

As individual media companies grow, integrate, and pursue global strategies, ownership in the media industry as a whole becomes more concentrated in the hands of these new media giants. There is considerable debate about the significance of this trend, but the trend itself is clear.

The concentration of media ownership is a phenomenon that applies to the industry as a whole rather than to a single media conglomerate. The fact that media conglomerates are getting larger does not necessarily mean that ownership is becoming more concentrated. Growth in media companies may just be a sign that the industry as a whole is expanding—as it certainly has in recent years. The real question is whether the revenues of the industry as a whole are being channeled to just a handful of companies.

When researchers analyze ownership patterns in any industry, they often measure concentration by determining the percentage of total revenue in an industry segment going to the top four and the top eight companies. These numbers are referred to as the *concentration ratio,* or CR, of an industry. CR4, then, refers to the ratio of revenue going to the top four companies in an industry. CR8 is a calculation of the same ratio for the top eight companies. A common threshold for

Exhibit 3.5   Ownership Concentration by Select Media Industry
Segments: CR4 and CR8 Ratios (1999)

	CR4	CR8
Recorded music	.98	1.00
Television networks	.84	.98
Filmed entertainment	.78	1.00
Radio stations	.77	.88
Consumer books	.77	.94
Consumer magazines	.77	.91
Cable systems	.61	.87
Newspapers	.48	.69
Television stations	.31	.51

Source: Albarran (2003).

Note: CR indicates concentration ratio. The common threshold for high concentration is
.50 for CR4 and .75 for CR8.

declaring an industry highly concentrated is if the top four companies
control 50% or more of the industry's revenue or if the top eight companies control 75% or more.

One such analysis of nine media industry segments by Albarran
found that, using the CR4 ratio, every segment in 1994 was highly
concentrated except for newspapers (which fell just short of the 50%
threshold) and local television stations (see exhibit 3.5). The same held
true for the CR8 ratio.[72] If the lobbying efforts to remove regulations
prohibiting cross-ownership between newspapers and television stations are successful, it is likely that ownership in these two industry
segments will also become highly concentrated.

In the various editions of his book *The Media Monopoly*, Ben
Bagdikian has also shown the dramatic increase in the concentration
of media ownership. Back in 1983, when the first edition of his book
was published, Bagdikian argued that 50 media firms controlled the

majority of all media products used by American audiences. Over the years, Bagdikian tracked the remarkable decline in the number of firms controlling the media. By the 2004 edition of his book (now called *The New Media Monopoly*), he wrote that just five global conglomerates— Time Warner, Disney, NewsCorp, Viacom, and Bertelsmann—"operating with many of the characteristics of a cartel, own most of the newspapers, magazines, book publishers, motion picture studios, and radio and television stations in the United States" (p. 3). According to Bagdikian, the steady increase in media power enjoyed by these firms has translated into "a steady accumulation of power in politics" as well (p. 28). He notes that such concentrated ownership "gives each of the five corporations and their leaders more communications power than was exercised by any despot or dictator in history."[73]

The highly concentrated nature of the media industry exists in large part because of the relaxation of ownership regulations discussed earlier in this chapter. The 1996 Telecommunications Act not only allowed companies to get bigger, it also allowed companies to dominate a larger share of the industry, thus increasing ownership concentration. For example, Patricia Aufderheide writes that with the introduction and passage of the law, national concentration limits on radio were eliminated entirely.

> Virtually overnight, an industry marked by relative diversity of ownership and formats, and low advertising rates, became highly concentrated. Within a year and a half, more than a quarter of U.S. radio stations had been sold at least once. Radio stock prices rose 80 percent in 1997, reflecting the new market power of group owners. The FCC calculated that two years after the Act the number of owners of radio stations had declined nearly 12 percent, while the number of commercial radio stations had increased 2.5 percent.[74]

Radio ownership went the way of other media outlets and became concentrated in the hands of major corporate chains.

It is clear that some forms of media are more concentrated than others and that the level of ownership concentration can change. For example, in the 1970s, the three major television networks collectively had more than a 90% share of all television viewers—and, thus, the associated advertising revenue. Television was enormously concentrated. (A program's *rating* is basically the percentage of *all* television households that are watching a program. Its *share* is the percentage of television sets *in use* that are tuned to the program.) Since the early 2000s, the share of prime-time television viewers who tuned in to the four major networks has routinely fallen below 50%. Networks still dominate, but the playing field has changed considerably. Cable television has become—collectively—a major competitor for the networks, even though no single cable channel comes anywhere near generating the ratings that even the lowest rated of the four major broadcast networks receives. A modestly rated program on network television often gets twice the audience that the very highest rated cable programs receive.

One of the reasons for variable concentration between media segments is the cost of entry. Publishing a magazine requires considerably less funding than launching a television network, to take just one example. As a result, large, big-budget media such as movies and television tend to be much more concentrated than lower cost media, such as various forms of publishing and radio.

However, as Aufderheide's observations about radio ownership suggest, low entry cost is not always a deterrent to concentrated ownership. One reason is that some forms of media still face conditions of scarcity. There is no limit to the number of newspapers that might compete in a city, but there is a practical limit on the number of broadcast television and radio stations that a location can accommodate because of the narrowness of the electromagnetic spectrum used to send broadcast signals. The FCC regulates broadcast licenses and assigns a spot on the radio or television dial to licensed broadcasters to prevent interference from overlapping signals. Although digital broadcasting compresses the amount of space needed to send a signal and thus allows for more signals in the same electromagnetic spectrum, populated areas still do not have enough space to meet interest and demand. The bottom line is that there are not enough broadcast slots to go around. Industry segments without this limitation are less likely to be concentrated.

❖ INTERPRETING STRUCTURAL CHANGES

The media industry, then, has been undergoing significant changes in recent decades as companies have grown, integrated, and become global players. There is little debate about these basic trends. However, the significance of these trends is a subject of intense debate. Market advocates see these structural changes as the normal evolution of a growing and maturing industry. However, the public sphere framework reminds us that media cannot be treated simply like any other industry. Furthermore, it raises serious questions about what these structural changes mean for diversity and independence in content and for the power of newly emerging media corporations.

The Market Perspective

From the perspective of the market model, the media industry is one that has enjoyed enormous growth in recent years. With that growth has come a repositioning of major players, the introduction of some significant new players, and an evolution in the basic terrain of the industry. This perspective tends to see this growth as a logical outcome in an industry that has become more integrated across media and more global in scope. To operate effectively in such a new environment, media corporations must develop new business strategies (to be discussed in the next chapter) and draw on the large capital resources available only to major global corporations. The structural changes of growth, integration, and globalization are merely the signs of companies positioning themselves to operate in this new media world. The concentration of media ownership, on the other hand, is the natural byproduct of a maturing industry, as young startups and older, underperforming firms are consolidated into the business plans of mature but innovative companies.

The rapid growth in media outlets, the constant shifts in consumer tastes, and the ever-changing terrain of the industry itself make any apparent domination of the industry by a few companies an illusion. No one can control such a vast and constantly evolving industry.

Market advocates note that we should not be nostalgic about the media era gone by. In reality, as recently as the mid-1970s, the media landscape was much more sparsely populated than it is today and consumers had far fewer choices, on the whole. Compared with this earlier period, market advocates point out, we have a cornucopia of media outlets and products available to us.

It is true that more communities had competing daily newspapers than today, but often the quality of those smaller local papers was mediocre at best. In contrast, today's papers may be local monopolies and part of larger chains, but by drawing on the resources of their owners, they are able to produce a higher quality product. Also, consumers have many more options for news—especially with cable television and the Internet—than they ever did in the days of more competing daily papers, making local newspaper monopolies less significant.

In the 1970s, many communities had only small local bookstores with very limited inventory and choice. Today, more and more communities have "superstore" booksellers with thousands of diverse selections of books and magazines. Rather than killing the old print medium, the Internet has been a shot in the arm for book sales, as online retailers such as Amazon.com offer hundreds of thousands of titles for sale at the click of a mouse. This has made books and other media products more widely available than ever.

In the 1970s, local movie theaters were beginning to feature more multiscreen offerings, but these were limited compared to what is available today. Video rentals were not readily available, because VCRs were still primitive in those days. Today, more multiplex theaters bring more options to moviegoers. By 2005, over 90% of U.S. homes had a VCR—though this technology was rapidly being displaced by DVD players, which were in two thirds of homes, and, increasingly, by digital video recorders such as TiVo. Titles for these devices were widely available for low-cost renting or purchase from brick-and-mortar rental stores or online rental services.

Radio was admittedly more diverse in terms of regional preferences years ago, but it is not clear whether a broader range of music was readily available to listeners then. Today, radio has become largely a chain-owned affair, with new standards of professionalism and high production values. In addition, online streaming in various formats is offering greater musical variety to listeners, and satellite radio has begun to establish itself as a major competitor to traditional broadcast fare.

Most striking is that 90% of the prime-time television audience in the mid-1970s was watching just three television networks. Cable television was not really an alternative because it was largely used to transmit the "big three" broadcast networks to homes in which reception was difficult. Satellite television, of course, was unheard of. Today, three new broadcast networks have joined the older big three. Almost two thirds of U.S. homes have cable, and over 20% have satellite television, each offering scores of channels.

Finally, the vast universe of the Internet is becoming available to more and more people. In 2004, the majority of U.S. households were online, with industry analysts estimating Internet access at two thirds of U.S. households.[75] The Internet, especially with broadband access, opened up unprecedented avenues for news, entertainment, and commerce.

In light of these rapid changes, as we have seen, market advocates have called for more deregulation of the industry to spur increased competition. Because of digitization, companies in fields that were previously separate can now compete with each other if regulations are lifted. On the delivery side, telephone companies, for example, can now offer Internet access as well, and cable companies can enter the telephone and Internet businesses. On the content side, companies that had traditionally been focused in one medium can now branch out to work in films, television, print, Internet, and other media. All of this, market advocates contend, means more choices and better media for the consumer; a regulatory system created in a far different era is obsolete in this new dynamic media environment.

Questioning the Market: Revisiting the Public Sphere Approach

Although the market approach may celebrate the new media environment, there are questions that this focus on markets and profits effectively obscures. The public sphere perspective suggests that the technological change and growth in the number of media outlets should not be accepted as an unequivocal benefit, especially if these outlets are linked to a growing concentration in media ownership.

The introduction of new media has never ensured quality content. History has shown that the great potential of new media forms has often been subverted for purely commercial purposes. Both radio and television, at various points, were touted as having profound educational and civic potential. That potential was never reached. Cable television has, in many ways, simply reproduced the formats and formulas of broadcast television. Because it is not covered by the same content rules that regulate broadcast television, cable has had more leeway to air raunchy, violent, sexually suggestive, and sensational entertainment. This type of entertainment can be seen in everything from adult-oriented cable movies to the funny, but foul-mouthed, animated prepubescent offerings of *South Park*. The popularity of such cable programming pressured broadcast television to seek increasingly wild and aggressive programs, leading many parents to despair about the lack of appropriate entertainment and educational television for their children. In recent years, complaints from conservative and religious groups has helped spur the FCC to issue a series of fines against both radio and television broadcasters who aired indecent programming.

More wasted potential seems to have plagued the growth of the Internet. Early discussion of the "information superhighway" was quickly supplanted by a focus on e-commerce. Here, too, adult-oriented sites proved to be very popular. There may be more media outlets, but we need to examine what these channels are delivering.

A concern for the health of the public sphere leads us to argue that media outlets are only truly beneficial if they serve the public interest by delivering content that is genuinely diverse and substantive. Early indications were that, to the contrary, much of cable television was delivering more of the same commercial fare that characterized broadcast television. Why could not some of these many channels be used to deliver innovative, diverse, and inclusive public affairs programming? Or alternative visions from independent filmmakers and other artists? Or programming that specifically spoke to the common challenges we face as a society? Instead, the fragmentary nature of the cable television world might even be exacerbating cultural divisions in society, as segregated programming targets separate demographic groups based on age, gender, class, and race. The Internet, too, has been used by major media companies primarily to sell products to consumers and to promote other media ventures, few of which have added significantly to a vibrant public sphere.

Finally, the blurring of boundaries between media, coupled with calls for deregulation, raise the specter of fully integrated, multinational media giants that can simultaneously dominate multiple media. Old monopoly criteria seem incapable of dealing with this new market reality. Despite the fact that it was promoted as a means of increasing competition, the 1996 Telecommunications Act has resulted in renewed consolidation in the media industry. Despite this continuing consolidation, market advocates still talk about the new "competition," and policy makers seem unwilling to examine the significance of an emerging media monopoly owned by a few giant firms.

Part of the problem is that the recent waves of media mergers have often brought together companies that have not been direct competitors in the past. So, for example, a phone company buys a cable company or an Internet provider buys a multimedia conglomerate. Using traditional market theory, antitrust law has had to show that a proposed merger would substantially reduce competition and that this reduced competition would enable combined companies to increase prices. However, as one *Wall Street Journal* reporter put it, "It is tough to show that rivalry could suffer where none exists, as with a merger between companies that have never competed against each other."[76] Recent mergers have often been across forms of media, but they nonetheless raise troubling questions. Although it was difficult for such deals to be challenged based on the traditional criteria of monopolies, who was to say that the blurring lines between, for example, cable, telephone, and Internet could not be exploited by just a few companies who would dominate all three?

On the content side, market theory promised diversity from an unregulated market, but the reality seems to be quite different, as the same old media content is being sold in new packaging, and underserved communities continue to be marginalized. Little that is fresh or independent seems to come from the new media giants. This, coupled with the growth in the sheer size of these corporations, raises the disturbing specter of concentrated corporate power capable of stifling diverse expression and exerting significant political power.

Thus, although the structural changes in the media industry are apparent, what these changes mean is not at all settled. Advocates of a market approach to media, the most visible perspectives in the public debate, see growth as positive evidence of a vibrant industry. From a public sphere perspective, however, it is clear that we need to look beyond economic criteria to assess the new media giants. Instead, we need to ask, What have the media corporations done with their newly acquired resources? What strategies have they pursued in this new media environment? These are the sorts of questions we examine in the next chapter.

4

Strategies of the
New Media Giants

The structural trends described in chapter 3 were made possible by a lax regulatory environment and changing technologies. Structural change is a means, not an end, for major media firms, however. Media companies grew, became more integrated, and developed a global presence to more effectively carry out some basic business strategies. Those strategies are the subject of this chapter.

Major media corporations pursue these strategies to accomplish three general goals. First, media giants seek to *maximize profits*. This simple truth is the heart of any analysis of business strategy within the media industry. Although the strategies discussed in this chapter have been popular in recent years, they will continue to be so only if they remain profitable. Structural changes have facilitated the use of new strategies that place a premium on profits. For example, different segments of the media industry have historically had significantly different profit margins. Publishing has never been as lucrative as television, for instance. However, with conglomeration, companies that once operated only in certain segments of the media industry are now owned by a single media conglomerate. As once-distinct media companies have been transformed into collaborative divisions of single corporate conglomerates, one effect has been increased pressure to improve profitability. What might have been a respectable profit margin in a particular segment of the industry may now be unacceptable when compared with other divisions of the company.

Second, some of the structural changes have enabled companies to *reduce costs* by improving efficiency and streamlining departments. Efficiency can improve when conglomerates more fully use and combine assets into an integrated media strategy. Also, announcements of mergers and acquisitions are often accompanied shortly thereafter by layoffs, as redundant personnel are cut after the consolidation of key functions. Keeping costs low in relation to revenue generated is a central goal of any for-profit business, including media companies.

Third, conglomeration has enabled companies to pursue various business strategies geared to *reducing risk*. In seeking to ensure continued profits, companies often try to control the environment in which they operate by reducing uncertainty and minimizing expensive competition. By doing so, they can better ensure lower costs and higher profits.

One or more of these three general goals lies behind all of the specific strategies discussed in this chapter. These strategies are usually not immediately obvious to the public. Primarily, what we see and hear from the media industry concerns their products, not their tactics. Thus we begin our discussion of corporate media strategies by briefly looking at an example of a familiar media form—a movie—that is the result of several key strategies used in the contemporary media industry.

❖ THE CASE OF *TITANIC*

In current dollars, *Titanic* was the highest grossing film of the 20th century and went on to become the best selling live action film in history.[77] At the time of its creation in 1997, the movie cost a staggering $200 million ($238 million) to make—just over $1 million for each minute of screen time. However, its box office revenue reached $2 *billion* worldwide, including more than $600 million in North America alone. That was just the beginning. Movie rentals worldwide brought in another $900 million. Television sales generated $30 million. The sale of 25 million copies of the movie's soundtrack album took in more than

$400 million. Videotape and DVD sales worldwide surpassed 30 million units, representing another $1 billion in revenue.[78]

With those kinds of sales, profits were enormous. The film was a coproduction of two media giants, News Corporation (through its Twentieth Century Fox studio) and Viacom (owner of Paramount Pictures). News Corporation is estimated to have made nearly half a *billion* dollars in profit from *Titanic;* Viacom's profits were more than $300 million.

The film's history was a bit unusual because, by Hollywood block-buster standards, it did not receive megamarketing prior to its release. There were questions about how well the film would do. The movie was more than 3 hours long, was initially aimed at adults rather than the lucrative teen market, and—partially to offset its huge special effects budget—it did not feature major stars, although some of the film's actors went on to become stars.

However, the film's immediate popularity had executives seeing dollar signs, and a virtual industry of *Titanic* promotions and merchandise quickly appeared. A Web site was devoted solely to selling officially licensed *Titanic* products.[79] By the time the film was ready to be released on video in September 1998, Paramount Home Video had spent $50 million to advertise it—at the time, an amount roughly equivalent to the entire budget of an average Hollywood movie.

The number of *Titanic* products and promotions was enormous.

❖ For sale were innumerable T-shirts, sweatshirts, tank tops, baseball caps, coffee mugs, and movie posters.

❖ HarperCollins, owned by News Corp., published the highly successful *James Cameron's Titanic,* a look at the film and its making, written by its director.

❖ FOX (also owned by News Corp.) broadcast a television special, *Titanic: Breaking New Ground,* which also featured commercials for the movie's soundtrack.

❖ Sony was licensed to produce the hit soundtrack for the film, creating a rarity: a classical music album at the number one spot in sales. Meanwhile, pop-star diva Celine Dion's own album (also a Sony property) featured the *Titanic* signature song "My Heart Will Go On," which also sold millions of copies. Dion's song was so popular that, in a partnership with Morley Candy, Sony launched a new series of celebrity chocolates in the shape of the singer's face.[80]

❖ A new line of Max Factor lipstick colors "inspired" by the movie was promoted with television and print advertising, free samples via the mail, 9 million brochures distributed door to door, and 60,000 *Titanic*-themed in-store displays. In one cross-promotional effort, consumers who bought the *Titanic* home video and $10 worth of Max Factor cosmetics could receive a free copy of the book *James Cameron's Titanic*.[81]

❖ In June 1998, more than 100,000 copies of the video were sold in just 1 hour on the home shopping channel, QVC. A month later, QVC featured *Titanic* memorabilia, including movie posters and film cels.[82]

❖ Several computer CD-ROMs appeared, including *Titanic: Adventure Out of Time* and *Titanic: A Voyage of Discovery*.

❖ *Titanic: A New Musical* was launched on Broadway, spawning its own set of promotional merchandise, including T-shirts, caps, an original Broadway cast CD, posters, lapel pins, and books.

Hundreds of unlicensed products, with tie-ins to the original *Titanic* disaster, emerged as well. They included everything from small lumps of coal from the wreck site of the original ship, to crystals etched with the *Titanic's* likeness, to reproductions of the ship's furniture. Dozens of old books about the disaster were rereleased, and even the transcripts from congressional hearings on the original disaster were sold. J. Peterman Company, the upscale clothing and accessories retailer, devoted part of its 1997 holiday catalog to replica, prop, and souvenir items related to the movie, including a necklace and Titanic stationery. They even offered a 13-foot anchor for $25,000. The company sold more than $3 million worth of merchandise in its first offering.[83]

Ironically, this movie about 1,500 deaths on a sinking ship sparked a surge in ocean cruises,[84] and two cruise lines announced plans to build full-scale replicas of the *Titanic*.[85] All of the hype and consumerism also stirred considerable backlash, including numerous Web sites devoted to mocking the film and its endless commercial tie-ins. Still, *Titanic* launched a mini-industry of promotional tie-ins that only contributed to the film's transformation into a pop culture phenomenon. It was a fad that media corporations rode all the way to the bank.

Titanic was soon replaced in our memories by a series of more recent Hollywood blockbuster movies. Although each film has brought with it unique stories and stars, as a group, blockbusters all represent the end result of a common series of corporate strategies.

❖ STRATEGIES OF THE NEW MEDIA GIANTS

The story of *Titanic* is just one illustration of several key strategies that media giants employ in their pursuit of profits. The scale and sophistication of these efforts has been made possible in part by the restructuring of the industry. We now examine some of the business tactics that have emerged as a result of this restructuring. Although we discuss various strategies individually, it is clear that these are often overlapping approaches that make up an overall integrated business strategy.

Size Matters: Cost and Economies of Scale

The most obvious change in the media industry's structure has been the growth of the major media companies. Although there are notorious difficulties involved in managing such vast global enterprises, companies also enjoy some distinct advantages when they grow to be such large media players.

One advantage is that they can afford to develop more expensive projects, because they control or have access to enormous amounts of investment capital. Only a select few companies can afford to put up the incredible $200 million that was needed to make *Titanic*. By 2003, the *average* cost of a single Hollywood film exceeded $63 million, and the average cost for that year's top seven movies topped $102 million.[86] As a result, even the major studios have struggled to cover the escalating costs of production and have searched for new strategies to lower costs and ensure profits. These strategies include coproduction with other media giants to reduce cost and risk; the use of younger actors, who command smaller salaries; and the growing practice of paying actors, directors, and writers a share of the profits instead of large, up-front salaries. The producers of *Titanic* used all of these methods.

Other very expensive areas of the media business—such as national television networks—are also accessible only to a few megamedia corporations. That means competition in some very lucrative areas of the media business is limited to only a few corporations, which develop huge war chests of resources. Such limited competition helps to ensure the profitability of these ventures, despite their enormous costs.

By getting bigger through mergers and acquisitions, today's large media corporations strive to enter this very elite world. Consequently, there tends to be a self-perpetuating cycle that emerges from major movie productions or other very expensive media projects. Only a few media giants can afford to produce and promote these expensive projects. In turn, a successful project can be enormously profitable, thus reinforcing the conglomerate's role as a dominant media corporation.

A second advantage of size is that media giants have the resources to advertise and promote a product with expensive, multifaceted campaigns, a topic examined more fully later in this chapter. For example, the cost of major advertising and promotion often amounts to 50% of a movie's entire production cost. For studios, therefore, it is important to carefully pick and choose the films that will receive big-time promotion. Usually, such support goes to films aimed at teens and young adults—the industry's best customers—featuring well-known box office stars. Studios launching such expensive projects cannot afford to experiment with risky, unproven efforts. Instead, major Hollywood movies tend to follow a few select formulas with records of past success, such as the action-adventure genre. Coupled with stars that are proven box office draws, such formulaic films are the trademark of a "Hollywood" production. In the end, studios hope a big investment, following a proven formula, combined with heavy promotion results in substantial profits. This strategy is largely unavailable to smaller competitors.

A similar strategy is used in other fields, as well. Publishers have increasingly turned to their own version of the blockbuster strategy, increasingly relying on "big name" authors and books. In recent years, as a direct result of consolidation in the media industry, pressure has increased to make book publishing as profitable as other forms of media. Mark Crispin Miller notes, "For decades, publishers thrived on annual profits of roughly 4%. But as major media conglomerates have bought out these independents, they have come to expect profits comparable to other parts of their media empires—12 to 15%."[87]

To achieve these profit goals, publishers have focused their resources and attention on a few titles they believe may become bestsellers. A handful of celebrity authors receive huge advances, while lesser known authors receive minimal pay. For example, Pope John Paul II received an $8.5 million advance for his book, former president Bill Clinton was paid $10 million for his memoirs, and suspense novelist Mary Higgins Clark signed a five-book deal for a $64 million advance. In turn, much as with the movies, publishers try to ensure they recoup these big investments by spending heavily on advertising and promotion for these few "big books." Meanwhile, as they focus on these big books, some publishers have been known to slash the overall number of books they publish and keep in print, especially reducing the number of "mid-list" books that can be costly to promote but are not likely to become bestsellers and "serious" titles that reach a more limited readership.

A third advantage of size is that companies can develop economies of scale. Traditionally, *economies of scale* refers to the fact that the cost of producing individual units of a product (books, CDs, etc.) declines as the volume of sales goes up. The investment in studio time, for example, remains the same whether a CD sells 3000 copies or a million copies. Even the per-disk cost of actually manufacturing the CD can go down if larger quantities are produced. The bigger the sales, the less per unit the production and manufacturing costs, because those costs are spread over many more units. That translates into more profit for the media company. This is one advantage of the global strategy pursued by the big media firms. For media conglomerates with the capacity to promote heavily, it is more efficient to develop and support major hits with sales in the millions than it is to produce many products with much smaller sales. Products that reach smaller niche audiences are not likely to be as profitable.

A fourth advantage of size is the ability to withstand short-term losses. Despite following previously successful formulas, the reality is that for every *Titanic,* there are dozens of movies—or books or other media products—that make little or no money. Here too, being bigger is an advantage. Only a major conglomerate can afford to absorb the cost of an expensive media flop and still keep on making movies while waiting for the next megahit. Smaller companies, of course, cannot afford such a capital-intensive strategy.

One of the features of the Internet touted by early proponents was that it could overcome all the inherent advantages of size because it eliminated the high-cost barrier of entering the media market. With the Internet, the argument went, the cost of entry was very low, and small producers could compete on an even playing field with major companies, potentially revolutionizing the media industry. The reality, however, proved to be less than revolutionary. Traditional media players bought out most early, promising ventures. As mergers and consolidation reached the Internet in the late 1990s, the early optimism for change faded. The cost of competition with the major media companies rose to millions of dollars, and large media firms dominated the Internet's most popular sites.

Jeff Bezos, CEO of online retailer Amazon.com, Inc., noted in late 1998 that with the increase in Internet mergers, "What is happening is that people are finally realizing that these Internet businesses are scale businesses." Being large—regardless of the medium—brought with it advantages of economies of scale. Small companies were at a distinct disadvantage when trying to survive in the Internet environment. The cost of promotion and advertising on the cluttered Internet also favored large businesses. As one *Wall Street Journal* report concluded, "Building a brand in crowded Internet markets will require ever larger spending on advertising and marketing."[88] Only the major media players had those sorts of resources, and they were showing a decided interest in buying up promising ventures. The Internet, too, became a medium in which having deep pockets provided a distinct advantage.

Synergy: Cross-Development and Cross-Promotion

On the announcement of Disney's takeover of Cap Cities/ABC, Disney CEO Michael Eisner told the press, "I'm optimistic that one [plus] one adds up to four."[89] What he was alluding to was the concept of *synergy*. As we have noted earlier, synergy is the idea that separate entities working together can achieve results that none could obtain individually—or, as Eisner's creative mathematics suggested, the whole is greater than the sum of its parts. Maximizing synergy, therefore, is taking advantage of multiple media holdings to develop or promote a single project with many different facets. In this way, media conglomerates seek to maximize the benefits they can obtain from owning many different media firms.

One element of synergy involves developing and packaging a single concept for various media. A children's story, for example, may be packaged as a comic book, movie, soundtrack, television cartoon series, and computer game—each adding to the popularity of the other. By doing this, media conglomerates can take advantage of simultaneous revenue streams, thereby generating as much profit as possible from a single idea. Indeed, new projects are often created specifically because of their potential to exploit synergy in this way. It is now routine for executives from a conglomerate's different divisions to meet specifically to develop ideas that can be used across media. In fact, some companies base executive bonuses in part on how well managers can create ideas that are exploitable in this way.[90] As a result, a book manuscript that might be transformed into a movie, television series, and computer game is likely to be much more attractive to a company than a book that is, well, just a book. The result is that project ideas now often live or die based on how well they can be exploited across media—rather than how "good" they are on their own terms.

Such thinking has even affected how journalists operate. In a world of synergistic development, the nature of news is being transformed. For example, the editor of the *Chicago Tribune,* a daily newspaper owned by the growing media conglomerate, the Tribune Company, once noted that "I am not the editor of a newspaper. I am the manager of a content company."[91] In this way, news becomes "content" that can be repackaged to fit with and be usable by the other divisions of the company.

A second aspect of synergy involves cross-promotion—promoting a single concept via various media. Turning the notion of artistic creativity on its head, companies now often strive to develop an idea that can be successfully marketed, rather then trying to market an interesting idea. For example, after Disney bought the ABC television network, periodically some of the plots for the network's· favorite sitcoms involved the characters vacationing at Disney's theme parks. During a 2004 episode of the *George Lopez* show, not only were the characters going to Disneyland, the audience was invited to spot hidden images of Mickey Mouse scattered throughout the episode. Viewers could send in their list of findings for a chance to win a family vacation at Disneyland and other prizes. Thus, Disney used one of its properties, ABC, to promote another of its properties, Disneyland—to the benefit of both, it was hoped.

Synergy can be seen most starkly in "blockbuster" media projects that can quickly seem to saturate society. The *Titanic* movie was one example. The Titanic concept was repackaged for the movies, television, magazines, CDs, Internet, computer software, and other media. Through heavy, synergy-driven promotion, a simple movie became a multimedia phenomenon, catapulting the film's stars to the celebrity stratosphere. In addition to the many examples cited here, the film's coproducers could take advantage of their other media holdings to help promote the movie relentlessly. Viacom, one of the coproducers, also owns MTV. It therefore could prominently feature a Celine Dion music video related to the movie in MTV's rotation and, in effect, run commercials for the film on MTV. News Corporation, the film's other coproducer, could use its network, FOX, to promote the movie via programming about the making of the film and specials on the real *Titanic*.

The popularity of a media product generated by cross-promotion can further be exploited by lucrative licensing deals with other companies. In a typical such process, Viacom translated its Nickelodeon cable children's hit *SpongeBob SquarePants* into related products such as videotapes and DVDs (produced by Viacom's Paramount Home Video), children's books (published by Viacom's Simon Spotlight), and a major motion picture (released by Viacom's Paramount Studios). The success of SpongeBob could then be marketed to other companies wanting to license the name and image of the character. As a result, Viacom received fees for the licensing of hundreds of SpongeBob products, including video games, toys, board games, computer software, radios, posters, charm bracelets, bathrobes, backpacks, bedding, T-shirts, clocks, furniture, and trading cards.

Consequently, conglomerates, with their enormous resources and diverse holdings, have an advantage in developing and promoting projects in ways that smaller competitors simply cannot match. Spending a lot of money on a project does not ensure that it will be popular and economically successful, but it does mean that it will be given every possible chance to succeed in an otherwise busy and overcrowded media marketplace. Projects without the backing of major media conglomerates do not enjoy such advantages.

Of course, synergy does not always work. When Japanese electronic hardware companies Sony and Matsushita Electric Industrial purchased Columbia Pictures and MCA, respectively, they tried in vain to develop successful cross-promotional strategies. Many industry observers believed such hardware-software synergy efforts were much less likely to succeed than those that focused on various forms of media content and delivery rather than on hardware.

That is not the only problem that can occur when trying to exploit synergy. Another problem some recently merged companies have discovered is that it can be difficult to coordinate efforts across various media—book publishing and movie making, for example—that sometimes have vastly different norms of operation and dramatically different industry cultures. The failure of the AOL Time Warner merger, discussed at the opening of this book, is one such example. Assumptions about the efficiency of synergistic relationships have also been challenged at times. Most often, this has occurred when a division of a huge conglomerate is forced to do business with another of the conglomerate's companies, even though the same work might be more efficiently done by an outside company. Still, despite such setbacks, the

profits associated with a successful synergy project are a strong induce-
ment for companies to keep trying. There can be little doubt that the
next big-budget movie, best-selling book, hit TV series, monster video
game, or smash music CD will be developed into products for various
media and marketed using the synergistic possibilities of a media
conglomerate.

Branding

Another practice closely associated with synergy and cross-
promotion is *branding*. Brand names, of course, are a staple of a consumer society. Whether Kellogg's, Abercrombie & Fitch, Chevrolet,
Apple, Nike, or a host of other company names, brands have proven to
be attractive to consumers overwhelmed with choices in a cluttered
marketplace. If a brand is associated with a quality or image that the
consumer likes, the consumer tends to choose the branded version of a
traditional product or try a new product from the same brand name.
Rather than risk an unknown brand, consumers often use a brand as a
shorthand way of making purchase decisions. Brands and brand loyalty also make it more difficult for new competitors to enter a market.

In some markets, products are very interrelated, which, again, promotes brand name loyalty. Such is the case with software, for which it
is crucial to have compatibility between operating systems and software applications, between different applications, and between PC-
based applications and other, non-PC electronic devices. Because these
systems, applications, and so on often use similar conventions, a consumer's familiarity with one company's software may reduce the time
necessary to learn how to use other applications from the same company. In such an integrated field, especially, a well-known brand such
as Microsoft is an incredibly valuable commodity.

Even in more traditional media fields, companies market their
goods with branding in mind. Specifically, branding strategies usually
include the following:

1. Distinguishing a product from others via real attributes or
   image creation

2. Maintaining high-profile marketing campaigns highlighting the
   brand name

3. Repeating the brand image and message across different media

It is easy to see, therefore, how branding relates to synergy and cross-promotion. Branding is a strategy that is available primarily to major media companies. Advertising insiders estimate that creating a new, nationally recognized brand costs from $20 to $40 million in television advertising in the first 4 months after launch alone.[92]

Media conglomerates, such as Disney, have learned the value of branding. Disney's corporate Web site noted that "The Walt Disney Company's objective is to be one of the world's leading producers and providers of entertainment and information, using its portfolio of brands to differentiate its content, services and consumer products."[93] Disney uses its brand name association with wholesome family entertainment to sell all sorts of products. It has theme parks, children's movies, a cable channel, books, Internet sites, toys, and even a cruise line for family vacations, all emblazoned with the Disney brand. Regardless of the content, a new animated movie, for example, enjoys an advantage over competitors if it is a new *Disney* animated movie. (This does not *guarantee* success, however. Disney's *Treasure Planet* is widely considered to be one of the biggest box office duds of all time, costing $140 million to make but earning less than $40 million at U.S. box offices.)

Other branding efforts abound. Disney owns ESPN, the popular all-sports cable channel, which itself is a popular brand name. The ESPN brand has resulted in cable spin-offs (ESPN-2, ESPN News, ESPN Classic, ESPN Pay-per-view, ESPN International), a publication (*ESPN Magazine*), ESPN radio, retail stores (ESPN–The Store), a Web site (ESPN.com), and sports-themed restaurants (The ESPN Zone).

To take another example, *Star Wars* was a popular 1970s science fiction film that became, in effect, a brand name licensed for use on a wide variety of products. The 1999 release of the fourth Star Wars film, *Episode One: The Phantom Menace,* marked the culmination of nearly a decade of careful marketing by Lucasfilm, the movie's creator, to revive the Star Wars brand that had been popular two decades earlier.[94] In the 1990s, products based on the Star Wars brand included a series of books aimed at adults, a comic book series aimed at kids, a number of computer games, video rerelease of the original *Star Wars* film trilogy, theatrical rerelease of special editions of the original *Star Wars* trilogy, *Star Wars Kids: The Magazine,* and piles of new *Phantom Menace* toys, accessories, and video games. Remarkably, all of this was done *before* the release of the movie. It was all possible because of the popularity of the Star Wars brand name. A similar strategy was used in advance of the 2005 release of a new Star Wars film. In this case, advance marketing included a new Star Wars video game and a 4-DVD boxed set of the special editions of the original films.

The Internet has proven to be susceptible to the same branding strategies that have marked other media. A few of the Internet's early commercial pioneers, such as Amazon.com, have so far survived and established valuable brand names, but most have been swallowed up by the traditional media conglomerates. The struggle for influence on the Internet often has been a battle of traditional brands. One of the central strategies for large media players in the 1990s was the development of major "portals"—sites that serve as a central hub for multiple Internet services. Smaller independent players were forced to spend extensively to buy up other companies to compete with giants such as Disney.

For example, Disney purchased a $70 million controlling share of Infoseek, a Web search site, and in 1998, it launched its "Go Network." In 1999, NBC, owned by General Electric, followed suit, buying Xoom.com and Snap.com and merging them into a new NBC Internet effort. As a business press report noted at the time, "Xoom.com and Snap.com are not currently top-tier players on the Web. But NBC is betting it can turn the whole stew into something more valuable by slapping on the NBC name and logo throughout NBC Internet and aggressively promoting it on the NBC broadcast network."[95]

Halsey Minor, CEO of CNET—an online news company—described NBC's promotion of Snap.com as "the first big salvo in what I think is going to become a very large marketing war pitting some fairly large media companies" against one another. This competition between media giants will crush many smaller competitors who do not sell out, all or in part, to the large conglomerates. Minor concludes, "It's going to be very, very expensive for those who don't have a partner to compete, given the amount of promotion NBC will be putting behind Snap."[96] Thus the competition for the Internet may well leave a few familiar media giants in control of the most lucrative Internet sites.

There is a dilemma, though, associated with branding. Some companies have become so large that placing their brands on everything they own might easily result in consumer backlash against a media "Big Brother." Imagine, for example, if the Viacom brand name were explicitly used on all of its properties listed in Exhibit 3.2. What would happen if *all* of Disney's holdings were labeled with the familiar corporate logo? If consumers were aware of the enormous tentacles of this media conglomerate, Disney's innocent image as a supplier of whole-some family entertainment might become suspect. To avoid this situa-tion, Disney and other major conglomerates have developed multiple brands that obscure their common ownership. Disney, ESPN, ABC, and the Go.com brands—although all owned by Disney—distinguish these various product lines from each other.

Segmentation and Specialization

Most companies that make consumer products operate in a single market: They produce goods that are sold to consumers. As we saw in chapter 1, however, media industries are different because they often operate in a *dual product market*. That is, they sell two separate prod-ucts to two completely different sets of consumers. The first market involves the selling of media content (books, videos, CDs, etc.) to audi-ences of readers, viewers, and listeners. The second market involves selling the attention of audiences (as measured by ratings, circulation, etc.) to advertisers. Because some media depend so heavily on them for survival, advertisers are by far media's most important customers.

Although consumers and advertisers are two separate markets, they are closely related. TV ratings are directly linked to advertising revenue. Attracting a large audience to a television program allows the networks to charge more for advertising time on that program. The bigger ratings numbers translate into more advertising dollars. Some advertisers paid $2.4 million for a 30-second commercial during the 2005 Super Bowl because, in recent years, more than 130 million people watched at least part of the game.

However, ironically, one of the ways that big media conglomerates can take advantage of their size is by thinking small. That is, rather than simply targeting large audiences, media giants are now more likely to use new technologies to develop niche products aimed at spe-cific market segments. In some ways, this strategy contrasts and con-tradicts the approach of exploiting economies of scale, where massive sales are the goal. Instead, through specialized media products aimed at smaller market segments, companies seek to piece together larger profits.

Niche audiences are important to media companies because they can be sold to advertisers at a premium. When advertisers choose where to place their messages, they are usually interested in reaching fairly large audiences. As a result, they pay more for advertising time on a television program or in a newspaper that has more viewers or readers. More important is that advertisers are interested in reaching the "right" audience—those with sufficient income in the demographic group most likely to purchase the advertisers' products. By using specialized media products to segment the audience into specific demographic groups, media companies can more efficiently meet the needs of advertisers. We explore the social impact of this strategy in chapter 6.

Some forms of media, such as magazine publishing, have long had significant niche audiences. As we saw in chapter 2, the magazine industry once had a number of major, general audience publications, such as the *Saturday Evening Post, Look,* and *Life,* but publishers have also offered a wide array of specialized magazines aimed at audiences with particular interests. Business publications, magazines for hobbyists of all sorts, sports magazines, fashion and beauty magazines, and many others have long been part of the industry. These special interest publications became the standard after the general audience magazines failed in the late 1960s and early 1970s.

However, some forms of media have always been wholly aimed at a single large mainstream audience. Television is a good example of an industry that used to rely on this approach almost exclusively. As we have seen, as recently as the 1970s, just three national networks were routinely attracting more than 90% of the viewing audience on any given evening. That meant that the audience for any particular show was more or less diverse, by TV-audience standards. It would include both men and women, people from all racial and class groups, a fairly broad age range, and with a wide variety of interests.

The widespread adoption of cable has significantly changed television marketing. Now the "big four" networks (ABC, CBS, NBC, and FOX) attract less than half of the viewing audience—and that is declining. Audiences have instead slowly migrated to cable, with its cacophony of competing channels with relatively low-cost programming usually aimed at niche audiences. Cable delivers channels devoted entirely to sports, movies, cartoons, comedy, music, shopping, home improvement, cooking, golf, and many more subjects. This requires a fundamentally different marketing strategy than the original networks used in the past.

The broadcast networks formerly relied on programming aimed at a large mainstream audience. They tried to develop programming that would appeal broadly but would not be offensive. Cable, on the other hand, often sought to program narrowly and focused on the interests of demographically specific niche audiences. As a result, cable networks could afford to ignore or even offend some segments of the mainstream audience, because these segments were not part of the audience targeted for the particular program. If you do not own a home or do repairs yourself, Home and Garden Television (HGTV) is unlikely to catch your attention. That is of little concern to cable channels, however, because advertisers on HGTV specifically want to reach home-owning do-it-your-selfers with ads for power tools, gardening accessories, and other home-related products. MTV and BET's sexually suggestive music videos and the adolescent chauvinism of Comedy Central's *The Man Show* are also partially byproducts of this difference in marketing strategy. Cable channels such as MTV, BET, and Comedy Central can push the line of industry decency standards and simultaneously appeal to a lucrative teen (and often male) audience because they are not particularly concerned about offending other viewers. Instead, their stock in trade is generating corporate profits by selling teens rebellious, "edgy" programming. Other channels are aimed at different lucrative demographic groups, such as the professional women targeted by Lifetime and the Oxygen Network.

One particular area of specialization that has experienced dramatic growth in recent years is that of foreign language television programs. Cable and satellite companies have been competing for this segment of the market by offering channels featuring programs from the native lands of recent immigrants. One provider, the Dish Network, has developed a particular strength in this area, offering more than 50 international or foreign language channels in dozens of languages.[97] With a rapidly growing Hispanic population in the United States, Spanish language television exploded in the early 2000s. By 2004, there were at least ten television networks with broadcast, cable, and satellite programming targeted specifically at Hispanic audiences (see Exhibit 4.1). The audience for such programs has been considerable: During the 2002-2003 season, the top 72 rated television programs in Hispanic households were Spanish language.[98]

For media companies, the strategy of focusing on specific niche markets can be financially risky because it places all of a company's eggs in one basket, so to speak. If music videos become less popular, and your company's cable channel plays only music videos, you are in trouble. However, the solution to such dangers comes, again, from conglomeration. Major media companies generally do not own *single* cable channels. Instead, they usually own many different channels, either wholly or partially. That way, the media company can profit from

Exhibit 4.1   Hispanic Television Networks in the United States
(2004)

Azteca America: Spanish language TV network owned by TV Azteca of Mexico

ESPN Deportes: Spanish language sports network launched by ESPN in 2004

Fox Sports En Espanol: Spanish language sports network operated by Fox Pan American Sports

Galavision: Spanish language cable network owned by Univision

mun2: Bilingual programming focused on young Latino audience, launched by Telemundo in 2001

Si TV: English language, Latino-themed channel focused on youth market

Telefutura Network: Spanish language network launched by Univision in 2002

Telemundo: Spanish language network owned by GE, operated by NBC/Universal

TuTV: Markets and distributes five international Spanish language TV networks to the American market via satellite

Univision Network: The largest Spanish language TV network in the United States

The Voy Network: English language, Hispanic-themed lifestyle network

---

specialized niche marketing via any single channel and simultaneously enjoy the security benefits of diversification because of the overall mix of audiences tuning into its collection of holdings. For decades, this has been the situation in the magazine industry, in which major media companies own an array of different titles.

Even the mainstream television networks have been affected by this movement in the media business toward audience segmentation. Networks still receive the lion's share of the audience, but as their viewers have migrated to cable, the networks have tended to focus on desirable demographics in their quest to maintain advertising revenue. They have, to a degree, imitated cable programming and targeted their attention more than ever on the desirable teen and young adult market— with an accompanying increase in violent, sexually suggestive programming, with adult language. Thus a series of full-page newspaper ads from the FOX network could tout: "FOX. The #1 Network. #1 in Adults 18-49. #1 in Teens."[99] FOX had focused on youth-oriented programs and wanted to share with potential advertisers their good news. Viewers more than 49 years old, apparently, were not a concern.

Older viewers, in fact, have long been neglected by television programmers interested in the advertising dollars that follow younger viewers. In a dramatic 1996 example of this fact, CBS canceled the longest-running detective drama in TV history, *Murder She Wrote,* despite the fact that it had been receiving solid ratings and was the highest rated drama series for nine seasons straight. As one industry reporter summarized, "Despite its sterling household numbers, the show was plagued by an inability to draw younger viewers, making it significantly less desirable to advertisers. Although its competitors in the Sunday night time period drew smaller household numbers, ABC and NBC were able to sell the time for more money than CBS, based on more attractive demos [demographics]."[100] This is a good example of how media markets sometimes meet the needs of advertisers, not viewers.

None of the individual cable channels attracts anywhere near the audience numbers that the broadcast networks do (see Exhibit 4.2). The ratings obtained on the most-watched cable programs would be considered relatively poor by network standards. For example, during the week of November 29 to December 5, 2004, the top-rated cable program was an ESPN broadcast of an NFL football game that received a 7.4 rating—by far the highest rated cable program that week. This means that 7.4% of the nation's 105.5 million households were watching this program—about 7.8 million households. The 10th-ranked cable program that week was another ESPN sports program, *Sportscenter,* which received a 2.9 rating. Overall, the top ten cable programs received an average rating of 3.7 during this particular week.

Compare these ratings with those of the broadcast networks, where that week's top rated show was CBS's crime drama *CSI,* with a

Exhibit 4.2   Top Ten Rated Network and Cable Television
Programs, Week of November 29 Through
December 5, 2004

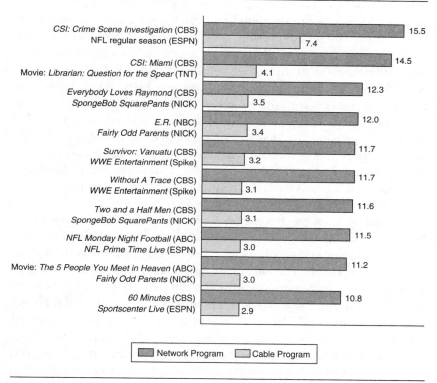

Source: Nielsen Media Research.

15.5 rating. The tenth-ranked program was the long-running CBS newsmagazine *60 Minutes*, which received a 10.8 rating—about 50% higher than the top ranked cable program. Overall, the top ten network broadcasts received an average rating of 12.3—more than three times the top ten cable average.[101]

If an advertiser is interested in appearing on a national stage, network television is still unsurpassed in delivering broad audiences. However, cable has emerged as an important alternative means of reaching niche audiences.

Specialization and audience segmentation have become part of the newspaper business too. Most daily newspapers in the United States have adopted the strategy of publishing special sections designed to attract advertiser dollars as much as readers. The result is a series of newspaper sections, usually featured on particular days of the week, that highlight the products and services of particular types of advertisers. In addition to the perennial real estate and automobile sections, which are nearly all advertising, most newspapers now have features under headings such as "Lifestyle" or "Weekend" that highlight dining and entertainment to attract advertisers in those industries. Advertisers from home furnishing, remodeling, and home repair businesses are offered sections with titles such as "At Home" or "Living." Advertisers targeting older readers are sometimes offered sections called "Prime Living" and "Golden Years," aimed at those consumers. "Food" sections are prime territory for ads from grocery stores and gourmet cookware and kitchen supply companies. "Computer and Technology" sections are full of ads from hardware manufacturers, computer stores, and software firms. The list goes on.

However, new technologies have allowed newspapers to go beyond such strategies and to specialize different editions of the paper to target different types of readers. Publishers most often do this by developing different versions of the paper aimed at people living in different areas. Increasingly, the local daily paper you read is likely to be different if you live in a suburb than if you live in the neighboring city. For example, the *Chicago Tribune* publishes eight differently zoned editions each day. What you see in the newspaper depends on where you live. As a result, people living in the suburbs are unlikely to read much about what is happening in the inner city and vice versa.[102] With this strategy, newspapers are able to entice readers by highlighting very local issues and concerns. In turn, they can sell such readers to advertisers interested in targeting readers in specific areas—especially in the more affluent suburbs.

News magazines have also employed this strategy, producing multiple covers for sale in different parts of the country, often highlighting stories of regional importance. The June 2004 edition of *Reason* magazine provided a good illustration of the extreme to which micromarketing can be taken. For that edition of the publication, all 40,000 subscribers received a personalized issue that featured a satellite photo of their particular neighborhood with their own house circled.[103]

Another way to exploit a niche market is by so-called *place-based media*. This is media that reach a particular audience because it is found exclusively at certain locations. *Channel One*, the ad-filled news broadcast aired in many schools, is perhaps the best-known example of this approach. It provides advertisers with a captive audience of teenagers, a demographic group that is lucrative but sometimes hard to reach. Other types of place-based media include a special version of CNN's news service aired on airport television monitors, allowing advertisers to reach travelers, and magazines and news broadcasts filled with health-related advertising that are available solely in doctors' waiting rooms.

The Internet offers advertisers the promise of being the ultimate medium for audience segmentation. Not only is the Internet highly fragmented with niche specialty interests, but a consumer's moves on the Internet can be electronically tracked via "cookies" and spyware placed on a user's computer that allow a Web site to identify return visitors and monitor their use of the Internet. Sites that sell items, such as Amazon.com, can track a user's purchases, enabling customized advertising based on an individual user's past purchases to be presented to that user when he or she next visits the site. Buy a couple of mystery novels at such a site and, on a return visit, you are likely to be greeted by suggestions and advertising for more books in this genre. Thus this technology allows for marketing based not on a person's demographic characteristics but on his or her specific interests and past market behavior. This is the ultimate in niche marketing, and it has even been applied to sites that customize news delivery. Users at such sites can see only headlines and information about topics in which they are already interested. Here, too, accompanying advertising is likely to be customized based on these interests. As the explosion of Internet sites continues, and as new television technologies usher in the 500-channel universe, these customized marketing strategies will be employed more widely.

The particulars vary by medium, but the basic dynamic in all of these segmentation and specialization efforts is the same: Offer a specialized media product to a particular audience segment to generate more interest from advertisers who want to reach this audience. The result has been an explosion in media products—cable channels, magazines, Internet sites—that obscures for consumers the concentration of media ownership. With so many choices available to consumers, it is usually difficult to realize that, more and more, a select few media giants are controlling these choices.

Diversification

One of the most popular forms of stock market investing is mutual funds. Individuals can invest their money with a fund that maintains a diverse portfolio of stocks in many different companies. These funds offer differing levels of risk. However, one of the reasons mutual funds are attractive to many investors is that their diversification better positions them to ride the ups and downs of particular industries. If the airline industry is doing poorly, to pick one example, not to worry—a mutual fund has investments in many other companies that, it is hoped, are doing better.

Conglomeration is, in some ways, a similar way in which to pursue risk reduction through diversification. Instead of buying stock in various companies, however, media conglomerates have simply bought the companies themselves. By having interests in many different aspects of the media business, conglomerates are better able to withstand downturns in particular market segments. If the movie business goes into a slump, for example, perhaps revenue from publishing or music recording will take up the slack. In a couple of years, the expansion and contraction of particular markets may shift, and movie revenue will be the cash cow that helps support other areas of the conglomerate.

Diversification is closely linked with horizontal integration, which we discussed in chapter 3, so we mention it only briefly here. Diversification is one strategic justification for integration as a structural change. If a corporation such as Viacom, coproducer of *Titanic*, were limited to only producing movies (as is its Paramount Pictures division) it would be taking an enormous risk with such an expensive production. However, as a huge integrated conglomerate, even a massively expensive production like *Titanic* becomes just one of a large number of concurrent projects. Dismal failure with such an investment would certainly hurt, but the continuing revenue streams from other diverse projects would help offset such losses. As we saw in the discussion of corporate size, by having many irons in the fire, a conglomerate such as Viacom can withstand losses on individual projects and maximize the odds of producing huge *Titanic*-like hits from time to time.

Globalization

Globalization, too, was discussed in the previous chapter and is thus mentioned here only briefly. As we noted earlier, to varying degrees, all the major media companies have become global media players. This has meant structural transformations in how the corporations are organized.

It has also produced significant changes in the strategies companies employ to achieve maximum profitability and reduce risk.

One basic change is the increasing reliance by media companies on international revenues. Back in November 1988, Time Inc. chairman Richard Munro said, "Every player in the media/entertainment business—at least every smart one—will be trying to do the same thing: to build enterprises that can lay off the risk of increased production costs over as many worldwide distribution systems as possible."[104] Thus international sales serve as a way of maximizing the economies of scale strategy outlined earlier in this chapter.

Six years after Munro's comment, Time had merged with Warner Bros., and the chairman and CEO of the new Time Warner, Gerald Levin, noted that in 1993, the company's publishing, music, and studio divisions generated about 40% of their income from outside the United States.[105] That percentage continued to increase, and by 2004, the company's latest CEO, Richard Parsons, was continuing the global theme, saying "we clearly have an interest in further internationalising our company."[106] For nearly two decades, then, globalization has been a consistent theme.

In addition to pursuing basic economies of scale via expanded global markets, media giants have also set their sights on international revenues because market expansion is likely to be greatest in countries outside of the United States. With its already well-developed media markets, the United States continues to be the single most important country in the world in terms of media revenues. The domestic market is essentially saturated, however, with a virtually endless menu of media products.

Meanwhile, there are portions of the globe where media corporations see much more potential for rapid expansion. For example, News Corporation has probably been the most aggressive in pursuing a global media strategy, becoming, in its own words, "the world's most international media provider."[107] Beginning with a base in newspapers in both Australia (where it owns more than 100 papers and controls more than two thirds of all newspaper circulation) and Britain (where it owns the prestigious *Times* and *Sunday Times*, as well as the tabloid *News of the World* and *The Sun*), News Corporation has expanded to all forms of media. Its U.S. holdings include, most notably, the FOX network, more than 30 television stations, Twentieth Century Fox studios, several cable channels (FOX News, FX, FOX Movie Channel, Speed Channel, National Geographic Channel, etc.), HarperCollins book publishers (with more than 20 imprints), DirecTV satellite television, *TV Guide*, and the *New York Post*, among many others. Its global media holdings are far more extensive. It has been especially successful in satellite television services, including full or partial ownership of the British Sky Broadcasting (BSkyB), Sky Italia, Sky Latin America, Australia's FOXTEL, China Networks Systems, and Japan's SkyPerfecTV, among others. News Corporation also owns all or part of 90 different television channels, including Sky TV channels distributed through much of Europe. It has TV and radio stations in the United States, Europe, and India; elsewhere, News Corporation owns publishing companies and other media interests. According to News Corporation's CEO, Rupert Murdoch, the company's satellite systems and television channels reach more than three quarters of the earth's population.[108]

News Corporation has also cashed in on the global love of sports by owning valuable broadcast rights to sporting events, sports channels, sports venues, and even some professional sports teams. FOX first made a big splash as a competitor to the big three networks in the United States by obtaining the rights to broadcast NFL football games. The company went on to own regional sports cable channels in the United States (FOX Sports Net), Star Sports (a set of sports channels in Asia), and FOX Sport Noticias in Latin America, among others. News Corporation's ownership of sports franchises has included the preeminent British First Division soccer club, Manchester United, and half of the Australian National Rugby League. In the United States, it owned (and later sold) the Los Angeles Dodgers baseball team, had minority ownership in both the New York Knicks NBA basketball team and the New York Rangers NHL hockey team, had options to purchase 40% of the Los Angeles Kings (NHL) and 10% of the Los Angeles Lakers (NBA), and owned 40% of Los Angeles' Staples Center.

News Corporation has used these vast holdings to develop a global strategy that reproduces a successful media model around the world. Thus its satellite television services, along with some of the channels distributed over those services, have become staples in Europe, Latin America, Asia, and elsewhere. News Corporation has also focused much of its attention on areas of the globe that have been less developed in terms of media infrastructure. It is in Asia, India, and Latin America that the company has staked its ground for long-term growth.

News Corporation represents one of the most developed examples of a global media strategy. However, a business approach without borders is now a common characteristic of the new media giants.

Joint Ventures

As mentioned earlier, in pursuing profits, companies try to reduce the amount of risk and uncertainty they face in their business environments. We have already seen various strategies, including diversification, that are used to reduce risk. However, to conduct business, companies depend on the cooperation of other organizations. They need other companies to supply necessary resources, key personnel, investment capital, technology, and access to distribution channels. If one company has control over a resource that is central for the success of another company, we can say that the second company is dependent on the first.

That is the essence of *resource dependency theory*, commonly used in the study of markets and business practices. The theory posits that to the extent one organization controls resources needed by another organization, it has power over that organization.

Conglomerates seek to reduce the uncertainty associated with doing business in multiorganizational environments. The most direct way to do this is simply to buy the other organizations on which a company depends. This strategy has often been employed and has resulted in the vertical and horizontal integration discussed in the previous chapter. By buying suppliers and competitors, media giants help to reduce the uncertainty that can arise from competition.

It is not always possible, however, to buy competitors. With the number of media conglomerates continually declining, each merger or acquisition between ever larger conglomerates gets more and more expensive. As a result, the last few remaining conglomerates rely increasingly on strategies of cooperation and joint ventures with their competitors as ways of reducing risk. As media scholar Ben Bagdikian puts it, "Financial news still is full of the sounds of clashes between giants. But the new media leaders compete only over marginal matters: their imperial borders, their courtship of new allies, and their acquisitions of smaller firms. Underneath these skirmishes, they are interlocked in shared financial ownership and a complex of joint ventures."[109]

Thus, although media conglomerates are competing in some areas, they have simultaneously developed an extraordinary level of collaboration and cooperation. The resulting set of strategic partnerships is often compared to the *keiretsu*, a Japanese business model characterized by informal, collaborative associations between companies in related fields.

The tangled web of collaborative ventures is constantly changing. It has been most extensive in movie projects, cable channels, and Internet ventures in which the largest of the media companies often cooperate through joint ownership of projects. For example, A&E Television Networks, which operates cable's A&E channel, the Biography Channel, and the History Channel, is a joint venture between network "competitors" NBC (General Electric) and ABC (Disney), along with the Hearst Corporation. The British version of these channels has an additional partner: NewsCorp, the parent company of the FOX network. Such cooperation, which some argue is more like collusion, has become a staple of the industry.

Sometimes the cooperation between media firms takes the form of more limited partnerships, rather than joint ownership. In recent years, news organizations have increasingly turned to such partnerships with competitors, signing deals that, for example, enable *Washington Post* reporters to appear regularly on NBC, CNBC, and MSNBC.[110]

Even more cooperation and joint ventures occur between the largest of the media conglomerates and some smaller second- or third-tier media companies. There are several important reasons for this. First, the smaller companies must often turn to larger partners for necessary infusions of capital. With their deep pockets, the media giants are able to buy into budding projects that smaller firms cannot adequately capitalize. Second, smaller firms must sometimes rely on the media giants for distribution agreements, especially in movies and recorded music. The vertical integration of the major media companies gives them control over distribution networks. If smaller independents want to enter national and international markets, they often must sign distribution agreements with the larger companies. Finally, smaller firms enter into joint ownership agreements to stave off—at least temporarily—wholesale takeovers.

Technology has played a role in the rise of collaborative ventures. As digitization and technological convergence have brought telephone, cable, Internet, and software companies into each other's businesses, they often choose to collaborate, rather than compete, on new ventures. Such developments can blur the distinction between media, computer, and telecommunications companies. In perhaps the highest profile of these ventures, software giant Microsoft teamed up with media giant NBC to create both a cable channel (MSNBC) and accompanying Web site (MSNBC.com). NBC was not alone. All of the television networks, to use one example, have collaborative agreements or joint ventures with Internet companies. Thus the new media of the Internet have become just as fertile ground for joint ventures as the old media.

❖ BEYOND MARKET STRATEGIES: THE SPECTER OF MONOPOLIES

In November 1998, Barnes & Noble, the country's largest book retailer, announced it would pay $600 million ($703 million) for Ingram Industries Inc., the country's largest book wholesale distributor. Compared to many media acquisitions, this one was modest in size, and most of the public had never heard of Ingram. Within the publishing industry, however, the deal drew considerable attention. Ingram was the distributor for many small, independent bookstores, as well as Barnes & Noble's major rivals such as Borders and Amazon.com—all of which compete directly with Barnes & Noble's superstores and Web site. When the intended purchase was announced, the American Booksellers Association immediately raised monopoly concerns, asking the Department of Justice and the Federal Trade Commission to examine the deal more closely. After its investigation, the Federal Trade Commission staff recommended that the agency block the sale, because it would stifle competition. Finally, to avoid a protracted battle, Barnes & Noble withdrew from the deal.[111]

Why did this sale raise such concern? First of all, the retail book market had already seen a great decrease in competition during the previous decade. In 1990, independent bookstores accounted for nearly a third of all book sales, but by 1998, they had lost half of their market share. Instead, giant discount retailers like Wal-Mart and Kmart sold nearly half of all books bought, and a few immense bookstore chains and Internet sites accounted for most of the rest.[112] Within this context, the specter of a single bookstore giant controlling the distribution of books to small, independent stores was very troubling. Such monopolistic control would be likely to reduce competition and create a vastly uneven playing field that would further handicap small, independent bookstores. For example, Barnes & Noble could use its control of Ingram to offer its own superstores and Web sites favorable pricing and distribution deals that would be unavailable to competitors. The potential for undermining market competition was so blatant in this particular case that regulatory hurdles indirectly derailed the deal.

An even more blatant monopolistic threat emerged in 2002, when one of the country's two satellite television providers, EchoStar, attempted to buy its only rival, DirecTV. The prospect of a single company with a monopoly over this emerging industry was too much for even the antiregulatory FCC to take. The deal became the first merger to be rejected by the FCC since 1969. (DirecTV was subsequently bought by NewsCorp.)

However, the resolution of these cases was an anomaly. The market impact of most media mergers has been less clear cut, and in recent years, regulators have usually rubber-stamped their approval with little hesitation. On the whole, the lax regulatory environment usually has allowed conglomeration and ownership concentration to proceed virtually unimpeded, creating conditions in which media giants undermine competitive markets.

The Role of Competition and the Threat of Monopolies

Even by the traditional standards of market advocates, the growth in media conglomeration and concentration in ownership present potential threats to the basic functioning of the market. The central threat is a lack of competition. In theory, one of the key ingredients of a well-functioning market is competition. Competition spurs innovation and keeps prices down, because consumers have choices and can take their business to a competitor if they find that one company is charging too much, not providing the products and services they want, or not keeping up with innovations in the field.

In reality, though, businesses do not like competition. In stark contrast to market theory, McAllister notes that

> Business, especially big business, abhors competition. When businesses face competitive situations, they face potential economic instability; organizations fight for the same dollars and some might bet more than others. If the situation is really competitive, it might even mean bankruptcy. In competitive situations, economic predictability becomes uncommon for industry. This is why businesses, if permitted, strive to eliminate competition through such means as vertical and horizontal integration, where they can control at least large sectors of the market, if not the entire market.[113]

Such control of a market raises the specter of monopolies. Monopolies threaten basic market dynamics. The lack of competition characteristic of monopolies reduces incentives for companies to operate efficiently, potentially resulting in higher operating costs that are passed on to consumers, who have little or no choice in a monopolistic situation. Producers can also artificially inflate prices and otherwise distort the market because there are no competitors challenging them. Producers have no incentive to invest in research and development or to try risky new ideas, because there are no competitors threatening to undercut sales via innovative products. Finally, monopolistic power in a key industry may be translated into political power, a topic we examine later in this chapter.

As we saw in chapter 2, the Justice Department's antitrust case against Microsoft, which began in the late 1990s, uncovered one example of how a company's dominance in the marketplace allowed it to pursue practices that were not in the interest of consumers. In particular, Microsoft dominated the personal computer operating system market with its "Windows" product. U.S. District Judge Thomas Penfield Jackson found that

> Microsoft enjoys so much power in the market for Intel-compatible PC operating systems that if it wished to exercise this power solely in terms of price, it could charge a price for Windows substantially above that which could be charged in a competitive market. Moreover, it could do so for a significant period of time without losing an unacceptable amount of business to competitors. In other words, Microsoft enjoys monopoly power in the relevant market.[114]

This ability to distort market relations is at the heart of monopolies.

In the Microsoft case, the court described three important characteristics of monopolies that it said were applicable to Microsoft. First, a monopoly has a very large and stable share of the market for a given product. In this case, Microsoft's share of the market for operating systems was 95% or more over a number of years. Second, a high barrier to entry for competitors protects a monopoly's market share. In the Microsoft case, the integrated nature of software and operating systems created a "chicken and egg" problem. No one is likely to buy a different operating system unless there is software available to run on it. On the other hand, no one would invest in developing software for a new operating system unless there was already a substantial customer base using that operating system. Third, customers do not have a viable alternative to the monopoly's product. Largely because of this chicken-and-egg dynamic, customers were stuck with Windows whether they liked it or not.

Microsoft was able to use its monopoly position to engage in a variety of unfair business practices. Government charges included the following:

- ❖ To restrict further competition, Microsoft made an illegal offer to divide the Internet browser market with Netscape, its major competitor.
- ❖ Microsoft tried to eliminate competitors by tying its Explorer browser to its Windows operating system. Because more than 90% of the world's computers already used Windows, this gave Microsoft an unfair advantage.
- ❖ Microsoft struck deals with the country's largest online and Internet service providers that required that they provide Microsoft's Internet Explorer as their exclusive or primary browser.
- ❖ Microsoft prohibited computer makers from changing the Windows desktop that featured an icon for Explorer.
- ❖ Microsoft used its monopoly power in the operating system market to convince computer companies to limit their use of Netscape.

In all of these cases, and others, Microsoft was accused of using its monopoly status to unfairly reduce competition and control the new Internet browser market. In his "finding of fact," Judge Jackson concluded that

> Microsoft has demonstrated that it will use its prodigious market power and immense profits to harm any firm that insists on pursuing initiatives that could intensify competition against one of Microsoft's core products. Microsoft's past success in hurting such companies and stifling innovation deters investment in technologies and businesses that exhibit the potential to threaten Microsoft. The ultimate result is that some innovations that would truly benefit consumers never occur for the sole reason that they do not coincide with Microsoft's self-interest.[115]

Given these findings, no one was surprised when in April 2000, Microsoft was found guilty of violating antitrust laws. The court ruled that Microsoft's marketing arrangements with other companies were *not* illegal. However, it agreed with the government's charges that Microsoft "maintained its monopoly power by anticompetitive means and attempted to monopolize the Web browser market" and that it unlawfully tied its Web browser to its operating system.[116]

Appeals in the case dragged on for years, and with a more friendly Republican administration in power, the Justice Department eventually dropped its effort to split Microsoft into two companies, as was first proposed. By 2005, Microsoft's domination continued, with Windows capturing over 90% of the operating system market and Explorer having over 80% of the Internet browser market. The company even faced a new—but extremely similar—suit from Real Networks, which claimed that the bundling of Window's Media Player with the Windows operating system was forcing Real Networks' Realplayer out of the market.

Monopolies, then, threaten the operation of markets in a variety of ways, and there is good reason for concern that the media industry has taken on monopolistic characteristics.

Reducing Risk by Reducing Competition

From a company's perspective, marketplace competition is a potentially negative thing, because it threatens profitability. Instead of constantly facing the threat of competitors who could undermine market share and profits, it is in the interest of companies to stabilize markets so as to reduce such risk. One way to ensure profitability, then, is to *reduce* competition or even achieve monopoly status, as did Microsoft.

Companies, of course, cannot publicly advocate reduced competition, and they often resist government regulation or other actions on the basis of free market principles of competition. However, sometimes companies' actions speak louder than their words. As we have seen, some mergers, joint ventures, and other cooperative agreements contribute to a market with reduced competition.

In fact, some forms of media are simple monopolies. In the United States today, all but a handful of local daily newspapers are monopolies. If consumers want a local daily newspaper in most U.S. cities, they have no choice. These papers have the entire market share, thus meeting the first criterion for a monopoly. Second, potential competitors usually face a high barrier to entry into this marketplace, because starting a significant daily newspaper from scratch is a capital-intensive endeavor with very high risks. Because newspapers are so dependent on advertisers for revenues, a new competitor must lure advertisers away from a well-established fixture in the community. Many local dailies are now also part of major regional or national newspaper chains. This allows them to pool resources as a cost-saving measure—one that would be unavailable to new independent local competitors. Third, for access to in-depth local news, citizens usually have few or no alternatives to the local newspaper. Compared to the depth offered by newspapers, local television and radio usually provide only superficial coverage. As a result of the rise of newspaper chains and concentration of ownership in the newspaper industry, then, many local newspapers clearly enjoy monopoly status.

Most cable systems are a sort of monopoly, as well. Although satellite dishes increasingly provide an alternative to cable, consumers usually have no choice of providers if they wish to have cable service. This has led to considerable consumer anger over ever-increasing cable rates. With only limited government regulation and no effective competition, cable companies have been able to raise rates with little fear of losing customers. In 1993, the country's largest cable company was caught being a bit too candid about its monopoly power. In an internal memo leaked to the press, an executive from Tele-Communications Inc. (TCI) told company managers to raise their prices via new charges and blame the government, regardless of what customers thought. The memo noted, "We cannot be disuaded [sic] from the charges simply because customers object. It will take a while, but they'll get used to it." Referring to new FCC rules about to take effect, the executive suggested that managers blame the government for the increases—even though the new rules were aimed at *limiting* price increases. He wrote, "The best news of all is, we can blame it on re-regulation and the government now. Let's take advantage of it!"[117]

The convergence of cable, telephone, and Internet technology means that companies in any one of those businesses often can use the same wires or cables to enter the other businesses. At first glance, this may seem to offer the prospect of *more* competition—and indeed, this was the rationale for deregulating these industries. However, the flurry of mergers and acquisitions that has accompanied the deregulation of the telecommunications industry has meant that cable, telephone, and Internet companies have been buying each other up at a rapid rate. When this consolidation process is through, the result is likely to be just a few major players providing all of these services. Increasingly, many households rely on a single company to provide all these media and communications services, opening the door for further market manipulation.

Single monopolies in the model of Microsoft or local newspapers are unusual. More common are markets in which there is some limited competition. As media corporations pursue merger and acquisition strategies designed to reduce risk and promote synergy, they often create such a situation. As we saw in chapter 4, the growth of media giants through mergers and acquisitions certainly reduced the number of major players in the market, thus decreasing competition. In some cases, it did so by eliminating existing competitors (e.g., Time Warner buying Turner Broadcasting). In other cases, it eliminated potential competitors. The latter occurs when, for example, a company primarily involved in production (such as Viacom or Disney) merges with a company known primarily for its distribution capacity (such as CBS, via its television network, or Capital Cities, via its television network and cable holdings). Such mergers preempted the possibility that Viacom or Disney would have developed their own distribution capacity or that CBS or Capital Cities would have substantially expanded their media production. The formation of media giants also makes it more difficult for still existing smaller companies or new entrants to compete—another feature characteristic of monopolies.

The impact of such potentially monopolistic situations has a ripple effect and can be seen in unlikely places. For example, after the restrictions on network ownership of television programs (fin-syn rules) were lifted, television networks could own their programs. (In 1998, NBC even tried demanding ownership stakes and perpetual licensing rights for *all* the programs it airs—even those it did not help to create.[118]) Such ownership arrangements raised the possibility of "sweetheart" deals. Take the case of the once-popular sitcom *Home Improvement*. The show was coproduced by Wind Dancer Productions (headed by the program's star, Tim Allen) and Walt Disney Co., the corporate parent of the ABC network on which the program aired. When the program came up for renewal, Disney gave ABC a favorable deal rather than trying to sell the show to the highest bidder on the market. While this was good for ABC and its corporate parent, the smaller Wind Dancer Productions lost potential revenue as a result of this fixed deal. Tim Allen and Wind Dancer Productions sued Walt Disney Co., and the suit was settled out of court in 1999 under undisclosed terms.

The *Home Improvement* case was just one in a line of similar suits. David Duchovny of the *X-Files* television show filed a similar suit against Twentieth Century Fox, as did Steven Bochco, producer of *NYPD Blue*. David Kohan and Max Mutchnick, producers of *Will and Grace*, also sued NBC for failing to negotiate a fair license fee for the show. In response to such suits, networks began inserting language into contracts that limited the ability of coproducers to sue. In all these cases, increased conglomeration distorted the workings of the market to the advantage of media giants and to the disadvantage of smaller players.

The music industry, too, has used limited competition to keep the prices of CDs artificially high. In 1996, the largest music companies, along with major music retailers, were subject to a class action lawsuit on behalf of consumers. The suit charged that the music companies had conspired to keep prices high, despite the fact that technological advances had made CDs cheaper to produce. After a 2-year investigation, the Federal Trade Commission ruled in May 2000 that the five biggest music companies (Time Warner, Sony, Bertelsmann, EMI, and Universal) had used illegal marketing techniques to artificially inflate prices and prevent retailers from offering discounts. The Federal Trade Commission estimated that consumers were overcharged by more than $500 million during a 4-year period. In a settlement, the companies agreed to refund $67.4 million to consumers; distribute $75.7 million in CDs to schools, libraries, and other nonprofit groups; and change the offending marketing practices.[119]

Reduced competition has also resulted from joint agreements with "competitors," as described earlier. Although these agreements do not create monopolies in the formal sense, they can stabilize markets, limit consumer choice, and create formidable barriers for new competitors who wish to enter the market—all characteristics associated with monopolies. Because most media companies are not formal monopolies, this model of limited competition is the one that reflects most segments of the media industry.

Monopolies in Perspective

A handful of media giants dominate the media marketplace—but is this really a new development? The significance of media monopolies depends, in part, on our frame of reference. First, we must remember that "the media" are not monolithic, and trends in one arena may not parallel those in another. Newspapers, as noted, have seen a drastic decline in competition, with the rise of newspaper chains that usually enjoy local monopolies. Radio ownership, too, has seen significant concentration, as the limits on the number of stations a single company may own have been lifted. The FCC has attempted to offset this concentration of radio ownership through the licensing of low-power radio stations that help meet community needs—a development strongly opposed by the commercial radio industry.

On the other hand, television and the Internet have seen an explosion in growth. From just three major networks and limited local choice, broadcast television, and especially cable, now offer many more channels. As an entirely new form of media, the Internet offers options simply unavailable a generation ago. Have the changes in the media, then, created conditions that seem to reduce competition? Yes, but this impact has varied from medium to medium.

We must remember that today's media giants have holdings in many different forms of media. That is one of the key characteristics distinguishing today's media empires from those of earlier eras. It is this unprecedented conglomeration and concentration of ownership that is most disconcerting. The resulting scenario is one in which decreased competition creates market distortions at the same time that consumers—at least temporarily—experience more media options.

❖ CONCLUSION

The restructuring of the media industry has allowed media conglomerates to pursue a series of strategies aimed at maximizing profits, reducing cost, and minimizing risk. The new media giants have used their size to pursue strategies not generally available to smaller competitors. They can access large amounts of investment capital for expensive projects, heavily advertise and cross-promote their products, generally take advantage of the efficiencies resulting from economies of scale, and absorb significant losses on some projects because a few major hits more than make up for these losses. The integration and globalization of these major firms has allowed them to exploit synergy by packaging content so it is usable in different media, by promoting products across media, and by developing well-known brand names. These firms have used recent technologies (cable and the Internet) to target lucrative niche audiences to attract advertisers' dollars. Finally, these media giants have sought to reduce financial risk in various ways, including diversification of holdings and increased use of joint ventures with competitors.

Corporate attempts to reduce risk can sometimes slip into strategies that violate basic market principles. In particular, competition is an essential element of healthy markets, but it is in the interests of corporations to reduce risk by limiting the amount of competition they face. This has led to situations in some parts of the media industry in which characteristics of monopoly behavior are evident. Thus, even by market standards, concentration of media ownership presents serious problems.

The concerns raised by the business strategies of media giants are only exacerbated when we use a public interest perspective to examine the social, cultural, and political impact of these tactics. For example, does an emphasis on "big hit" media products squeeze out important, although less profitable, forms of cultural expression? What happens to news organizations absorbed into vast media conglomerates concerned with maximizing profits? Do segmentation and niche marketing spell the end of a cultural common ground? Should joint ventures between an already dwindling number of media giants raise the concern that control of our public ideas, information, and culture are concentrated in too few hands? It is to such difficult questions that we turn our attention in chapters 5 and 6.

PART III

Neglecting the Public Interest

Media Conglomerates and the Public Sphere

5

How Business Strategy
Shapes Media Content

I n Part II, we examined how the structure and strategies of the media
business have changed in recent years. In market terms, these
changes have been beneficial for media companies insofar as they have
produced large profits for these rapidly growing media giants.
However, the same changes have resulted in a concentration of media
ownership and a potential loss of competition that is troubling even by
market standards.

As we argued in chapter 1, the market approach may be helpful in
understanding business dynamics, but profits are just one yardstick for
measuring media performance. The public sphere approach identifies a
different set of concerns by asking whether changes in the media industry serve the public interest. To consider such a question, our field of
vision must widen dramatically beyond bottom-line concerns, to
include how changes in the business of media may shape media content
and influence society more broadly. In this chapter, we look at how business strategies shape media content; in chapter 6, we assess the influence that changes in the media industry have had on broader social life
and politics. In both chapters, we focus on public sphere concerns.

❖ CONSIDERING THE PUBLIC INTEREST

Before embarking on our discussion of the impact of media changes, it is helpful to review the concept of *the public interest*. Denis McQuail reminds us that

> As an adjective, the word "public" indicates what is open rather than closed, what is freely available rather than private in terms of access and ownership, what is collective and held in common rather than what is individual and personal.[120]

Thus *the public sphere* suggests those spaces in society that are open, accessible, shared, collective, and common. Assessing media in terms of their contribution to the public interest suggests that media are fundamentally intertwined with matters of the common good rather than just with private profit. When we talk of media and the public interest, we need to look beyond public service media, because these usually are limited to publicly owned communications systems. Indeed, public interest standards can be applied to all major media, regardless of ownership structure.

In chapter 1, we noted the considerable disagreement about just what constitutes the public interest. For the purposes of discussing media content, however, we propose that media in the public interest have at least four basic characteristics:

1. *Diversity.* In a democracy, media should reflect the range of views and experiences present in a diverse society. Citizens using the media should be able to find cultural representations and political expressions that are both reflective of their own views and experiences and that diverge considerably from those views and experiences. In contrast, homogenized media lack this range of diversity.

2. *Innovation.* The impressive technological capacities and capital resources of the media industry should be coupled with creativity and innovation in form and content. We should expect our culture and entertainment to be imaginative, fresh, creative, and original, reflecting the vibrant nature of our society. In contrast, imitative media rely on tried and true formulas.

3. *Substance.* Light entertainment is akin to sugary snacks; everyone loves them from time to time, but they do not constitute a healthy

diet. A healthy democratic society must have media that include substantive news and entertainment addressing significant issues facing society, presented in an engaging manner that promotes civic participation. In contrast, trivial media focus excessively on sensationalism, celebrity, and similar fare.

4. *Independence.* Citizens of free societies abhor the notion of concentrated power controlling information and culture. Media should provide citizens with information and views independent of such concentrated power—either governmental or corporate. In contrast, censored media succumb to economic and ideological pressures to limit the range of issues and perspectives they feature.

Of course, evaluating media on these terms requires subjective interpretations—but so do judgments about freedom, human rights, fairness, justice, and a host of others. Important ideas and values are never simple or clear-cut. However, we must not let the complexity associated with the idea of serving the public interest deter us from doing our best to construct a media system that can achieve this lofty goal.

The reality is that contemporary mass media have often fallen far short of this public interest ideal. Although the media industry employs thousands of talented artists, craftspeople, and other professionals, the structural constraints created by the primacy of business concerns have frequently prevented them from meeting their full potential. Instead of media that are diverse, innovative, substantive, and independent, the recent structural and strategic changes in the media industry have too often led to content that is homogenized, imitative, trivial, and constrained. We examine each of these overlapping limitations in the following sections.

A Note on Elitism

One of the dangers in evaluating the media in a public interest framework is that it can easily take on an elitist tone. For some people, talk of media in the public interest invokes visions of dreary offerings of opera and esoteric, intellectual discussions (not that we have anything against intellectual discussions, although we confess that we are not avid opera fans). Such narrow and highbrow programming is not the foundation of public interest media, although it may be part of a diverse media menu.

When we invoke the public interest, we are not suggesting some single vision for the cultural or political content of media. Quite the contrary: We are calling for more inclusion and variety in media's form and content. We are not proposing that any centralized, elite group be the judge of media value. Instead, we are calling for more voices and perspectives to be included in our media, to reflect a more dynamic range of interpretations of what is important and valuable. Finally, we recognize the importance of media that are sometimes silly and just plain fun. Playfulness is part of the human experience, and it should be part of our media fare, as well.

The argument that serving the public interest is elitist is often based on the assumption that our current media system is democratic in giving people what they want. As we have already seen, however, media are usually giving *advertisers* what they want and responding to the interests of demographically desirable audiences. If anything, this market-oriented approach might itself be labeled elitist, because it favors those with more money. Despite the appearance of a large number of options, the business dynamics of media usually limit audience choice to variations on a few profitable formulas developed to meet advertiser needs.

Ultimately, the core principle underlying a public interest approach to media is the radical notion of democracy, because it values widespread, equal, and diverse participation over centralized power and anointed spokespeople. There is no doubt that broader democratic participation in the media is a threat to those who benefit from current economic and social arrangements. However, we believe enhanced participation and a media more oriented toward the public interest are necessary steps for reinvigorating our culture and democracy.

❖ HOMOGENIZATION AND IMITATION

A common strategy that parents use to get their young children to eat their vegetables is to give them a choice—broccoli or carrots, for example. Of course, the choice is somewhat deceptive, because either way, the menu has already been determined by the parent. You *will* eat your vegetables.

Mainstream media companies do something similar with audiences. Certainly audiences are faced with many media choices, but if the options are somehow all similar in some way, then choice is an illusion. Audiences have learned that, ironically, an explosion in the *quantity* of media outlets and products does not necessarily mean more diversity or better *quality*. In fact, some media executives readily admit that media outlets are redundant. Speaking about the future of television, then–HBO chair Michael Fuchs once acknowledged, "Everyone says 500 channels. . . . Those 500 channels are going to be reconfigured old channels. There'll be eight HBOs, multiplexed. There will be 100 pay-per-views and there will be 10,000 shopping channels."[121] (Fuchs understated the case; by 2004 there were actually 10 HBOs.)

The real issue in media choice is the amount of differentiation among various products. Recall from our chapter 1 discussion that two key dimensions of market structures are the number of supplying firms and the level of product diversity (see Exhibit 1.1). We have already seen that the number of firms supplying media products is declining as a result of the concentration of media ownership and the development of joint venture agreements. There is also reason to suspect that media firms pursuing similar business strategies reduce the level of product diversity. Rather than leaning toward the market ideal of diverse competition, our media system too often tilts in the direction of a homogenized monopoly, with a few giant firms producing remarkably similar media fare.

Homogenization can be the unintentional outcome of companies minimizing risk and maximizing profits. As media giants pursue their synergistic strategies and try to reduce risk, they face limited competition from other media giants. The frequent result is very little innovation and a great deal of imitation. By following tried and true, standardized formulas, Hollywood movies, television entertainment, and other types of media have become formulaic and resistant to new ideas. Despite the potential for quick profits, this kind of media is not likely to serve the public interest.

Imitation and Formulas

Homogenization is often the byproduct of imitating previous successes to minimize risk associated with new products and to take advantage of known and profitable trends. For example, major music labels often intentionally sign bands precisely because they are *unoriginal;* they sound like whatever is "hot" at the time. Rather than risk potential loss with something new, innovative, and untested, companies tend to cash in on the latest wave of whatever is popular. As one *Billboard* article starkly put it, "A&R folks [talent scouts] run in packs, desperate to sign flavor-of-the-month acts, many of whom are just learning how to tune their instruments."[122]

Once signed, however, bands usually have to produce adequate sales almost instantly. The idea of an artist maturing and gradually building a following is not one that short-term, profit-conscious corporations favor. Weak sales for an initial CD often mean the end of the contract. This practice contrasts with what used to happen in the music industry. Promising artists were more often allowed to develop their talents over several years, despite poor sales of their early albums. Some of these artists with poor initial sales, such as Bob Dylan and Bruce Springsteen, eventually achieved both critical acclaim and massive commercial success.

Now, musicians who do succeed face yet another type of homogenizing pressure. A label's attitude toward a successful new artist is usually summed up in two words: "Don't change." Companies want artists to repeat their success by creating new music that is similar to their earlier work. This makes it easier to market the band as a predictable commodity. As a result, musicians are usually discouraged from experimenting with new sounds or genre-crossing work for fear that this might alienate an already established (and profitable) audience. The results are artists whose catalogues grow stale and repetitious—while their labels' A&R people search for the *next* hot trend.

Finally, in a process similar to that in book publishing (described in chapter 4), major labels tend to put big money behind a select few acts that have proven to be popular, shelling out huge multialbum advances and supporting massive promotional tours. A few veteran mainstream performers have enjoyed this royal treatment, but most other musicians languish from neglect by the very label that signed them. As a result, audiences tend to hear and learn about the same few mainstream groups.

The homogenization process is similar in other fields. Independent film producer Barbara Maltby argues,

Media mergers in Hollywood are just a step in the progression toward the homogenization of filmmaking. . . . The creative act is merely something that's used to make money. . . . Narrative is information, and Hollywood is in the business of making narratives, and those narratives have a powerful informational impact on us. The more that they are reduced to the most simplistic formulas the more we as a culture are reduced.[123]

Peter Bart, editor in chief of *Variety* and a former Paramount Pictures executive, agrees. With conglomeration, he says,

The studios are if anything more risk averse. They are desperate to hedge their bets. It's the nature of bureaucratic self-protection. Every unit of a multinational corporation has to meet its numbers. That pressure is reflected in the kind of pictures that get made.... The old-time studio bosses followed their hunches. Today, these green-light decisions are very much a question of committees, focus groups, rule by consensus. Not exactly a recipe for art.[124]

There are artists who consciously choose alternatives to the corporate giants to maintain creative control over their work and avoid this homogenization pressure. One such artist is Ian MacKaye, member of the band Fugazi and founder of Dischord Records, which is based in Washington, DC's punk scene. Noted for its do-it-yourself ethic, much of punk music, MacKaye notes, was based in a "sense of self-definition and also sort of playing music for music's sake and being part of a family for family's sake." He observes, "Major labels didn't start showing up really until they smelled money and that's all they're ever going to be attracted to is money."[125]

Another artist, Ani DiFranco, plays a very different type of music, folk-rock, but shares the general attitude. Despite repeated contract offers from major labels, she has chosen to release her more than a dozen CDs through her own independent label, Righteous Babe Records, which she created in 1990. Such a strategy reduces the potential sales of DiFranco's albums, because they do not receive the advertising campaigns and promotional support offered by major labels. However, like other artists who choose this route, she believes her independent efforts are important. "I don't think the music industry is conducive to artistic and social change and growth," she commented in one interview.

It does a lot to exploit and homogenize art and artists. In order to challenge the corporate music industry, I feel it necessary to remain outside it. I could be selling a lot more albums. Life could be a lot more cushy. But it's much more interesting to try and hammer out an alternative route without the music industry and maybe be an example for other musicians. You don't have to play ball.[126]

Numerous experiments with making the music of unsigned bands available via the Internet have given many hope that the do-it-yourself spirit will be able to survive.

Declining Localism

Homogenization is sometimes related to another phenomenon resulting from the concentration of media ownership: loss of localism in media. Localism has two important elements: local control and local content. The concentration of media ownership has, obviously, shifted ultimate control of local television stations, newspapers, and radio stations to the corporate headquarters of media conglomerates. To varying degrees, budget and other key strategic decisions—if not outright editorial direction—are made by executives with little or no connection to the local community. In short, control of much local media has migrated to the national corporate offices of a few media giants.

This trend has been particularly dramatic in the newspaper industry. By the late 1990s, only about 300 of the nation's more than 1500 daily newspapers were independently owned, and most of these were very small papers with less than 10,000 circulation. Most dailies, and nearly all major papers, are now part of larger newspaper chains. In 2002, the 10 largest newspaper chains accounted for over half of the nation's weekday (51%) and Sunday (56%) circulation.[127] As one analyst in the *American Journalism Review* concluded, when an independent paper gets bought out by a larger corporation, "some get worse, a few get better, and most get homogenized."[128]

One potential consequence of decline in local control is the loss of local content. Newspaper groups, as noted earlier, sometimes pursue the efficiencies of chain ownership by developing regional news services that feed standardized stories to all of the chain's papers. In this way, a reporter's single story can be used in a number of papers, resulting in significant savings in the cost of gathering and reporting the news, as fewer journalists are needed. In many cases, the more your morning newspaper is made up of such standardized chain content, the less likely it is to cover local news substantively.

Radio, too, has followed suit by consolidating staff and resources for both news and music programming. The result has been the standardization of much commercial broadcasting, leaving little that reflects the unique characteristics of the local community. With radio stations increasingly part of regional or national ownership "groups," it is common practice for radio companies to broadcast the same programming on many stations, regardless of their location.

A dramatic event crystallizing this trend took place in 2002 in Minot, North Dakota.[129] On a January night, a train derailed in Minot, spilling a cloud of suffocating anhydrous ammonia fertilizer over the state's fourth largest city. Police called the radio station that was the designated emergency broadcaster, but there was no answer, leading to a lengthy delay in warning the public about the imminent danger. One person died in the incident and 300 people were hospitalized.

Emergency officials had such difficulty because all six of Minot's radio stations were owned by giant Clear Channel Communications, which was piping in a satellite feed from elsewhere to the local stations. In the wake of the incident, media accounts told of other consequences of life with a single media owner. "The old radio stations used to cover the local news," the police chief of Minot noted. "We very seldom hear local news anymore." Another thing that disappeared with the arrival of Clear Channel was ratings. Because Clear Channel was the only game in town, they no longer bothered to tell their advertisers about ratings.

FCC Commissioner Gloria Tristani had earlier warned about the loss of localism before a group of Texas broadcasters. She noted that the 1996 Telecommunications Act had resulted in "an unprecedented wave of consolidation that has dramatically reshaped the radio industry." Such changes, she noted, raise the danger that "consolidation could lead to lots of formats but only one voice." It also risked the loss of localism, which, she argued, is "the bedrock of our broadcast system." Localism, she noted, "means covering local issues, reporting local news, doing local programming, providing an outlet for local voices." However, as Tristani remarked, consolidation often leads to homogenization:

> Eventually, the danger is that with national play lists, nationally syndicated programming, and outsourced news, everything ends up sounding the same . . . many stations have already been turned into "virtual stations" that have no announcers of their own but just run prerecorded feeds from distant announcers. Sure, costs are down and earnings are up. That makes Wall Street happy. But at what price on Main Street?[130]

The question is an important one. It starkly pits the market values of profits against the public interest value of diversity.

❖ TRIVIALIZATION AND SENSATIONALISM

If homogenization results in media that all start to look alike, what is that look? Rather than being substantive, today's media—especially broadcast media—have become increasingly sensational and trivialized.

Fluff and Stuff Just Short of Snuff

The rule in both entertainment and news is that a certain amount of shock value draws attention—and advertisers. The list of media fare that is cheap to produce and generates considerable audiences and advertiser revenue is lengthy. It includes programs featuring videos of wild animal attacks, tabloid gossip shows, fist-fighting dysfunctional families on daytime talk shows, the sexual scandals of politicians, wrestling thespians in makeup and costumes, "reality" programs featuring accidents and arrests, sensational and bloody crime reports on local news broadcasts, risqué programs pushing the boundaries of sexual explicitness, get-rich-quick game shows, radio "shock jocks," and many others. Sex, violence, spectacle: These sorts of programs are the logical end products of the corporate pursuit of profits. They are relatively cheap to produce and, like an accident on the highway, they predictably draw a regular audience. What these programs lack, however, is any sense of serving a larger public interest through providing substantive content. As media concentration results in more corporate emphasis on bottom-line profits, to the detriment of any public service mission, we can expect more such programming reaching new heights of sensationalism.

On television, advertisers who want audiences to be in a relaxed "buying mood" as they watch their commercials usually welcome such "fluff" programming. As Ben Bagdikian has put it, "Serious programs remind the audience that complex human problems are not solved by switching to a new deodorant."[131] The result has been more fluff, more raunch, and more self-proclaimed garbage. In recent years, perhaps no media product exemplified this trend more than daytime talk shows, epitomized by the *Jerry Springer Show*. Repeatedly accused of being phony and staged, Springer's programs often featured dramatic revelations of infidelity followed by a near-obligatory fist-fight. Springer himself made repeated disclaimers that his show was nothing more than mindless entertainment, and he expressed shock that anyone would watch such "garbage." Even so, WMAQ in Chicago moved to introduce Springer as a commentator on its once respected evening newscast, blurring the boundary between raunchy entertainment and news. As a result of the move, both anchors of the newscast resigned on principle, and the station suffered a significant drop in ratings. The title of a journalism review article about the incident posed the question everyone was asking: "How Low Can TV News Go?"[132]

Springer was not alone in the swampy ground of daytime talk shows. In 1994, *The Jenny Jones Show* gained dubious notoriety when one man killed another after being humiliated on the program. He had been surprised on the air by a "secret admirer" who turned out to be another man. When the program was sued over the murder, the host's televised courtroom testimony became fodder for another round of tabloid journalism on *Court TV* and other programs.

Another prominent genre has been the so-called reality show, originally popularized by the FOX network in the 1990s. A blend of "real" people and dramatic excess, these programs became a staple of the network's schedule. Some, such as *Cops*, were tightly edited productions subject to the approval of the police departments being filmed, raising concerns that the programming was little more than hour-long commercials for police. Some of the programs were dubbed "shockumentaries" and featured titles such as *When Animals Attack* and *World's Wildest Police Videos*. Referring to their often explicit depiction of violent and bloody encounters, NBC West Coast President Don Ohlmeyer referred to these shows as "one step short of a snuff film."[133]

Although they drew good ratings, these programs eventually alienated advertisers, who did not want to be associated with their increasingly raunchy or gruesome content. By the end of the decade, FOX decided that it had relied too heavily on these shock programs. Peter Chernin, president of News Corp., FOX's corporate parent, compared the network's reliance on the genre to a heroin fix injected whenever FOX needed a boost in the ratings.[134] Feeling the pressure from critics, FOX scrapped its planned *Celebrities Out of Control* and a show featuring the broadcast of an unmanned jet crash in the desert.

Nevertheless, television did not abandon "reality" programming. FOX moved in the direction of what producer Erik Nelson called "deranged game shows." However, one of its early ventures in this direction, *Who Wants to Marry a Millionaire?*, was a fiasco when the "millionaire" in question turned out to be an accused spouse batterer and the "marriage" was clearly done to cash in on the publicity; it was annulled almost immediately.[135]

Still, other networks followed the formula. For example, in the summer of 2000, CBS launched the first of its wildly successful *Survivor* series, in which contestants faced physical hardships on an island and each week had to vote to eliminate one contestant. The last remaining "survivor" was awarded $1 million. The program became an ugly variation of a prime-time soap opera, as members of the group lied, schemed, and deceived their way through the dog-eat-dog battle for the money. It was not too surprising that the two finalists were revealed to have criminal charges against them, one for using a stolen credit card, the other for child abuse.

Not only did *Survivor* return in various popular incarnations, but a slew of similar programs began to populate prime-time television. The names varied—*Big Brother, Fear Factor, The Apprentice, American Idol, The Amazing Race*—but the formula was largely the same: Put "real" people in "real" contests where losers were gradually eliminated and winners could walk away with a substantial paycheck. The biggest winners, however, were the networks, who could dramatically slash the cost of their prime-time programming by filling them with unpaid actors.

News Lite: Scandal and Entertainment

Mindless entertainment may be written off as just that, but news is supposed to be an oasis protected from sensationalism and trivialization. As we have seen, however, this has not always been the case. A century ago, the "yellow press" of the early media moguls moved journalism into the world of scandal and sensational storytelling in pursuit of a mass audience. Joseph Pulitzer, owner of the *New York World,* told his staff, "Heretofore you have all been living in the parlor and taking baths every day. Now I wish you to understand that, in future, you are all walking down the Bowery."[136] The Bowery—a New York symbol of grimy derelicts and street criminals—was to be the new figurative home of yellow journalism.

Less known is the fact that the early print media moguls coupled their sensational storytelling with open disdain for concentrated wealth and power. As Madeline Rogers notes,

> The early titans' sympathy for the common people was fueled not only by a desire for circulation and profits, but by a hatred of the excesses of the Gilded Age, which they felt were inimical to the republic. Pulitzer created his own 10 commandments for his

New York World, which included a promise to "always oppose privileged classes and public plunderers." Hearst was a self-declared enemy of "reactionary interests and predatory corporations"; Patterson, who dedicated his *New York Daily News* to Abraham Lincoln's "common man," was a socialist in his youth.[137]

Times have changed, as the pursuit of profit by today's media moguls is more likely to be coupled with a veneration of "the good life" and a cozy relationship with those in power.

Yellow journalism was only one tradition in the news industry, however. Other news outlets, both print and broadcast, later developed professional norms that committed journalists to providing independent information to serve the public interest. Although carried out within the framework of profit-generating networks, broadcast news was for decades widely considered to be the network's public service contribution. News divisions had to stay within their budgets, but they were not expected to generate significant profits for the corporate owners. Instead, as "loss leaders," respectable news divisions added prestige to the national networks.

All of this began to change with the commercial success of CBS's *60 Minutes*. The newsmagazine program showed corporate executives that public affairs programs in prime-time television could be profitable. By the 1980s, the consolidation of media ownership put businesspeople, rather than journalists, in ultimate charge of news divisions. Their primary concern was profits, and this orientation was applied to news as well. Because *60 Minutes* had shown that news could make money, the networks all imitated the formula with countless "newsmagazine" shows, most of which failed in both journalistic and commercial terms. Staff and expenses at the network news divisions were cut, and pressure to generate higher ratings and profits increased. Soon, this "respectable" branch of the news industry was borrowing strategies from the playbook of yellow journalism.

The expansion in the number of media outlets, coupled with corporate pressure for profits, has pushed today's media—at an ever-accelerating pace—toward blending journalism with entertainment. A major survey of national and local journalists by the Pew Center for the People and the Press asked if they believed increased bottom-line pressure was "seriously hurting the quality of news coverage." In 1995, when the question was first asked, 41% of national and 33% of local journalists said yes. When the same question was asked in 2004, the percentages had gone up dramatically; now 66% of national journalists and 57% of local journalists felt this way.[138] As one reporter at an Illinois daily newspaper put it, "If a story needs a real investment of time and money, we don't do it anymore." Instead, he said, "In assignment meetings, we dream up 'talker' stories, stuff that will attract attention and get us talked about, tidbits for busy folks who clip items from the paper and stick them on the fridge. . . . Who the hell cares about corruption in city government anyway, much less dying Bosnians?"[139]

Local television news, especially, has developed a reputation for featuring little hard news, almost no investigative news, and lots and lots of entertainment, poignant human interest, sports, and weather. Crime is the subject for about a quarter of all local news stories—double the second most common topic, accidents and disasters.[140] In fact, what constitutes "news" at many of these stations consists of little more than crime, accidents, and fires—the latter making for dramatic video from the station's helicopters. "If it bleeds, it leads" has become the informal mantra of such stations. This approach has been promoted by teams of news consultants who are hired by stations to revamp their sets, choose their on-air personalities, poll their audiences, and—most of all—boost their ratings.

It is not only local news in which this change has occurred. Arthur Kent was an NBC news correspondent from 1989 until he left in 1992 after he clashed with the network's weak commitment to hard news. He argues that "the people who constitute the conscience of the broadcast news discipline—working journalists—now have less real influence on the daily news agenda than ever before, and they face harsh treatment from management if they speak out."[141] It is business managers, not journalists, who wield power in today's newsrooms. As we will see, this has resulted in a situation in which journalistic integrity is increasingly undermined by the quest for profits.

The competition between media outlets has led to a slippery slope in terms of standards. When there were fewer media outlets and a smaller news "window," the news stayed more focused on substance. The advent of several 24-hour news channels, the Internet, and more outrageous tabloid journalism has resulted in pressures to include more sensationalism and fluff—even in the traditional news programs. While he was still *CBS Evening News* anchor, Dan Rather noted:

Fear runs in every newsroom in the country right now, a lot of different fears, but one fear is common—the fear that if we don't do it, somebody else will, and when they do it, they will get a few more readers, a few more listeners, a few more viewers than we do. The Hollywoodization of the news is deep and abiding. It's been one of the more important developments of the last 20 to 25 years, particularly the last 10 to 15, that we run stupid celebrity stories. . . . It has become pervasive, the belief that to be competitive, you must run a certain amount of celebrity news.[142]

The trend toward entertainment stories has led many to refer to network news as "news lite." This trend has also affected another form of media that has been traditionally associated with more substantive content: book publishing. In 1999, the former head of Pantheon Books, Andre Schiffrin, examined the spring catalogues of three major publishers—HarperCollins, Simon & Schuster, and Random House. He found that out of a list of more than 400 titles, only four books had been published about current political issues. Instead, the list had "an increasing reliance on television and movie tie-ins, seen most dramatically in the launch of HarperEntertainment, which is scheduled to publish 136 books in its first year along the lines of the *Jerry Springer Picture Book.*"[143] Here the pursuit of profits through synergistic strategies seems to be edging out the substantive ideas and discussion that would be more valuable to the health of the public sphere.

❖ MEDIA CONSTRAINT I: COMMERCIAL INTERESTS

The notion of censorship conjures up images of government authorities protecting themselves from criticism by removing objectionable material from media content—the antithesis of a free and independent press that is a pillar of democracy. Censorship, and broader constraints on the media, need not come from government, however; they can come from other powerful sources. Today, constraints on media in democratic societies are more likely to come from corporations, for economic purposes, than from governments, for purely political purposes. This section and the next focus on how changing media business has resulted in constraints and various forms of media censorship.

The first section examines how the quest for profits has eroded the foundation for independent media by inserting commercial considerations into many different forms of news and information media. The next section, which is closely related, examines censorship and conflicts of interest.

The Disappearing Line Between Journalism and Commerce

Instead of developing independent media content, current practices often result in media that are severely constrained. One type of constraint occurs when commercial interests pervade decision making about media content. Although this practice can have a negative impact on the quality of entertainment media, it is especially disturbing when the content is news and information.

Some constraints that result from the primacy of commercial interests are built into the very routines of newsgathering and are certainly not new. Commercial news organizations would like to produce credible news coverage at the lowest possible cost. This leads to practices in which journalists rely on outside sources to feed them stories. Routine news material from government and the private sector efficiently helps news organizations fill their broadcasts and newspapers. Reliance on such sources, however, also means it is more difficult for those outside the corridors of power to gain access to the news media. It also means that news organizations are less likely to pursue costly investigative journalism that requires greater investments of time and resources, with no guarantees of suitable stories at the end. Better to use the pre-arranged press conferences, written press materials, and video press releases that flow from the public relations and information offices of corporations and government agencies. As one comprehensive analysis of the state of the media in 2004 concluded, "Those who would manipulate the press and the public appear to be gaining leverage over the journalists who cover them."[144]

Thus the business logic of lowering expenses and increasing profits results in news that is limited in its range of ideas, favoring those entities that have the resources to aid journalists in their work.[145] As such cost-cutting logic is carried to its conclusion, we are seeing more and more collaborative news efforts, in which "competing" media conglomerates pool their newsgathering resources to produce lower cost news. The result for citizens will be an even smaller number of news providers.

Beyond the economic concerns that underlie newsgathering routines, there are new economic pressures on journalism caused by the recent changes in the media business. In newsrooms, the "church-state wall" refers to the traditional separation between the business side of news and the editorial content. Analogous to the separation of church and state in politics, "the wall" in journalism has long been a sacrosanct element of journalistic integrity. To maintain their credibility with citizens and their integrity as professionals, journalists must remain independent of advertisers' wishes or the strictly business concerns of their employers. That independence is aided by the tradition of the "wall."

In myriad ways, big and small, the recent changes in media have eroded, if not completely dismantled, the protective church-state wall. In its place, a bottom-line mentality has crept into decision making. "When MBAs Rule the Newsroom," as one journalist titled his exposé of these practices, making profits can take precedence over good reporting.[146] The result can be feel-good, watered-down, sensational-ized news that may attract readers and audiences but leaves citizens with little of substance. Citizens wind up with "news" that serves com-mercial interests rather than the public interest. Managers are rewarded for increased profitability and journalists are left wondering what has happened to their profession.

The Case of the Los Angeles Times

One of the more dramatic examples of this change in attitude about the wall occurred at the *Los Angeles Times,* beginning in 1997.[147] An economist and former General Mills cereal marketer, Mark Willes, had become chairman and CEO of Times Mirror Company—owner of the *Los Angeles Times.* His controversial cost-cutting measures, which included thousands of layoffs (earning him the nicknames "cereal killer" and "Captain Crunch") and the closing of *New York Newsday,* contributed to dramatic improvements in the financial picture of the company. The value of its stock nearly tripled in just 2 years, and Willes was awarded a $1.35 million bonus in addition to his nearly $800,000 annual salary. In the fall of 1997, Willes named himself publisher of the *Los Angeles Times* and announced that he was dismantling the wall between the paper's business and editorial departments, saying he would blow it up with a bazooka if necessary. Willes contended that the two could work together to help the paper without allowing adver-tisers to influence news decisions. Many journalists were skeptical. Petitions protesting the actions circulated in the newsroom, and when that failed, a string of resignations followed.

The new system in place at the *Times* called for collaboration and cooperation between advertising salespeople and journalists, to market the paper like any other consumer product. Business managers (referred to as "product managers")—whose responsibility was prof-itability—were teamed up with the editors of each of the paper's sections—whose responsibility was content—to help develop story ideas and plan long-term strategy. In contrast to the usual practice at newspapers, individual sections now had to account for their profits or losses, with most expected to turn a profit. Targets and goals for revenue and readership were developed. Reader focus groups were also enlisted to help plan the direction of each section. The goal of Willes's plan was to increase the paper's circulation by as much as 50%, attract more advertisers, and increase profits. Those enthusiastic about the changes looked forward to creating a more vibrant paper that better met readers' needs. Critics argued that it was an open door to business decisions influencing content. Either way, the wall had come tumbling down.

One of the first visible signs of the change at the *Los Angeles Times* was its new Monday "Health" section, based in part on reader surveys and focus groups, along with advertiser interest. Reactions were mixed at best. One observer in the *Columbia Journalism Review* described the new effort as

> a bright, photo and graphics laden package of six or eight pages [that] wraps literally dozens of snippets from medical books and journals around two fitness profiles each week—one celebrity and one ordinary person—several advice columns and a lead feature that seems intended to hold readers more with its chatty tone than eye-opening reporting.

The author goes on to note that

> what's lacking in the section is . . . hard news of the world of health care, from HMOs and managed care to fraud and government action. Also lacking is any sophisticated treatment of new advances in science and medicine. . . . to judge by its content, Health was founded on a very low estimation of the readers' intellect and attention span.[148]

The section, however, is designed to attract readers and, more important, advertisers who know their message will appear in the context of a light, news-you-can-use environment. Early indications were that advertisers loved the new section.

The elimination of the church-state wall began to produce major embarrassments. Most notably, in October 1999, the *Los Angeles Times* devoted its entire Sunday magazine to stories about the Staples Center, a new sports arena and entertainment venue that was just about to open in downtown Los Angeles. What readers—and even journalists who worked on the stories—were not told was that the *Times* had secretly agreed with the Staples Center to split the advertising profits from that project. After the deal was revealed by another publication, more than 300 *Times* journalists signed a petition protesting this conflict of interest and flagrant breach of basic journalistic independence. Their petition noted that they were "appalled by the paper entering into hidden financial partnerships with the subjects we are writing about" and called for an apology to readers and review of all the paper's financial relationships. The *Times* newsroom was in "open revolt"—a term later used by the paper itself to describe the situation.[149]

The revolt by journalists and widespread outrage over the breach of trust led to public apologies from the paper's editor and publisher. It also led the *Times* to launch an internal investigation that culminated 6 weeks later in an extraordinary 14-page story written by the paper's media critic, David Shaw. He began the lengthy story by putting the controversy in the context of the earlier changes at the *Times*, writing that "for several years, pressures for higher profits had reduced the size of the news staff and the space available for news in the paper. Increasingly, business concerns seemed to be influencing editorial decisions in ways long forbidden at the *Times* and at all respectable big city newspapers." Shaw acknowledged that the Staples Center affair constituted a flagrant "conflict of interest and violation of the journalistic principle of editorial independence."

Worse, Shaw's investigation found that many staffers saw the Staples Center controversy as "the very visible and ugly tip of an ethical iceberg of ominous proportions—a boost-the-profits, drive-the-stock-price imperative that threatens to undermine the paper's journalistic quality, integrity, and reputation." The changes under Willes had led to a situation in which, as a managing editor put it, "Money is always the first thing we talk about. The readers are always the last thing we talk about." Even the editor of the paper's book review section was affected. He had been repeatedly encouraged to pay more attention to books with big advertising budgets, such as those in the windows of Barnes & Noble. At the time, the *Times* had a deal with Barnes & Noble. The bookseller paid the newspaper a 6% commission on book sales originating with a buyer clicking on the Barnes & Noble ad on the *Times'* Web site.

The investigation and its revelations led to the adoption of new principles reestablishing some of the traditional separations between the business and content sides of the paper. Shaw, however, ended his investigation on a note of skepticism, asking rhetorically, "Will the guidelines be followed diligently only until profit margins fall again and pressure for new revenue intensifies? Will the heightened sensitivity recede once the Staples Center controversy begins to fade?"

The string of controversies and embarrassments took its toll at the *Times*. By the time of the Staples Center affair, the paper's stock had significantly declined in value in the midst of a booming economy. Willes had used some of the paper's own cash reserves to buy back some of its stock. Willes's efforts left the paper enmeshed in controversy, flush with cash, and struggling to maintain its stock prices. That made it ripe for a takeover. Early in 2000, the Tribune Company—owners of the *Chicago Tribune* and other papers, 22 television stations, four radio stations, and other media—bought the *Los Angeles Times*. Mark Willes, the man who wanted to blow up the wall between the business and editorial departments, was replaced.

The Influence of Commerce Elsewhere

Although the drama at the prestigious *Los Angeles Times* may be better known, it is not a unique story. Newspapers and magazines across the country—big and small—are increasingly blending the responsibilities of business managers with those of newsroom executives. The managing editor of the *Free Lance-Star* of Fredericksburg, Virginia, summarized it this way:

> Five or ten years ago, your focus could be pretty much solely on content, and the question always was, "Is this a good story?" Now I have to think, "Is this a story that will connect with my readers' particular lifestyles?" That's marketing, and it's something I never had to think about before.[150]

Journalists themselves are often quite concerned by the subtle—and not so subtle—changes that have taken place at media outlets where turning profits for the corporate parent has become more important than ever. Doug Underwood examined the effect on journalism of bottom-line profit concerns taking priority over journalistic news judgment in his book *When MBAs Rule the Newsroom*. In it, he writes:

Reporters . . . note that the character of investigations is changing as well as the atmosphere in the newsroom where they are trying to do their work. It is increasingly difficult, they say, to question authority out in the world when they themselves are being pressured to become loyal corporate soldiers inside their organizations. Michael Wagner, formerly an investigative reporter for the *Detroit Free Press*, says that . . . "the appetite these days is for fairly safe, less controversial, sociological investigative stories. . . . If you look across the country, you see papers doing a great job of covering prisons and juvenile crime and child abuse. But you don't see people asking how Exxon got to be bigger than five or six countries in the world." Or as [Brad] Bailey, formerly of the *Dallas Morning News*, puts it, "Do you see a corporation that's in the business of making money going out and investigating other corporations? I don't."

In this way, the business imperative influencing newsroom decisions can act as a censoring device, leading news organizations to avoid certain types of stories.

In some cases, the blurring of content and marketing is even more extreme. At the *Oregonian*, the advertiser-friendly home and auto sections are simply written by the ad department. The *Denver Post* turns over the production of its skiing, gardening, casino gambling, and other sections to its advertising department. In some cases, reporters are being asked to play more promotional roles. At the *Kansas City Star*, for example, journalists were encouraged to take part in panels and workshops at newspaper-sponsored public forums on personal finance and women's issues. Advertisers and other companies selling products were invited to set up booths at these events. Some journalists feared they were being used to lend credibility or even implicitly endorse the advertisers' products. Their complaints led to the creation of a new ethics committee to review such practices.[151]

Newspapers are not alone in this blurring of information and commerce. In 1996, cable's History Channel—co-owned by Disney, General Electric/NBC, and Hearst—invited major corporations to pay to have themselves profiled on the channel's *Spirit of Enterprise* series. The companies would retain veto power over the programs. DuPont, Boeing, AT&T, and others agreed to the deal, but when the arrangements were leaked and subjected to scathing criticism, the History Channel decided to drop the plans.[152]

In 1999, a CBS-owned Chicago television station, WBBM-TV, rented its journalistic credibility to advertisers by producing a series of commercials for a local hospital. The spots were taped in the style of newscasts and featured the station's former anchor and consumer reporter. The station had previously aired similar, news-style commercials for Hawaiian tourism that featured another former local reporter. That time, the "reporter" even ended the commercial with the station's ID: "I'm Lonnie Lardner for CBS 2 Chicago." Robert Feder, *Chicago Sun-Times* media critic, noted, "The pertinent question no longer is whether such commercials cross the line. The question is whether there is a line anymore."[153]

The Web site of the Seattle TV station, KIRO, featured a section called "experts"—who offer advice on everything from home repair to health care. Oddly, though, despite labeling them "experts," a small disclaimer at the bottom of the page cautioned, " KIRO7 does not endorse any expert nor is it responsible for information provided by its experts." That was because the "experts" were actually advertisers, who paid up to $1000 a month to be listed. Only after the situation was exposed in the local newspaper was the word *expert* replaced by *advertiser*—in the disclaimer only.[154]

Even more blatantly, one local television station literally put its journalistic integrity up for sale. WDSI, a FOX station in Chattanooga, Tennessee, faxed a flyer to prominent local businesses offering to produce a series of three "positive" news segments about "your company," lending its "most credible programming for the image of your company." For $15,000 the segments would be aired on their morning, midday, and evening news broadcasts.[155] Even obituaries—long a public service function—are becoming profitable ventures for some newspapers, which are now charging readers to run them.[156]

The blurring of the line between information and marketing permeates the Internet world, where a more subtle, but perhaps more pervasive, blend of journalism and commerce has taken place. In a development known as "transaction journalism," information that is presented in a journalistic form is directly connected to the promotion of a commercial product. For example, next to its book reviews, the online edition of the *New York Times* (and other papers, including, as we have seen, the *Los Angeles Times*) carries a direct link to an online bookseller, in this case barnesandnoble.com. If a review sparks readers' interest in a book, they can buy the book with just a few clicks of the mouse. The *New York Times* gets a percentage of the book's sale price for having brought the consumer to the barnesandnoble.com site. Because a negative review is unlikely to generate sales, the newspaper now has a financial interest in promoting—rather than just reviewing—a book. Under these circumstances, reviewers are no longer entirely independent voices to which readers can look for guidance.[157]

In 1999, AltaVista became the first major Internet search engine site to offer advertisers the opportunity to have their Web sites listed at the top of search results. Some search sites, such as Overture.com, consist entirely of paid listings.[158] Sites such as Amazon.com sell publishers the right to prominent reviews of their books, something they euphemistically call "supported placement." For various fees, publishers can have their titles described on the Amazon Web site under headings such as "Destined to be Classic," "What We're Reading," or "Our Customers Recommend."[159] Reviewers themselves sometimes work for a percentage of the revenue generated by the books they review on the site and thus have a financial interest in maximizing sales.[160]

At "cobranded" sites, advertisers partner with a Web site's content provider. The advertiser provides material about its products, which is presented alongside other "independent" information on the site. A Web site that provides information on health issues, for example, might include advertising from a drug manufacturer. That manufacturer's products then are mentioned (presumably in a favorable light) in relevant stories on the site.[161]

In all of these cases, commercial considerations have come to influence or dominate the development of media content.

❖ MEDIA CONSTRAINT II:
    CENSORSHIP AND CONFLICTS OF INTEREST

As we have seen, the critique of corporate media ownership is not about smoke-filled rooms populated with conspirators who are out to control the world. Instead, it is a critique of market logic as it applies to the world of culture and ideas. Corporate entities pursue profits for their shareholders because that is what they are expected to do. Those who manage such institutions tend to interpret events in the outside world in terms of whether they aid or hinder the company's pursuit of profits. There is nothing necessarily conspiratorial about any of this. It is the logic of the market system.

The pursuit of profits is not a value-neutral exercise, however. Regardless of the rationale, the pursuit of profits can have the effect—intended or not—of constraining the range of ideas and voices routinely found in the media. In conducting their business, corporations do not want to promote information or views that contradict their goals. As a result, the views that dominate in corporate media tend to be those that are compatible with a corporate worldview. This is most blatant in news coverage of the economy—where business programs and Wall Street analyses prevail and labor and consumer perspectives are rare—but it also spills over into coverage of a wide range of issues.[162]

The bottom line is that placing profits above all else has political implications and places real constraints on media content. For example, during preparations for the 2003 U.S. invasion of Iraq, MSNBC announced the cancellation of its prime-time *Donahue* program, noting that the program's host, Phil Donahue was "out of touch with the current marketplace." According to an internal MSNBC report, programming executives believed *Donahue* was "a difficult public face for NBC at a time of war." Referencing the growing audience of rival FOXNews, MSNBC executives feared the market consequences of news programming that might upset audience members, outlining a potentially disastrous scenario in which *Donahue* became "a home for the liberal antiwar agenda at the same time that our competitors are waving the flag at every opportunity."[163] In this case, profit concerns, expressed as a fear of audience responses to potentially unpopular perspectives, led MSNBC to take its most prominent critic of the impending war off the air.

Our discussion of these constraints is loosely organized by the source or nature of constraint, beginning with journalists themselves and moving outward to external sources of pressure. We start by looking at the phenomenon of self-censorship, in which journalists and others alter their own behavior for various reasons. Second, we discuss corporate censorship, in which managers and executives constrain the efforts of their own employees. Third, we look at conflicts of interest between different portions of single conglomerates, which can result in corporate censorship or self-censorship. Finally, we consider external pressures on media firms from advertisers.

Self-Censorship

Self-censorship occurs when organizational norms or the perception of likely criticism from powerful players leads to changes in media content. In such cases, there is no need for overt intervention to achieve desired results. We use the term here to refer to individual self-censorship. However, it is also possible that what we later term *corporate censorship* is another form of self-censorship, because the pressure for change is coming from within the corporation, rather than from outside sources. We treat corporate censorship separately because in those cases, the pressure exerted by someone higher up in the organization's hierarchy often leads to overt conflict rather than internalized self-censorship.

Unless someone later admits to what they have done, self-censorship is virtually impossible to document, because it occurs covertly. *Newsweek* columnist Jonathan Alter notes that self-censorship is a subtle process. "In a tight job market, the tendency is to avoid getting yourself or your boss in trouble. So an adjective gets dropped, a story skipped, a punch pulled. . . . It's like that Sherlock Holmes story—the dog that didn't bark. Those clues are hard to find."[164] As Andrew Jay Schwartzman, head of the Media Access Project, puts it, what has changed with growing consolidation is "not a question of misreporting. It's not a question of false reporting. It's a question of not reporting."[165]

There are no dramatic conspiracies here. Journalists want to keep their jobs. Editors know what the company's interests are. Little or nothing needs to be said about what is or is not acceptable in reporting. The smoking guns revealing the impact of corporate influence are few and far between. Instead, it is the cumulative effect of small daily decisions that results in homogenized, corporate-friendly media.

Although it is difficult to document, self-censorship in journalism is commonplace. For example, in one study, more than 40% of journalists and news executives surveyed admitted that they had engaged in self-censorship by purposely avoiding newsworthy stories or softening the tone of stories. With media organizations trying to attract more readers and larger audiences, market pressures were most often cited as the reason for such self-censorship. Almost 80% of those surveyed said important stories that are seen as dull are sometimes or often avoided, and just over 50% said important but complex stories are sometimes or often ignored. More than a third of all respondents said news that might hurt the financial interests of a news organization is sometimes or often ignored. More than one third said they censored themselves because of personal career concerns.[166] The journalists who are most likely to retain their jobs and advance to more influential positions are those who have best internalized the organizational norms of self-censorship.

Corporate Censorship and the
Pursuit of Organizational Interests

Corporate censorship involves cases that usually pit organizational interests against individual journalists or public interest principles. The censorship is still imposed from within the media organization, but it is more likely that there will be dissent about such a move. When corporate censorship abrogates journalistic standards and democratic ideals, it is not generally the result of political motivations or aspirations for power (although there are certainly exceptions). In most cases, the cause is the desire to most effectively pursue the primary goal of the corporation: profit making.

For example, in 1995, CBS's *60 Minutes* dropped an interview with an executive of Brown & Williamson Tobacco because the network was afraid of a potential lawsuit. The executive accused the company of hiding the truth about the addictive and harmful effects of tobacco from the public. Although the veracity of the story was well-founded, the president of CBS News flatly told the executive producer of the report that "the corporation will not risk its assets on the story."[167] However, news of the cancellation was leaked, creating a firestorm of criticism, resulting in the later airing of the interview. Industry observers noted that, because CBS was said to be up for sale (Westinghouse bought it shortly thereafter), an outstanding lawsuit would have made the network a less attractive property for potential buyers. In addition, the principal owner of CBS at the time was Laurence Tisch—the major stockholder in another tobacco company, Lorillard. This created a potential conflict of interest, a subject to be explored more fully later. Finally, RJR Nabisco and Philip Morris, conglomerates that are both tobacco companies and major food and beverage producers, are among the biggest advertisers on CBS and other television networks.

It certainly would have been in the public interest for CBS to broadcast their story about the deceptive practices of the major tobacco companies. From a corporate perspective, however, the possibility of a lawsuit could have threatened future profitability. When faced with a choice between protecting profits and serving the public interest, CBS followed the money. It was not the first time. In an earlier incident of this sort involving ABC's *Day One* newsmagazine, the network actually publicly apologized to Philip Morris, resulting in the discontinuance of a defamation lawsuit.[168] As the producer of the contested *60 Minutes* interview concluded,

Executives of the network news divisions say that they will report any story of public interest and import without fear or favor, without considering its potential commercial consequences. They say that, but do not believe it. The menu of what stories will be initiated, what enterprise reporting will and will not be done is formed by the networks' commercial interest. The idea of committing resources to do stories that in and of themselves are clearly in the public interest is dead.[169]

Although the *60 Minutes* and *Day One* incidents themselves raise serious concerns, they also suggest the possibility that many other similar decisions have been made without the public ever finding out about them. Such visible cases also increase the likelihood that future journalists will use self-censorship to avoid such controversy.

Despite the fact that many incidents of corporate censorship are unlikely to become public, there are a number of cases that have become part of the public record. These have occurred in many types of media. For example,

❖ The Walt Disney Company blocked its subsidiary, Miramax, from releasing Michael Moore's critical documentary *Fahrenheit 911* in 2004, despite Moore's substantial commercial success with his prior film, *Bowling for Columbine*. Moore charged that Disney dropped the film because of concerns that the film's criticisms of President Bush would jeopardize Disney tax breaks in Florida, where President Bush's brother, Jeb, is governor. Although Disney denied those allegations, it made clear that the decision not to release *Fahrenheit 911* was a business decision—with one Disney executive arguing: "It's not in the interest of any major corporation to be dragged into a highly charged partisan political battle."[170] Even when such business decisions are not politically motivated, they can have substantial political consequences. Other major U.S. film studios also shied away from the controversy, but Canadian studio Lion's Gate agreed to distribute the film, which subsequently broke box office records in the United States for documentary films.

❖ In 1998, one of News Corp.'s publishing holdings, Harper-Collins, dropped plans to publish a memoir by Chris Patten, the last English governor of Hong Kong. HarperCollins' top editor, Stuart Profitt, described the book as "the most lucid and intelligent" he had ever read by a politician and he felt sure it would be a bestseller.

However, News Corp. was attempting to expand its global satellite TV empire into China, and Patten's book criticized the Chinese government, which might potentially have caused problems for News Corp.'s profitable plans. The head of News Corp., Rupert Murdoch, ordered Profitt to tell Patten that his book was not acceptable. Profitt refused and was then suspended from his job.[171]

❖ Stephen Brill had been the founder of *Court TV* and several legal publications, but he sold his portion of the company to the majority owner, Time Warner. After his departure, it was revealed that Brill had written a memorandum to senior Time Warner executives complaining about repeated attempts to limit his editorial freedom. On one occasion, Time Warner executives tried unsuccessfully to get Brill to kill an article critical of an official of the Federal Trade Commission. The reason? The FTC was about to decide whether Time Warner could merge with Turner Broadcasting.[172]

❖ Investigative reporters for WTVT, FOX's Tampa Bay affiliate, discovered that—despite promises to the contrary—supermarkets were selling milk produced with rBGH, a synthetic growth hormone developed by Monsanto. Critics of the practice contend that the hormone is indirectly linked with increased risk of cancer in humans. When word of the ongoing investigation reached Monsanto, they sent a letter to the head of FOX News, Roger Ailes. In turn, the reporters' story was postponed and a long series of demanded revisions, cuts, and conferences with lawyers ensued. The reporters say it was clear management was not worried about the accuracy of the story; they were worried about a possible lawsuit. When the reporters resisted story changes that they believed were false and misleading, they were told by the station manager, "We paid $3 billion for these television stations. We will decide what the news is. The news is what we tell you it is." Further discussions about revisions dragged on, with the station even offering to pay the reporters $125,000 to go away and never tell anyone about the dispute. Eventually, with no resolution forthcoming, the reporters were fired.[173]

❖ Jim Hightower is a Texas populist and rare liberal voice on talk radio's otherwise conservative terrain. His popular radio commentaries feature sharp-tongued critiques of the political system (The political spectrum's not left-to-right, he argued, "it's top-to-bottom, and the vast majority of people aren't even in shouting distance of the economic and political powers at the top") and a satirical sense of humor

("Like NASCAR race drivers or PGA golfers, why not require each of the [presidential] candidates to cover their clothing, briefcases and staff with the logo patches of their corporate sponsors?"). His ideas reached some 1.5 million listeners on 150 stations nationwide. When Disney bought Capital Cities/ABC, the company that owned and distributed Hightower's program via the ABC Radio Networks, it was not amused by Hightower's continued critiques of corporate America and even Disney itself. In September 1995, he criticized ABC for backing down and apologizing to tobacco companies to avoid a lawsuit, noting that ABC "had just merged with the Mickey Mouse empire of Disney, Inc." The next day he was told his program was being dropped by ABC.[174]

❖ Even satirical treatment of corporate censorship can be subject to corporate censorship. In March 1998, NBC's long-running comedy program *Saturday Night Live* aired a short cartoon clip inspired by articles on media conglomeration in *The Nation*, an independent liberal journal of opinion. Modeled after *Schoolhouse Rock*, an old Saturday morning feature with catchy tunes about educational topics, the new cartoon poked fun at the concentration of media ownership. The cartoon included corporate logos with octopus tentacles altering the news and endlessly selling products. The song accompanying the cartoon included these lines:

> You mean Disney, Fox, Westinghouse and good ol' GE?
>
> They own networks from CBS to CNBC
>
> They can use them to say whatever they please
>
> And put down the opinions of anyone who disagrees. . . .

General Electric, corporate owner of the NBC network on which *Saturday Night Live* airs, was reportedly not amused. When the program was repeated a few months later, the cartoon was removed. The program's executive producer, Lorne Michaels, said it had been deleted because he "didn't think [the cartoon] worked comedically." However, others at the network told reporters that NBC's president and GE officials had been upset.[175]

One of the most disturbing incidents of corporate censorship (or self-censorship) occurred in the months prior to the passage of the 1996 Telecommunications Act (discussed in chapter 3). The act, which was the most sweeping change in telecommunications law in more than 50 years, fundamentally altered how the media industry is structured.

The media industry lobbied heavily for passage of this act, which, among other things, allowed larger conglomerates to form by removing or relaxing various media ownership limitations.

Yet most Americans knew virtually nothing about the act. That is because there was remarkably little coverage of the proposed legislation. For example, one study found that in the 9 months between the introduction of the bill and its passage in February 1996, the three major television networks had only 12 stories about the proposed legislation, totaling just 19.5 minutes of coverage.[176] In addition, much of this limited coverage focused on the introduction of new television content ratings and the V-chip that allowed viewers to block programs with sex and violence. The news largely ignored the bill's dramatic changes in ownership rules that would lead to further concentration of media ownership. Most citizens learned of these provisions only after the act passed.

Rather than learn from this dismal performance, the mainstream commercial media repeated it in 2003 when the FCC again reviewed media ownership rules. Despite the significance of the issue, a detailed review of coverage by the *American Journalism Review* concluded that as the FCC moved to significantly alter ownership regulations in "a plan that would greatly benefit a handful of large companies, most newspapers and broadcast outlets owned by those companies barely mentioned the issue."[177]

Conflicts of Interest

The inadequate news coverage of FCC actions that benefit the media industry—and some of the examples of corporate censorship discussed earlier—suggest the existence of a built-in conflict of interest. The major media companies stood to benefit directly from changes in FCC regulations and were instrumental in lobbying for their passage, even crafting some of the language of the 1996 Telecom Act. Reporting fully on the views of critics of these changes would have run counter to the economic interests of the industry. The result was woefully inadequate coverage. As Republican Senator John McCain put it while on the floor of the Senate, "You will not see this story on any television or hear it on any radio broadcast because it directly affects them."[178]

Newspapers are not much different. With conglomeration, many print media outlets are owned by corporations that also own television and radio stations, placing them in the same conflict of interest position as their broadcast counterparts. One study examined the newspapers that editorialized about the Telecommunications Bill's provision to give digital spectrum licenses to traditional broadcasters. It found that the newspapers with corporate owners that did not receive significant TV revenue editorialized against the bill, but those with corporate owners that *did* receive significant TV revenue editorialized in favor of the giveaway.[179] A similar pattern existed with coverage of subsequent FCC actions in 2003.

The problem of potential conflicts of interest, however, extends well beyond legislation or issues dealing directly with the media industry. The fact that media conglomerates are, by definition, involved in many different types of businesses creates the very real possibility of conflicts of interest in a variety of fields. This is especially true when one of the conglomerate's businesses is journalism. The responsibility of journalism to report fully and fairly on events of the day has the potential to clash with the interests of corporate parents in promoting their businesses and minimizing any negative news about their operations. In addition, because their business interests are so broad and far reaching, there are very few economic or legislative initiatives that do not affect some part of a media conglomerate.

It is not hard to imagine why major media conglomerates would not want to pursue certain stories. Why should we expect, for example, NBC—owned by General Electric—to aggressively pursue stories critical of its corporate partner, Microsoft? Why should we expect ABC to investigate issues that might be detrimental to the corporate interests of its parent company, Disney? In fact, in a 1998 interview, Disney head Michael Eisner said, "I would prefer ABC not to cover Disney. . . . I think it's inappropriate for Disney to be covered by Disney . . . by and large, the way to avoid conflict of interest, is to, as best you can, not cover yourself." Within days of this interview, ABC News dropped a *20/20* investigative report about pedophilia and lax security at Walt Disney World. The network said it was not influenced by the fact that the proposed story was about its corporate parent. Nevertheless, the incident exemplified the worst fears about conflicts of interest among the media giants.[180]

Evidence of those fears appears from time to time. In a 1989 incident, the *Today* show aired a segment on defective bolts but failed to mention that its corporate parent, General Electric, used these bolts in its nuclear reactors; the GE connection was only mentioned later in follow-up after critics pointed out the issue. A 1990 segment on the same program focused on consumer boycotts but failed to mention that the largest boycott at the time was one aimed at General Electric. In fact, one source interviewed for the story was cautioned by the program's producer not to mention the GE boycott. Subsequently, after public criticism of this incident, NBC has aired stories on GE scandals.[181]

In some cases, corporate censorship is not tied to a specific company interest but is instead linked to generalized promotion of a corporate-friendly worldview. For example, one study examined press coverage in the *New York Times* and the *Washington Post* of the debate over the North American Free Trade Agreement (NAFTA) during a 4-month period. NAFTA was supported by major corporate interests but opposed by labor, environmentalists, and others. The study found that despite the unpopularity of NAFTA among the general public, pro-NAFTA sources used by the press outnumbered anti-NAFTA sources by three to one, and not a single labor union representative was quoted during this period. The newspapers' boards of directors were filled with businesspeople whose companies stood to gain from the passage of NAFTA.[182]

Conflicts of interest can also occur because of the interconnected nature of corporate management. For example, in Liberty Media's 1995 annual report, Peter Barton, the president of its TCI subsidiary, commented on TCI's connections to other companies:

The six executives at Liberty Media sit on more than 40 corporate boards. Their function is to act not just as watchdogs for our investments but also as relationship managers with our partners. In this way, we can link pieces of our portfolio to create strengthened alliances, new businesses, and shared economics.[183]

This intertwined network of corporate boards raises additional questions about the ultimate independence of news media. For example, the *New York Times* coverage of the debate over health-care reform in the mid-1990s tilted heavily in favor of the "managed competition" option, which would have been profitable for larger health-care corporations. Other proposals for reform, such as the Canadian-style single-payer program, were either ignored or harshly criticized. Four members of the *Times*'s board of directors also sat on the boards of major insurance companies, and two were on the boards of pharmaceutical companies.[184] When key individuals in media companies have vested interests in the outcome of public debates because of their connections to other corporations, citizens have a right to question the independence of such media accounts.

Advertiser Influence

So far we have only mentioned efforts to influence coverage that emanate from within media companies. However, in some cases, advertisers have also sought to suppress media content or punish media companies for already published material.

Advertisers have long had substantial influence over what is and is not emphasized in the media. Usually this pressure is fairly subtle and indirect. For example, it has long been media's practice to offer advertisers a "heads up" about editorial content that might reflect badly on the advertiser. Oil companies, for example, generally are given the opportunity to reschedule their ads if the evening news features a story about an oil spill. Airlines are allowed to do the same if there is a plane crash. More recently, advertisers have begun demanding advance warning of content that might be controversial—whether or not it is related to their industry—so they have the opportunity to remove their ads. For example, Chrysler Corporation—at the time the nation's fourth largest advertiser—informed the magazines in which it advertised that

> It is required that Chrysler Corporation be alerted in advance of any and all editorial content that encompasses sexual, political, social issues or any editorial that might be construed as provocative or offensive. Each and every issue that carries Chrysler advertising requires a written summary outlining major theme/articles appearing in upcoming issues.[185]

Such requirements potentially create a "chilling effect"—and the danger of self-censorship—because they discourage magazines from publishing anything that might result in a loss of advertising revenue.

Sometimes, advertiser pressure is more direct. In a classic case dating back to 1980, *Mother Jones*, an independent liberal magazine, considered publishing a series of articles examining the link between cigarettes and cancer. At the time, the magazine accepted ads from tobacco companies, and staff were concerned about the economic repercussions of publishing such a series. To its credit, the magazine went ahead with the series and, as feared, angry tobacco companies pulled their advertising. For a decade and a half after this incident, mainstream publications continued to steer clear of stories too critical of tobacco and continued to receive the industry's substantial ad revenue.

Today, advertiser pressure has, in some ways, actually increased. One survey found that about 30% of journalists and news executives believed self-censorship sometimes or often occurred because of concern about advertisers.[186] The pressure is much worse for investigative reporters. One survey of investigative reporters and editors at commercial television stations found that nearly three quarters said advertisers had "tried to influence the content" of news at their stations. More than half said advertisers tried to kill news stories. More than two thirds said advertisers had threatened to withdraw their advertising because of their displeasure with a news story, and more than 40% said advertisers actually did withdraw their ads. Fifty-nine percent said there had been "pressure from within" their stations "to not produce news stories that advertisers might find objectionable." Conversely, 56% said they had been pressured from within the station "to produce news stories to please advertisers."[187]

Automobile dealers have often been cited as the most frequent source of advertiser pressure on local media. In one 1996 incident, a well-known consumer reporter, David Horowitz, was fired by his KCBS-TV employer in Los Angeles after advertisers complained about his stories on car safety. According to Horowitz, he was fired only after management first tried to get him to stop his stories by telling him, "I'm concerned about the story not because it's right or wrong, but because it may cost us advertising."[188]

Ironically, in one case, concern about advertisers led television networks to refuse advertising. In 1997, the Media Foundation tried to purchase ad time to promote "Buy Nothing Day," an event meant to bring attention to excessive consumerism and its environmental costs. The networks refused to sell them ad time. CBS wrote that a day without shopping was "in opposition to the current economic policy of the United States." NBC noted, "We don't want to take any advertising that's inimical to our legitimate business interests." Kalle Lasn, of the Media Foundation, found the refusals ironic, noting, "I came from Estonia where you were not allowed to speak up against the government. Here I was in North America, and suddenly I realize you can't speak up against the [corporate] sponsor. There is something fundamentally undemocratic about our public airways."[189]

❖ CONCLUSION

Changes in media structure and practices have had a significant impact on media content. The quest for profits often leads to media that are homogenized and trivial, and the boundaries between commerce and information are rapidly disappearing. Making profits the first priority also has political implications for what is and is not routinely included in the media.

We should not romanticize a "golden era" of journalism when reporters were staunchly independent. The reality is that commercial forces have long influenced the profession of journalism and the content of the news. However, the new business of media has resulted in additional direct and indirect pressure to increase profits and protect the company's interests. As media critic Ben Bagdikian puts it,

> The reporting of news has always been a commercial enterprise and this has always created conflicts of interest. But the behavior of the new corporate controllers of public information has produced a higher level of manipulation of news to pursue the owners' other financial and political goals. In the process, there has been a parallel shrinkage of any sense of obligation to serve the noncommercial information needs of public citizenship.[190]

The impact of these recent changes will only become fully apparent as a new generation of writers and reporters comes of age within media conglomerates led by savvy businesspeople—with virtually no experience in journalism or the arts. As one observer noted, "Future leaders of these media companies will be trained under their corporate bosses, who will likely teach them that their responsibility is to the shareholders, not necessarily to the citizenry."[191]

Changes in media content are the most obvious effect of changes in the media industry. However, changes in business structure and strategy have had a wider impact on society. To those effects we now turn.

6

How the Media Business Influences Society

The precise impact of media on society is notoriously difficult to establish. Media are pervasive and diffuse, making them virtually impossible to study using experimental methods. The influence of media on society is most likely to be slow and cumulative in nature, making it difficult to study by traditional social science techniques. Still, few would dispute the observation that a society inundated with media is likely to be affected by that media. In fact, despite the complexities involved in studying the relationship between the media and society, a large body of research has documented various media effects.[192]

If we accept that the media influence society (and are in turn influenced by it), then we can understand how significant changes in media structure and practices can alter not only media content but also the nature of the media's influence on society. In other words, if the media change, their impact is likely to change as well.

We have already looked at the impact of media industry changes on the content of media. This chapter focuses on the impact of these changes on broader social and political life.

❖ SOCIAL INFLUENCES

In this section, we briefly note some of the ways that media influence society. We are not concerned here with the specific content of the media but rather with how the media's very presence has influenced how we understand ourselves and our world.

Ubiquity of Commercial Media: All the World's a Sale

It may be that the commercial media's greatest impact on society has been its successful colonization of social space. In a manner unprecedented in human history, our daily lives are saturated with media. Television, radio, magazines, Internet, newspapers, books, and recorded music have taken up an ever-growing amount of our time and attention. In the pursuit of increased profits, the media have expanded dramatically into virtually all arenas of public and private life, bringing with them the commercial imperative that drives the industry.

Commercial media have been the vehicles for the introduction of advertising into virtually every facet of daily life. The media are commercial enterprises in two fundamental ways. First, media content is advertised and sold to consumers as products (e.g., music CDs, magazines, etc.). Second, media are vehicles for more advertising that sells other products (e.g., television commercials, magazine ads, billboards, etc.). Everything, it sometimes seems, is now a product and everything is a potential advertisement.

One of the great myths of mass media is that the media just give the people what they want. Paying attention to audience tastes as measured by ratings and readership is, of course, important for the industry to remain profitable. However, audiences have been remarkably persistent in avoiding one aspect of media content: advertising. In this area, the media are clearly *not* giving audiences what they want. Instead, the industry must find new and ingenious ways to load more and more advertising into the daily media diets of resistant consumers.

More than anywhere else, this is occurring on television. About 17 minutes of every prime-time hour of television broadcasting is devoted to commercials and promotions. During the daytime, it is about 21 minutes. Viewers, however, try to avoid ads whenever possible. The remote control gave viewers unprecedented power to avoid commercials. Digital video recorders have proven to be a huge hit, in part because of the feature that allows viewers to quickly skip commercials.

In response, the media and advertising industries have developed new ways of delivering ads to a resistant public. The result has been an onslaught of commercial advertising and media products that seem to know no limits.

Captive Audiences

One technique media companies use is to feed media and ads to audiences who cannot avoid them. This growth in "captive audience" (or "place-based") media is taking place in public spaces where individuals cannot control the flow of media advertising. One of the early efforts at place-based media appeared in middle and high schools, where students have been forced to watch *Channel One,* a television news service complete with advertising, in their classrooms. In recent years, *Channel One* has beamed news into 350,000 classrooms in more than 12,000 schools in the United States, with an audience of more than eight million students. Participating schools receive the daily news program along with additional educational video material, television sets for each classroom, two VCRs, and a satellite link. In exchange, schools agree to show *Channel One* to students as a required part of each school day. In this trade, schools are delivering a highly sought youth audience to *Channel One,* and the attention of these teens is sold to youth-oriented marketers at premium advertising rates.[193]

In addition, corporate ads are showing up in schools on everything from supplemental reading materials to Web sites designed specifically for use in the classroom.

- ❖ Companies from Calvin Klein to Nike distribute thousands of book covers—complete with corporate logos—to students.
- ❖ Companies sponsor writing contests that extol the virtues of their products. In 1996, Snapple even invited students to write a commercial for the company.
- ❖ Some schools play special music broadcasts—complete with 10 minutes of commercials per hour—in their hallways, courtyards, and cafeterias.
- ❖ Schools across the country are giving exclusive "pouring rights"—and accompanying advertising—to the soda company that is willing to pay the most. Some contracts are written with incentives for the school to sell their kids more soft drinks. Some schools have approved large colorful ads for soft drinks on the sides of school buses. One Texas school actually has a Dr. Pepper billboard on top of the school.

❖ Companies sponsor specific curricula featuring their products. For example, Hershey developed the "Chocolate Dream Machine," which offered lessons in math, science, geography, and (ironically) nutrition. Procter & Gamble's entry, "Planet Patrol," promotes environmental thinking in this way: You can create less waste by using its Pert Plus combination of shampoo and conditioner.

❖ One type of high-tech corporate curriculum is the "virtual field trip" in which corporations sponsor the voyages of real-world adventurers, create related Web sites for use in schools, and get their corporate messages into the classroom.[194]

Other cases of captive audiences abound. Most airports now prominently feature television sets feeding a stream of news, weather, and advertising. Audiences who have paid to attend a movie are often subjected to several advertisements before the film begins. The magazines and television sets of doctors' waiting rooms have been targeted as a place to feed advertising to captive audiences. The elevators of upscale hotels now routinely feature television sets complete with advertising. Gas station pumps, banks, and grocery checkout lines have all been turned into opportunities for advertisers. Even specialty apparel stores catering to young, fashion-conscious consumers are part of the act. In recent years, record companies have been promoting their artists by providing their music free of charge to music-programming companies who, in turn, supply background music played in apparel stores. The result is "stealth advertising"; the customer is not even aware of it. In all of these cases, advertisers are able to reach a particular audience (students, travelers, patients, hotel guests, customers, etc.) under conditions in which it is difficult to avoid the ad.

Saturation

Another way to make an impression on consumers by advertising is to make ads so conspicuous that audiences cannot possibly miss them. Various exclusive sponsorship deals, for example, ensure that one corporation's ads dominate a television program, sporting event, or other venue. Another approach is called "station domination," in which advertisers saturate the public space at transit stations with their advertising. As one news account summarized, "Pure station domination banishes all competing ads, and passersby can't change a channel or flip a page." For example, a campaign at New York's World Trade Center featured 138 simultaneous ads for the same company. In addition to the usual billboard space, marble walls were covered in ads and ads were embedded in the floor and escalators. As one salesman of such space enthused, "Literally anywhere anyone would look, they are bombarded [by the ads] . . . We call it surround sound for the eyes."[195]

Blurring Advertising With Content

Yet another approach used to advertise to reluctant audiences is to merge ads with media content. There are many different variations of this technique. Saturday morning cartoon programs aimed at kids popularized this approach years ago. Toy manufacturers discovered that animated programs based on their toy characters served as half-hour ads for their products. In those days, kids watching *GI Joe, Smurfs, He Man and the Masters of the Universe,* or other cartoons based on toys were, in effect, watching a half-hour commercial for the toys and accessories. MTV, the first music video channel, used a similar approach. Its video programming, featuring popular bands playing their latest releases, was an endless stream of ads promoting new music releases. The content was the ad, and the ad was the content.

A different, although related, approach involves placing advertising or products in the media content so that if a person wants to see the content, they must also see the ad. Perhaps the best example of this strategy can be found in sports. Professional sports in this country have always had a business element, but in recent decades, the merchandising and selling of sports teams and players has reached new heights. An enormous and growing sports merchandising industry sells every conceivable product stamped with team logos. Hats, banners, and jerseys are just the beginning. Teams license computer mouse pads, watches, cooking aprons, stuffed animals, wallpaper, CDs, memo boards, toys, banks, and much more.

More significantly, however, sports themselves have become opportunities for advertising. Playing surfaces and even players' uniforms are routinely plastered with corporate logos and advertising. Professional auto racing is where this occurs most blatantly. If race fans want to watch a race—either in person or on TV—they are subjected to dozens and dozens of ads covering virtually every inch of the cars and racetrack walls. Hockey, too, has advertising covering most of the boards and parts of the ice. Even the names of stadiums—which used to be reserved to honor the community or local figures—now read like a veritable who's who of corporate advertisers, in the process generating more revenue for the stadium owners (see Exhibit 6.1).

(Text continues on page 201)

Exhibit 6.1   Corporate Names of Select Sports Stadiums (2004)

Stadium Corporate Name	Home Team (League)	Avg. $/Year	Expires
Air Canada Centre	Toronto Maple Leafs (NHL) Toronto Raptors (NBA)	1.5 million	2019
Alltel Stadium	Jacksonville Jaguars (NFL)	620,000	2007
American Airlines Arena	Miami Heat (NBA)	2.1 million	2019
American Airlines Center	Dallas Mavericks (NBA) Dallas Stars (NHL)	6.5 million	2031
America West Arena	Phoenix Suns (NBA) Phoenix Coyotes (NHL) Phoenix Mercury (WNBA)	866,667	2019
Ameriquest Field	Texas Rangers (MLB)	2.5 million	2034
Arco Arena	Sacramento Kings (NBA) Sacramento Monarchs (WNBA)	750,000	2007
Bank of America Stadium	Carolina Panthers (NFL)	7 million	2024
Bank One Ballpark	Arizona Diamondbacks (MLB)	2.2 million	2028
Citizens Bank Park	Philadelphia Phillies (MLB)	2.3 million	2028

Stadium Corporate Name	Home Team (League)	Avg. $/Year	Expires
Comerica Park	Detroit Tigers (MLB)	2.2 million	2030
Conseco Fieldhouse	Indiana Pacers (NBA) Indiana Fever (WNBA)	2 million	2019
Continental Airlines Arena	New Jersey Nets (NBA) New Jersey Devils (NHL)	1.4 million	2011
Coors Field	Colorado Rockies (MLB)	N/A	Indefinite
Corel Center	Ottawa Senators (NHL)	878,142	2016
Delta Center	Utah Jazz (NBA) Utah Starzz (WNBA)	1.3 million	2011
FedEx Field	Washington Redskins (NFL)	7.6 million	2025
FedEx Forum	Memphis Grizzlies (NBA)	4.5 million	2023
Wachovia Center	Philadelphia 76ers (NBA) Philadelphia Flyers (NHL)	1.4 million	2023
Fleetcenter	Boston Celtics (NBA) Boston Bruins (NHL)	2 million	2010

(Continued)

Exhibit 6.1 (Continued)

Stadium Corporate Name	Home Team (League)	Avg. $/Year	Expires
Ford Field	Detroit Lions (NFL)	1 million	2042
General Motors Place	Vancouver Canucks (NHL)	844,366	2015
Gillette Stadium	New England Patriots (NFL)	N/A	2017
Heinz Field	Pittsburgh Steelers (NFL)	2.9 million	2021
Invesco Field at Mile High	Denver Broncos (NFL)	6 million	2021
KeyArena	Seattle Supersonics (NBA) Seattle Storm (WNBA)	1 million	2010
Lincoln Financial Field	Philadelphia Eagles (NFL)	6.7 million	2022
M & T Bank Stadium	Baltimore Ravens (NFL)	5 million	2018
MCI Center	Washington Wizards (NBA) Washington Capitals (NHL) Washington Mystics (WNBA)	2.2 million	2017
Mellon Arena	Pittsburgh Penguins (NHL)	1.8 million	2009
Miller Park	Milwaukee Brewers (MLB)	2.1 million	2020

Stadium Corporate Name	Home Team (League)	Avg. $/Year	Expires
Minute Maid Park	Houston Astros (MLB)	6 million	2030
Nationwide Arena	Columbus BlueJackets (NHL)	N/A	Indefinite
Office Depot Center	Florida Panthers (NHL)	1.4 million	2013
Pepsi Center	Denver Nuggets (NBA) Colorado Avalanche (NHL)	3.4 million	2019
Petco Park	San Diego Padres (MLB)	2.7 million	2026
Phillips Arena	Atlanta Hawks (NBA) Atlanta Thrashers (NHL)	9.3 million	2019
PNC Park (PNC Bank)	Pittsburgh Pirates (MLB)	2 million	2020
Qualcomm Stadium	San Diego Chargers (NFL)	900,000	2017
Safeco Field	Seattle Mariners (MLB)	2 million	2019
SBC Center	San Antonio Spurs (NBA)	2.1 million	2022
SBC Park	San Francisco Giants (MLB)	2.1 million	2024

(Continued)

Exhibit 6.1 (Continued)

Stadium Corporate Name	Home Team (League)	Avg. $/Year	Expires
Staples Center	Los Angeles Lakers (NBA) Los Angeles Kings (NHL) Los Angeles Clippers (NBA) Los Angeles Sparks (WNBA)	5.8 million	2019
St. Pete Times Forum	Tampa Bay Lightning (NHL)	2.1 million	2014
Toyota Center	Houston Rockets (NBA)	N/A	N/A
Tropicana Field	Tampa Bay Devil Rays (MLB)	1.5 million	2026
United Center	Chicago Blackhawks (NHL) Chicago Bulls (NBA)	1.8 million	2014
U.S. Cellular Field	Chicago White Sox (MLB)	3.4 million	2025
Xcel Energy Center	Minnesota Wild (NHL)	3 million	2024

Source: ESPN (http://espn.go.com/sportsbusiness/s/stadiumnames.html).

College sports arenas and stadiums have followed suit and are taking on corporate names, as well as making millions annually selling corporate retailers the merchandising rights to their teams. More recently, cash-strapped public schools have begun selling naming rights to corporate sponsors for everything from gymnasiums to football fields.

With digital technology, broadcasters now can maximize advertising revenue by showing television viewers virtual ads during sporting events. These ads appear to be on soccer fields or the walls of baseball fields but are, in fact, electronically generated and visible only to television viewers. The same technology has been used to show a virtual first-down line in football telecasts.

Most sports broadcasting is a seamless web of advertising with the name of a corporate sponsor attached to replays, highlights, pregame shows, halftime reports, stars of the game, and even college football bowl names—and that's not counting the "real" commercials. When FOX broadcast the World Series, it even sprinkled stars from its most popular programs in the stands. During lulls in the game, viewers were treated to more stealth advertising when cameras zoomed in on the stars of shows that just happen to be on FOX.

The Internet has followed suit in interspersing ads directly with content. Most commercial Web sites include "banner ads" and other promotional material that cannot be avoided by visitors to the site. Often, online articles are laid out in sections, so that the reader is forced to click to numerous pages—each with paid advertising—to finish the story, even if it would otherwise fit in one or two pages. "Pop-up" ads that appear in separate windows are even more intrusive, because they require users to click on these windows to close them. Free online gaming also comes with strings attached—ads that must be viewed before the game will start.

The introduction of no-cost access to the Internet continues this trend. To access the Internet "for free," users subject themselves to advertising that they cannot turn off. Similarly, offers of "free" e-mail or home pages on the Web come with a catch; most have advertising that pops up unsolicited on the screen, and users must provide personal information valuable to advertisers. Every e-mail message also carries an ad for the company providing the "free" service.[196]

Sneak Attack Ads

Another way to reach ad-adverse consumers with corporate logos and advertising is to use unexpected places where ads are not usually found. This "sneak attack" approach has included advertising messages on stickers stuck to fruit in the grocery store, popcorn bags in movie theaters, the walls of toilet stalls, gas pumps, the arms that sweep away toppled pins in bowling alleys, sidewalks, the backs of store receipts, the bottom of golf cups, tickets to theaters and sporting events, and church bulletins. However, this technique may soon lose popularity. With the proliferation of advertising, there are fewer and fewer places where ads are unexpected, so such ads are not as effective.

Product Placement

A more subtle way of integrating advertising with content has been product placement, especially in television and movies. The next time your favorite actor is shown driving off in a Ford automobile, drinking a can of Coca-Cola, or using a Macintosh computer, you can be fairly sure that the item's appearance is a paid product placement. When a recognizable product is part of the story line of your favorite "reality" show, it's almost certainly a product placement. To reduce costs, production studios like to use free and authentic props provided by manufacturers. In return for these props and sometimes a substantial advertising fee, manufacturers can display their products and associate them with popular film and television stars. The audience is usually unaware that the movie or television program has become an ad for the featured products. Snapple did it with *Seinfeld;* the Pottery Barn did it with *Friends;* Visa, Doritos, and Mountain Dew did it with *Survivor.* Now almost all programs have built-in stealth advertising.

Variations on such deals abound. For example, GM obtained first rights to place its vehicles in Warner Bros. films. In exchange, Warner Bros. gave GM the right to use logos of Bugs Bunny on a limited edition "Chevy Venture Warner Bros." minivan. One episode of the popular reality show *The Apprentice* featured contestants competing to develop a new ad campaign for a Pepsi product. Of course, the story line was itself part of a new ad campaign for Pepsi. In one of the most hyped product placements ever, Oprah Winfrey gave away a Pontiac automobile to each of her 276 studio audience members. The cars were donated as part of a publicity campaign by Pontiac. Everyone from candy companies to clothiers pays to have products inserted into popular video games (see Exhibit 6.2). Even DVD "Easter eggs"—hidden features that were once whimsical additions—have become places to hawk products. Excessive product placement can backfire, however. James Bond movies have become so notorious for their numerous and

Exhibit 6.2   Selected Examples of Video Game Product Placement ("In-Game Advertising"), 2004

Advertiser	Game
7 UP	SSX3
Best Buy	Need for Speed Underground 2
Burger King	Need for Speed Underground 2
Cingular Wireless	Need for Speed Underground 2
element skateboards	Tony Hawk Underground 2
Home Depot	Nascar Thunder 2004
Honda	SSX3
Intel	The Sims Online
Jeep	Tony Hawk Underground 2
McDonald's	The Sims Online
NAPA Auto Parts	Nascar Thunder 2004
Old Spice	NCAA Football
Oreo	Nascar Thunder 2004
Palm PDAs	Splinter Cell
Pepsi	Nascar Thunder 2004
Puma	True Crime: Streets of LA
Quiksilver	Tony Hawk Underground 2
Samsung	Enter the Matrix
SoBe	Tony Hawk Underground 2
Sony Ericsson Smart Phones	Splinter Cell

Sources: Wong (2004), Loftus (2004), Duncan (2005).

flagrant product placements that some critics began referring to the Bond franchise as having a "License to Shill."[197]

New technological convergence promises only to exacerbate the stealth advertising trend. Someone watching a television drama on digital TV, for example, will simultaneously be watching a commercial for everything on the program. Do you like the sunglasses the police officer is wearing? Find out more about them—and how to buy them— with a quick click. Are you impressed by the car the villain is driving? Click for specs and information. Do you enjoy the music playing in the background? Download the soundtrack song with a couple of clicks. That appears to be the future of commercial media: an endless shopping spree with no boundaries between ads and content.

Another technological development marshaled in the service of stealth advertising is computer-generated product placement. Unlike regular product placement, this variation features only virtual products or ads inserted in a television program or film after production is complete. Similar to virtual ads in sports, this allows advertisers to alter the virtual ad depending on the markets. Audiences in different parts of the country watching the same popular television series could see different product placements, depending on which advertisers in their regions paid for the placement.

Promos and Brand Names and Ads, Oh My!

It is difficult to overestimate the potential impact of this incessant commercialization. Children's entertainment is one example. Children learn about their world, in part, through play and entertainment. For centuries, children read or heard folktales that simultaneously entertained and taught life's basic lessons. Now, however, for the first time, children's entertainment is primarily—and almost exclusively—aimed at selling them products. Disney characters have replaced folktales. The stories told to children are chosen by corporate executives in part because of those tales' effectiveness in selling related products. From *The Lion King* to *SpongeBob SquarePants* to *Harry Potter*, children's entertainment is about selling. Even when there may be educational stories inherent in the products, the metalesson is one about consumption.

And the lesson starts early. The average American child now recognizes corporate logos by 18 months. By the first grade, children can identify about 200 brands. In 2004, American children were the target of $15 billion of advertising, a stunning 150 times the amount of a decade earlier.[198] As Norma Odom Pecora notes of children's entertainment,

> The material culture represented by the media cultivates a way of thinking, consumption and the acquisition of "things" is encouraged, and particular assumptions about the world are promoted. Our children learn to equate happiness with trips to McDonald's. Attending the movies is not a simple experience but an event relived through an array of coloring books, computer games, and pajamas. Toys demand less imagination when the generic teddy bear is replaced by a *Lion King* who comes with a history by Disney. . . . The shopping mall is the playground, and the video is the storyteller.[199]

Pecora notes that while marketing to children dates back to the early part of the 20th century, "what has happened more recently is the acceleration of the process and the takeover of all aspects of children's play and imagination. . . . Borders between storytelling and advertising and worldly possessions blur."[200] With a loss of emphasis on public service, and a corresponding growth in appealing to children as consumers, media conglomerates now treat children as just another target demographic for advertisers.

The ubiquity of advertising has cumulatively produced a society in which the commercial imperatives of buying and selling pervade both public and private life. Everything is for sale. Everything is a pitch. Nothing in a society saturated with advertising seems particularly real or authentic. The spokesperson selling perfume, the athlete selling a brand of sneakers, and the politician promoting a social policy all begin to blur in our hypercommercialized world. Everything takes on the trappings of the marketplace. It becomes difficult for anyone to operate outside of this commercial space.

The problem is not that we are gullible believers in advertising—just the opposite. Advertising fosters a skeptical, or even cynical, "buyer beware" view of the world in media-savvy consumers. Advertising engages us with humor, music, sex, and flashy visuals. At the same time, we know it is not to be believed, because, ultimately, advertising has an ulterior motive. Thus we are likely to develop a skeptical or cynical view of these messages. As a result, in our society, saturated as it is with commercial media, speaking of values or beliefs that are not tied to products and profits can seem quaint and out of date.

Still, societies do not function by products alone. They depend on a shared collective vision that articulates the values and beliefs underlying the ideas of a good society. Notions such as justice, responsibility, community, and compassion must be articulated and promoted in society. These crucial ideas have nothing to do with promoting and selling products. As our public spaces and our private lives become more and more places for commercial advertising, we are left with a much narrower public sphere for ongoing and serious discussions and debates about ideas and issues, challenges and goals—the kind of deliberation that is a foundation for a just and productive society.

Audience Fragmentation

As commercial media have proliferated and new technologies have evolved, advertisers have developed new techniques for reaching particular demographic groups. For most of human history, media were marked by scarcity. Books were expensive and difficult to acquire. Radio was limited to a handful of stations. Television emerged in the United States with three major networks dominating the airwaves. The result was that people who read, listened to, or watched media often shared a similar cultural experience.

In recent decades, however, industrialized nations have experienced a rapid increase in the number of media outlets. People now have more choices in radio, television, publications, the Internet, and music than ever before. Much about this expansion has been positive.

However, this cornucopia is somewhat illusory, in that it is built on the commonality of commercial media. Despite the proliferation of channels, nearly all of them ultimately do one thing: make money for their owners and advertisers. Indeed, advertisers have driven much media growth in specific directions. The expansion of media outlets, coupled with the advertising emphasis on targeted demographics, has produced an increased specialization in media content. For example, unlike the old television networks that tried to reach a vast, broad audience, today's cable channels are usually "narrowcasting" instead of broadcasting. They are trying to attract very specific audience segments (golfers, young black professionals, investors, etc.) that can then be delivered efficiently to advertisers. The audiences for these specialized cable channels are tiny compared with audiences who watched network programming in its heyday. Audiences, therefore, have become more fragmented. They share less and less of their media experiences. Instead, characteristics such as income, race, age, and gender determine what they are exposed to.

One study found that in an average week, typical American viewers watch only about one quarter of the television channels available in their homes. Also, the amount of time spent watching each channel has declined over the years. In 1950, a typical U.S. household watched television for an average of 32.5 hours per week and spent an average of 11.6 hours with each of the available channels. By 1996, total viewing time had jumped to 50 hours per week, but on average only 4.9 hours were spent on each channel.[201] Such trends towards fragmentation have continued.

The result of these developments, according to some observers, is that commercial media are contributing to the fragmentation of society. Joseph Turow, in his book *Breaking Up America,* argues that advertisers and media are creating "the electronic equivalents of gated communities," within which small segments of society essentially talk only among themselves.[202] He notes that there always have been various forms of specialized media that have helped define and affirm the identity of particular segments of society, but at the same time, there also have been what Turow calls "society-making" media that can provide communication bridging various elements of society. Recent trends in advertising, media, and technology, however, have dramatically weakened the status of society-making media, leaving us with more specialized media and a more fragmented society. This, too, is a disquieting development for the future of our multicultural society.

In an extreme version of pandering to niche audiences, the different international versions of Microsoft's *Encarta* multimedia encyclopedia have had different—and contradictory—information on many issues. For example, the U.S., U.K., and German editions listed the inventor of the telephone as Alexander Graham Bell. But the Italian edition of the software gave credit to Antonio Meucci, a poor Italian-American candlemaker who—according to this version of history—beat Bell by 5 years.[203] If companies producing supposedly authoritative information such as encyclopedias are comfortable generating multiple versions of history to appeal to different markets, then what is to prevent them from doing the same to court domestic audiences? Will corporations in the future produce different versions of history or current events for different advertising demographics?

Media audiences are not only fragmented by advertisers but also stratified. Newspapers, for example, try to attract affluent readers and sometimes intentionally discourage low-income readers to generate demographics that are more appealing to advertisers. One report by the Newspaper Association of America made this point clear. "Good business decisions are not always volume driven," it noted. "More is not necessarily better; better is better."[204] That is, the goal of newspapers, according to the report, is not to reach more people, but rather to reach "better" people—those who are of greatest interest to advertisers. The report recommended that papers target readers who do not need a discount to subscribe (i.e., more affluent readers) and suggested eliminating "fringe circulation." The latter term sometimes refers to people who live too far away to be of interest to local advertisers. It also includes those with low incomes, who are unlikely to purchase advertised products.[205]

A Media-Saturated Society: Fish in Water

The changes in the media industry in recent decades have resulted in the colonization of public spaces by commercial media and advertising. Although some dimensions of this expansion still seem unusual to us, younger people raised in such a hypercommercial world are likely to take the presence of such media and advertising for granted. Like fish in water, we tend to ignore what makes our environment distinctive. In the 21st century, commercial media have come to saturate our social environment. At this rate, it will not be long before the everything-for-sale approach epitomized by commercial media becomes so commonplace that we no longer even take note of it.

❖ POLITICAL INFLUENCE

In addition to the cultural influences on content and the broader social influences (described earlier), media giants have developed considerable political influence. This influence results from both the impact of the media properties owned by these conglomerates and from industry lobbyists and campaign contributions; that is, behind-the-scenes activities.

Media Corporations and the Political System

Like other corporations (and other interest groups), the media industry relies on lobbying efforts and campaign contributions to promote its agenda. Every segment of the media industry has its own lobbying arm—such as the National Association of Broadcasters and the Motion Picture Association of America—which promotes the interests of particular parts of the industry. With the growing integration of media, telecommunications, and computers, it is increasingly difficult to discuss the "media industry" as a distinct entity. A few years back, the National Cable Television Association changed its name to reflect this new reality: It is now the National Cable and Telecommunications Association. Therefore, if we are to consider the political clout of the media industry, we need to include such players as software giant Microsoft (video game consoles, interactive TV, and Internet access), local phone giant SBC Communications (DSL and Internet access), and Comcast (cable television). The lobbying and electoral efforts of such firms are impressive (see Exhibit 6.3). Time Warner, for example, spent $3 million dollars in lobbying expenditures in 2000 and donated nearly $2.7 million during the 2004 election cycle.

In addition to the direct lobbying and campaign contributions, the media industry holds fundraisers for friendly politicians, hosts receptions at both parties' political conventions, and hires well-connected lobbyists—often fresh out of government. For example, two recent Senate majority leaders, Republican Bob Dole and Democrat George Mitchell, both went to work for the lobbying firm that represents NBC and other media companies. At one point, the Newspaper Association of America, the National Association of Broadcasters, and CBS all had Anthony Podesta on their payrolls representing their interests. Podesta was a major Democratic Party fundraiser and campaign strategist whose brother was Bill Clinton's deputy chief of staff.[206] When it became a radio giant, Clear Channel Communications made a splash by hiring Andrew Levin as its senior vice president of government relations. Levin had been Minority Counsel of the House Committee on Energy and Commerce, the body that hears almost all broadcast legislation. Perhaps the poster child for this revolving door between government and industry has been Marsha MacBride, who went from being a communications lawyer with industry clients to serving as an attorney for the FCC, then left to take a job with the Walt Disney Company, only to return to the FCC as Chief of Staff, only to leave again to serve the National Association of Broadcasters.[207]

The industry's ongoing efforts to influence government got some rare attention in 2003 when the Center for Public Integrity released a report showing that, over an 8-year period, FCC officials had taken

Exhibit 6.3 Lobbying and Campaign Activity of Selected Media-Related Organizations

Organization	2000 Lobbying Expenditures	2004 Campaign Contributions[a]	Percentage to Democrats	Percentage to Republicans
Microsoft Corporation	$6,360,000	$2,695,889	60	40
Time Warner	$3,000,000	$2,462,902	76	23
SBC Communications	$7,208,000	$2,284,771	33	66
Viacom Inc.	$1,000,000	$1,160,598	78	22
Comcast Corporation	$620,000	$953,396	49	51
Walt Disney Company	$3,860,000	$872,385	71	29
News Corporation	$380,000	$832,766	62	38
National Cable & Telecommunications Association[b]	$5,920,000[b]	$795,994	49	51
Clear Channel Communications	N/A	$764,318	33	67
National Association of Broadcasters	$5,700,000	$519,873	38	62

Source: Campaign for Responsive Politics (http://www.opensecrets.org).

a. Includes contributions from political action committees, soft money donors, and individuals giving $200 or more to federal candidates and parties during the 2003-2004 election cycle, as released by the Federal Election Commission on October 25, 2004.

b. In 2000, known as the National Cable Television Association.

2500 business trips across the globe, most of which were paid for by media and telecommunications companies that the agency is supposed to regulate. In light of harsh public criticism that followed the report, the FCC later announced that it would try to dramatically reduce its reliance on industry for travel.[208]

The issues on which media lobbyists work may not be front-page news, but they can translate into millions of dollars for corporate media giants. During the 6-year period between 1998 and 2004, when the FCC was reviewing broadcast ownership regulations, the industry spent $222 million in its lobbying efforts. In 2004, when a conservative congressman suggested that cable subscribers should be able to get "a la carte" programming—paying just for the channels they actually want instead of being forced to buy a bundle of channels they may not want—the industry sprang into action and had the measure defeated.[209] In 1998, when Walt Disney Co. faced the expiration of its copyright on its Mickey Mouse character, it went to Washington and got the law changed, getting a 20-year extension on all copyrighted works. Even the music industry has used its political clout in unexpected ways. The Recording Industry Association of America lobbied for new limitations on who could file for bankruptcy. This association complained that too many performers were using bankruptcy as a way to get out of long-term contracts they had signed before they became famous.[210]

Sometimes, as with the 1996 broadcast spectrum giveaway, a successful lobbying effort can literally mean *billions* of dollars for the media industry. When the prospect of digital television first emerged, the FCC set aside spectrum space to allow broadcasters to simultaneously broadcast in both traditional analog and the newer digital signals during a transition period from the old standard to the new digital format. This would avoid making all existing TV sets immediately obsolete once the new digital signals were used. However, as the digital technology was further developed, engineers discovered that digital signals needed only about one sixth the amount of spectrum space as the old analog signals. Because the airwaves are a limited public resource, not unlike water, many believed that licenses to use the additional spectrum space would be auctioned off to the highest bidder. Older, less desirable, spectrum space had already sold for more than $10 billion, and the FCC estimated that this newly available spectrum space would generate upward of *$70 billion.*

The broadcast industry had other plans. They wanted to keep the additional space—for free. Media corporations lobbied successfully to keep *all* the additional spectrum space it had originally been allocated—even though five sixths of it was no longer needed for its original purpose. Instead, the industry wanted to put six different digital channels into this new space, filling it with multiplexed television and other lucrative commercial content.

Despite limited media coverage about this issue by broadcasters, the spectrum giveaway was an event of stunning proportions. *New York Times* columnist William Safire wrote,

> The rip-off is on a scale vaster than dreamed of by yesteryear's robber barons. It's as if each American family is to be taxed $1,000 to enrich the stockholders of Disney, G.E. and Westinghouse. . . . Network news shows that delight in showing waste of thousands of taxpayer dollars fall silent before the giveaway of the spectrum on which they will digitize their shows.

Even conservative Republican Senator Bob Dole thought Congress had gone too far, calling it "a big, big corporate welfare project."[211] One broadcast law scholar, Thomas Krattenmaker, called it "the greatest land grab since they lined the wagons up in Oklahoma. At least there, everyone had a chance."[212]

Sometimes the political efforts of media corporations run directly into issues of journalistic ethics. Shortly after General Electric bought NBC, a GE executive announced the company's plans to raise money via a political action committee to promote the company's agenda in Washington. In a memo, the executive noted that "employees who elect not to participate in a giving program of this type should question their own dedication to the company." Some employees saw this as a thinly veiled threat. Only after other media outlets reported on this effort did the president of NBC News announce that news employees would be exempt from contributing.[213]

Media giants use the political system in ways similar to other industries. However, the media industry can influence politics in unique ways as well. At the heart of this media power is the fact that the media have control of the information about public figures. As far back as 1927, people have been concerned about this aspect of the media's power. As one congressman put it at the time, "Publicity is the most powerful weapon that can be wielded in a republic." He warned that if control of the media was concentrated in a few hands, then "woe be to those who dare to differ with them."[214] Seventy years later, former

FCC Chair Reed Hundt made essentially the same observation. "TV and newspapers are the gatekeepers of public perception and can make a politician popular or unpopular. . . . Politicians know that in their bones; the only ones who don't are the ones who didn't get elected."[215]

Abuse of this media power is always a potential problem. This is most likely to happen in cases in which the financial interests of the industry are at stake. The woefully inadequate coverage of the 1996 Telecommunications Bill and later ownership deregulation efforts is a now-classic example of media influence by omission. By simply marginalizing a potentially explosive story, the media industry helped pave the way for legislation that was lucrative for the industry. Much of the public was none the wiser.

However, with the growth of media empires, there is an opportunity for even more flagrant abuse of media power to influence the political process. Such blatant interference has occurred only in relatively isolated incidents, but in many circles, Rupert Murdoch has come to symbolize this potential threat. As one profile said,

> He wields his media as instruments of influence with politicians who can aid him, and savages his competitors in his news columns. If ever someone demonstrated the dangers of mass power being concentrated in few hands, it would be Murdoch.[216]

Murdoch is the Australian-born head of News Corp., the largest television network operator in the world. He counts among his holdings dozens of major U.S. media outlets (including the FOX network, HarperCollins publishers, more than 20 television stations, and the *New York Post*), several British Sunday and daily newspapers (including the prestigious *Times* of London), and the biggest network of broadcast satellites in the world. He has gained a reputation as a take-no-prisoners businessman willing to gamble big to expand his empire.

Along the way, Murdoch has also repeatedly used his media holdings to advocate his conservative views and to promote or punish politicians. In 1975, he had his Australian newspapers slant the news so blatantly in favor of his conservative choice for prime minister that Murdoch's own journalists went on strike in protest. His British newspapers played a crucial role in the 1979 election of British conservative Margaret Thatcher as prime minister. One of his papers even used its front page to tout the role it had played in getting Thatcher elected. Later, Thatcher supported Murdoch with troops as he fought to break the labor unions in his paper's printing plants. Murdoch's HarperCollins book publishers later reportedly paid Thatcher more than $5 million for her memoirs.

In the United States, Murdoch's *New York Post* successfully threw its support behind Republican Mayors Ed Koch and Rudy Giuliani (whose wife, Donna Hanover, worked as a correspondent for the local FOX TV station). Murdoch also bankrolled new conservative media efforts, including *The Weekly Standard,* a high-profile conservative magazine whose editors are often featured on television public affairs programs. Murdoch's HarperCollins offered sitting U.S. House Speaker Newt Gingrich a $4.5 million book deal. (Gingrich returned the money in response to scathing criticism.) In his largest such effort, Murdoch started a 24-hour news channel, FOXNews, and put political conservative Roger Ailes in charge. Ailes, a former media advisor for Ronald Reagan, was also the executive producer of ultraconservative Rush Limbaugh's radio talk show. FOXNews has gone on to become the unabashed voice of conservatism in American television news.

The Politics of Content: Antidrug and Promilitary

Another type of political influence occurs when corporate media team up with government to insert certain messages into media content. From the corporate side, this is done primarily for economic reasons; from government's perspective, the commercial media offer a new avenue through which to distribute its messages to the public. Although government and corporate media do not team up often, there are some notable cases.

For example, early in 2000, it was revealed that major television networks had been working with the White House to insert antidrug messages into some prime-time programs.[217] The arrangement stemmed from a 1997 deal between the White House and the networks. Because the networks' donations of free public service announcement time had been significantly reduced, the White House Office of National Drug Control Policy committed to buying $1 billion worth of antidrug advertising time over 5 years. In return, the networks agreed to sell the time to the government for half the regular price. However, as the economy boomed in subsequent years and dot.com companies began buying up more network advertising, the networks were looking for ways to get out of their deal with the White House and sell their ad time at higher rates. White House officials gave the networks the option of putting antidrug messages in their prime-time programming as a substitute for their half-price ad deal.

In the agreed-to system, officials in the White House Office of National Drug Control Policy reviewed scripts and advance footage of more than 100 episodes of programs such as *ER, Beverly Hills 90210, The Drew Carey Show, Chicago Hope, 7th Heaven, The Wayans Bros., The Practice,* and *Sports Night.* If the programs were deemed to have sufficient antidrug messages in their plots—or could be altered to conform to government antidrug messages—networks were awarded credit based on a complicated formula that reduced the number of ads the network owed the government. Airtime that would have otherwise been devoted to the government's half-price antidrug ads could then be sold by the networks to regular advertisers at full price. In the 2 years the program existed, the networks earned approximately $25 million in additional advertising revenue from the arrangement. The deal meant more money for networks, more access for government, and serious questions for viewers left wondering about this new form of collusion. The article that originally reported on the arrangement said it all in its title; it was called "Prime-Time Propaganda."

Government-media collaborations are routine and uncontroversial, however, in another part of the media industry—the movies. Again, corporations watching the bottom line turn to a government interested in promoting certain ideas to the public. In this case, the collaboration usually involves the military. In filming war scenes and military movies, the media industry looks to the government for access and equipment that make the film much more realistic—and keep costs down. The price, however, is a close review of the script by government representatives. The government cooperates only when the film portrays the military in a positive light. In doing so, as one observer put it, "The Pentagon gets a promotional bonanza that reaches millions of taxpayers and potential recruits, all of whom see the military in its glory, with heroic soldiers and awesome weapons on display."[218]

The military has been involved in promoting itself through movies for years, with its influence peaking during World War II. Beginning with the 1986 hit *Top Gun,* the military's influence in films started growing again. Today's Hollywood operations officers in the military do not wait for filmmakers to come knocking, however. Instead, they take the initiative, attending Hollywood trade shows and industry workshops, advertising in movie industry publications, and speaking to film students in universities—all at taxpayer expense. They "knock on doors, propose the use of equipment, suggest characters or plotlines, and sometimes even push movie ideas . . . the military is less concerned with strict accuracy than it is with burnishing its image."[219] Well-known films such as *Armageddon*, *Air Force One*, *A Few Good Men*, and *Blackhawk Down* received extensive help from the military—after script changes were negotiated. Films that present a critical or unflattering portrayal of the military, however, are not given this assistance.[220]

Not to be outdone, other government agencies have worked with movie and television studios to ensure a positive image of their work. Like the Pentagon, the CIA provides support and access for films it believes paint a positive picture of the agency. In 2004, the Department of Homeland Security assisted in the television portrayal of its work in *D.H.S.: The Series*.[221]

❖ THE SPECIAL ROLE OF NEWS MEDIA

No discussion of the political impact of the media on society would be complete without mention of the special role of the news media. In the wake of the 9/11 attacks, Americans were reminded of the news media's public service role. Still, although the news media were widely applauded for their coverage of 9/11 and its immediate aftermath, public skepticism and mistrust of the media returned only shortly thereafter. The media's failure to scrutinize the Bush administration's erroneous claims regarding weapons of mass destruction in Iraq and the implied connections between Baghdad and terrorism, along with the Pentagon's ability to coopt journalists through its "embed" program, were widely regarded as major errors on the media's part.

A series of events in early 2005 raised new questions about declining public trust in the news media. Three journalists acknowledged that they had received money from the Bush Administration for their support of various administration initiatives, but they did not disclose these financial connections to either their editors or the public until reporters revealed their ties with the Administration.[222] The most high-profile case involved news commentator Armstrong Williams, to whom the U.S. Education Department paid $241,000 to support the Bush Administration's "No Child Left Behind" act in his newspaper column and radio program.[223] In addition, the Government Accountability Office released a report in January 2005 scolding the Office of

National Drug Control Policy for distributing antidrug messages in the form of prepackaged news stories, along with suggested anchor remarks, to local television stations for broadcast on the evening news. The Government Accountability Office's report concluded that "ONDCP's prepackaged news stories constitute covert propaganda in violation of the fiscal year 2002, 2003, and 2004 publicity or propaganda prohibitions"—and the report also noted that these prepackaged stories were broadcast on almost 300 television stations and reached more than 22 million households.[224]

Nevertheless, one of the most revered elements of American democracy continues to be its ideal of a free press, as enshrined in the First Amendment. Because its public service responsibility is so intertwined with the health of democracy itself, the press is the only business explicitly protected by the Constitution. Despite the fact that, as we have seen, much media content has become trivial and sensational, most citizens still believe the news media should serve the crucial role of informing the public. Even now, when market concerns dominate the media, the profession of journalism still contains a commitment to uphold public interest values. As we saw in chapter 1, every contemporary professional code of ethics for journalists speaks of the primary importance of serving the public.

American citizens face an interesting dilemma. This society, inundated with mass media of all sorts, also has extremely low voter turnout, limited knowledge of public affairs, and general disengagement from civic activity. Although certainly not the only cause, the media's inattention to its public interest role has contributed to generalized cynicism and alienation.[225] In particular, several of the media's characteristics are often cited for their corrosive effect on the public sphere.

Drama. The news media tend to focus on dramatic stories, such as scandals, to attract readers and viewers. We know the business rationale for such a focus: A certain amount of sensationalism has proven to be profitable for media companies. When it comes to news, however, this approach is also a recipe for civic disaster. When news is equated with scandal, citizens become tired of the sordid details and tune out political news altogether when it appears to be an endless series of stories about corruption and depravity. News coverage of the 1998 Clinton-Lewinsky scandal and the subsequent impeachment of the president is a prime example of this phenomenon. MSNBC's round-the-clock coverage of the scandal helped to establish an identity for the fledgling

24-hour cable news channel. MSNBC adopted an "All Monica, All the Time" approach to its programming and generated the channel's highest ratings to date and a constant stream of publicity. Still, there are consequences to such scandal-driven news coverage. Journalists relied heavily on anonymous sources, rushed to get the newest revelations on the air, and featured lots of heated arguments about the scandal.[226] Although audiences tuned in for the titillating revelations, it is no wonder that citizens became increasingly cynical about both the news media and the political system.

One of the reasons the media was praised for its post-9/11 coverage was that, in contrast to its usual fare, it generally took a serious and sober look at the event and its aftermath. However, claims that nothing was the same after the attack proved to be vastly overstated, as the media returned to its usual dose of scandal and sensationalism just months later. Indeed, some critics argue that the subsequent "war on terror" itself became just another sensationalized media story.

Negativity. The nature of news results in an emphasis on stories that have a "negative" tone. More broadly, the news seems to focus on shocking, disturbing, and sometimes depressing events, such as conflict, crises, and disasters—and rarely gives citizens a sense that there are practical solutions. Although such events are certainly newsworthy, their overemphasis can also lead citizens to despair and pessimism about the possibility of effective change. Susan Moeller argues that the nature of the news media's coverage of international events—focusing on images of pestilence, famine, death, and war—have helped to produce "compassion fatigue" among American citizens. The source of compassion fatigue, according to Moeller, is the news media's formulaic, sensationalistic, and image-driven coverage, which "helps us to feel overstimulated and bored all at once."[227] The result is a growing sense that there is nothing we can do about these faraway crises, which seem to disappear from the news media's radar screen as quickly as they appear. More generally, the news media's tendency to highlight dramatic problems with little context can discourage participation in public life and engagement with current affairs.

Events Instead of Issues. The format of the contemporary news media—especially broadcast media—lends itself to coverage of spectacular *events,* not enduring *issues.* Brevity and drama often seem to be the watchwords of media coverage. What readers and, especially, viewers experience is a parade of isolated incidents full of dramatic images. Rarely are people engaged as citizens with a role to play in the unfolding drama. Instead, they are invited merely to watch the spectacle.

Personalities Instead of Policies. The media often focus on personalities, not policies. It is easier to deliver drama through the personal lives of public figures or the personal tragedies of victims. This human interest approach has a place in journalism, but it has displaced more substantive analysis and examination of public policy and social issues. Coverage of political life often focuses disproportionately on issues of style, and enduring issues, such as crime, are treated as an endless series of tearful interviews with family members. The key issues of election campaigns or the underlying conditions contributing to crime, for example, require more substantive treatment than most media outlets give them. The potential impact of this type of coverage is to leave citizens poorly equipped for civic participation. Again, 9/11 serves as an interesting example of a story full of drama and stunning visual images, which many news outlets handled well. However, most media largely failed with the more substantive questions regarding the causes of terrorism and the U.S. policies that have led some to target America.

Fragmentation and Superficiality. The news media's coverage of events tends to be fragmented and episodic, with little depth or context. Again, because of the type of media formulas often used, news can be little more than a series of isolated events. The news spotlight wanders across the landscape, briefly illuminating certain events before moving on to the next ones. The average readers and viewers of such media coverage rarely see substantive, continuing coverage. It becomes almost impossible to understand what any of the fleeting coverage means, because news stories contain little or no context explaining why the events occurred. This is especially true of foreign news. Citizens may have little background information with which to fill in the picture. As a result, citizens are likely to feel unqualified to take part in discussions of public affairs.

Lack of Relevance. The news media often do not address the concerns of average citizens, focusing instead on "insider" politics and economic information for the investor class. Most people who pay no attention to the news media probably do so because what is routinely presented seems to have little relevance to them. Although it may be admirable to educate oneself about current affairs simply to become well-rounded, most people pay the greatest attention to the news when they believe it is relevant to their lives. Because, as we have seen, news media are often interested in reaching only the particular desirable demographic groups that advertisers covet, many news media outlets do little to engage broader groups of citizens or educate them about the significance of civic affairs. The result is likely to be further alienation and disengagement from public life.

Strategy Over Substance. A great deal of political news focuses on the "game" of politics, highlighting the strategic actions of various public figures. This emphasis on political strategy, calculation, and tactics generally diverts attention from the substance of political actions and policies. The emphasis on the *why* deflects attention from the *what*, and, as a consequence, coverage of substantive issues is often neglected. Citizens get the message that politics is a strategic game and that news is the "program" by which to assess the moves of the key players. However, the strategic game of politics usually appears removed from the experience of most Americans, because it focuses on the efficacy of political tactics and not on the consequences of public policies for citizens. In addition, political news generally employs a "two-sided" approach, covering the regular debates between the Democrats and Republicans. When media regularly focus on such "insider" politics— and rarely present voices from outside the Washington beltway— citizens may well conclude that these fights are only about "politics" in its most derogatory sense. The routine nature of these ongoing battles between the same two sides may also suggest intractability in the political world and promote a sense of paralysis among citizens about which of the predetermined two sides is preferable. This may well encourage cynicism and apathy, rather than engagement.

In sum, the news media generally address people as consumers and spectators, not active citizens. Except for the anemic get-out-the-vote messages around election time and occasional calls for charitable involvement, the news media do little to foster a commitment to civic participation. News does little to help teach citizens about how government works or why they should care. It rarely spotlights the impact of ordinary citizens in effecting change. It usually does not show concrete opportunities for civic involvement. All of these would be more prominent in a news media that paid closer attention to its public interest role.

The news media cannot be solely—or even primarily—blamed for the discouraging state of civic engagement today, but news has too often been part of the problem rather than part of the solution. Furthermore, the changing business of media has exacerbated these deleterious aspects of the news media's influence on political life.

❖ CONCLUSION

Changes in the business of media have had broad effects on society as a whole. The ubiquity of media and advertising has transformed social experiences in daily life. The growing importance of media has given the industry significant political influence, and the news media, especially, has helped influence political culture in our society.

Many of the changes described in this and other chapters paint a picture of a neglected or even endangered public sphere. This situation is not inevitable, but what can be done to revive the public interest role of media? We turn to this important question in the final chapter.

7

Choosing the Future

Citizens, Policy, and the Public Interest

In the early years of the 21st century, general trends in the media business are complex but relatively clear. Ownership consolidation continues, as a handful of global conglomerates merge with or acquire their former competitors. Technology advances, with satellite and broadband promising more media outlets, faster access, and more interaction—all at lower prices. Convergence accelerates, as digitization erases the lines between different media. Commercialism expands, as the industry develops increasingly sophisticated advertising techniques that better target consumers and generate record profits. Measured against the standards of just 20 years earlier, the scale of this expanding media business seems almost unimaginable.

Still, there is something missing in all of this. Most of the enthusiasm about the new media world focuses on the benefits to *consumers*, who will gain from new innovations, lower prices, growth in outlets, and new methods of shopping. With rare exceptions, the discussion of these benefits has little to say about what the new media landscape means for *citizens.* By confining the discussion to costs and benefits for consumers—a useful, but limited, approach—broader questions about community, power, participation, and the public interest are either neglected or reframed so that consumers and citizens are defined as one and the same.

However, *citizen* and *consumer* are *not* synonyms; they represent different aspects of human experience. Consumers pursue privatized, personal goals by buying various products, services, or experiences. Because of their differing buying power, consumers are not equal. Citizens, on the other hand, are connected to communities and participate in ongoing deliberations that constitute shared civic life. A fundamental assumption of democratic societies—distinguishing them from markets—is that citizens are equal, regardless of their consumer capabilities. In a participatory democracy, citizens do much more than vote in occasional elections. They are involved in the process of debate, compromise, and decision making that affects their communities. To participate effectively in this deliberative process, citizens need access to a wide variety of information and perspectives—both in terms of news and culture. Thus, the media play a vital role in providing resources for an active citizenry.

Many recent developments in the media industry have been beneficial to some consumers, especially those who are of greatest interest to advertisers—the young and the prosperous. However, developments that deliver benefits for consumers do not, by definition, serve the needs or interests of citizens. The media's growing commercialism, the concentration of media ownership, and the increasing pressure to merge information with entertainment are all examples of how a *consumer*-friendly media industry is indifferent to the needs of *citizens.* The result is a diminished public sphere—the discursive space that is a central component of a democratic society—and a weakened democracy.

In market-oriented societies such as the United States, the consumer identity looms very large, often crowding out notions of citizenship. Focusing solely on consumer concerns tends to narrow our vision so that we do not even ask larger questions about the impact of the media on the quality of our public lives. As we have tried to show in this book, these are precisely the questions we *need* to ask if we are to understand the significance of the media business. These are also the issues to keep in mind in looking at the future of media.

This chapter begins to map out the contours of a media landscape that promotes citizenship and nourishes a healthy public sphere. On the one hand, we have tried to avoid sweeping utopian visions, although we do not shy away from ideas that may not be politically viable immediately. On the other hand, we have avoided detailed discussions of policy minutiae, although we do provide a few more detailed examples. The chapter starts with public policy issues, briefly mentions professional concerns, and concludes with a discussion of some recent citizen activist initiatives.

❖ REGULATORY POLICY AND THE PUBLIC INTEREST

Over the years, different media have been subjected to different forms of regulation in the public interest. The First Amendment declares that the government "shall make no law . . . abridging freedom of speech, or of the press," and, as a result, print media have been largely unregulated. However, public policy has been used *to support* the print media. The U.S. Post Office, for example, subsidizes some print media via its reduced rate for mailing periodicals.

Broadcast media (television and radio) have been more actively regulated because they use a scarce public resource, the airwaves. Since the Communications Act of 1934, the legislation that provided the framework for the development of the media industry in the United States, broadcasters have been required to serve "the public interest, convenience and necessity." Cable television represents yet another type of regulatory target, because it does not use the airwaves but is a local monopoly. It, too, has been subject to various regulations in the public interest, from "must carry" rules about local broadcast channels to price restrictions.

Regardless of the medium, the meaning of *the public interest* has been both contested and dynamic. Now, as the digital media evolve, blurring distinctions between each medium, a new task of regulatory policy is to clarify not only what we mean by the public interest but to whom such standards apply.

What does it mean to serve the public interest in the new digital media world? The principal policy document of this new era, the Telecommunications Act of 1996, defines the public interest as competition in the media industry—a definition from a market perspective. The act begins by noting that its purpose is "to promote competition and reduce regulation in order to secure lower prices and higher quality services for American telecommunications consumers and encourage the rapid deployment of new telecommunications technologies."[228] This orientation marks the wholesale adoption of a market framework concerned about consumers rather than citizens. In fact, the word *consumer* appears 24 times in the text of the act. Excluding references to "citizens band radio," the word *citizen* appears only twice, including once in a technical discussion about residency requirements. The only time the word is used in the context that we have used *citizen* in this book is to praise the Internet. "The rapidly developing array of Internet and other interactive computer services available to individual Americans represent[s] an extraordinary advance in the availability of educational and informational resources to our citizens."

In lifting various ownership restrictions and abolishing regulations that barred companies from participating in multiple sectors of the telecommunications industry (telephone, cable television, Internet), the act's writers ostensibly intended to unleash new innovations and lower prices for consumers. With the act's implementation, various entities— telephone companies, cable companies, broadcast networks, film studios, and music labels, among others—were expected to cross into new markets, offering new products and services and developing new technologies and applications.

Instead of unleashing new competition, however, the Telecommunications Act produced a wave of mergers in the media and telecommunications industries, as the major companies took advantage of the deregulatory environment to preempt new competitors. Ironically, rather than encouraging a more competitive communications environment, the act helped to strengthen the major media companies, cementing the oligopolistic structure of the industry. Thus, even by market standards, the act has been problematic at best. More important, the increased concentration of media ownership resulting from this approach and the neglect of nonmarket public interest concerns made the Telecommunications Act a step in the wrong direction.

Part of the reason this act harms the public interest is that the public was never a part of its development. As broadcast historian Robert McChesney has shown, there has been virtually no public participation in media policy making since the early 1930s.[229] The 1996 Telecommunications Act passed without any significant public involvement in the deliberations leading to it and with little news coverage of its roots or consequences. Instead of news aimed at stimulating broad public conversation about how best to regulate the emerging media industry, most news media framed the Telecommunications Act as a business story, largely neglecting the political and cultural significance of this restructuring of media policy. In what may be a hopeful sign, the subsequent round of deregulatory action by the Federal Communications Commission in 2003 produced significant public opposition that opened up a broader discussion about the merits of deregulation and, more generally, the media policy-making process. Such citizen participation needs to be part of any future media policy debate.

❖ MEDIA AND PUBLIC POLICY

The primary mechanism by which citizen interests are protected is through public policy. Our discussion of policy is loosely divided into efforts aimed at media content and those aimed at media access.

Content-Based Regulations

Over the years, many advocacy groups have argued that federal regulations should apply to the content of various media, defining what material promotes or undermines the public interest. This can be very sticky terrain, as long-standing cultural contests about the appropriateness of images become intertwined with regulatory policy. For the most part, the media industry opposes regulation of media content, arguing that this regulation is either unconstitutional, violating First Amendment rights of free expression, or is unnecessary, or both. Media industry opposition to content regulations often accepts the underlying premise that media content and the public interest are connected—indeed, that some media may enhance and others may damage the public interest. Instead of government regulations, however, representatives of the media industry generally argue for self-regulation, whereby private industry "polices" itself.

There are two basic approaches to regulating media content. One approach calls for limits on certain types of content or for restrictions on who has access to certain types of media. Pornography involving children is illegal, for example, as is the sale of pornographic magazines or videos to minors. A second, lesser known approach calls for the mandatory inclusion of certain types of content. Broadcasters are required to air some children's educational programming, for example. For reasons discussed later, we generally find the first approach troubling but are generally supportive of initiatives using the second approach.

Restricting Content

Supporters of regulations that limit content want federal regulators to restrict or prohibit certain types of images or language deemed to be harmful or inappropriate. The most obvious examples are media that include sexually explicit content. Ongoing debates exist about when and how media with "obscene" or "indecent" content should be regulated. For example, one component of the Telecommunications Act of 1996, the Communications Decency Act (CDA), outlawed the transmission of sexually explicit and other indecent material on the Internet. In response to a legal challenge by free speech advocates, the Supreme Court ruled the CDA unconstitutional.

Although the court struck down the CDA, efforts to regulate the Internet continue, particularly efforts limiting the availability of sexually explicit materials online. In 1998, President Clinton signed the Child Online Protection Act (COPA), a much narrower version of CDA. COPA required all Internet sites with material deemed "harmful to minors" to institute age confirmation checks (such as credit card registration) to help ensure that only adults were accessing the material. Criminal penalties were established for Web sites that made such material available to minors. The American Civil Liberties Union and a coalition of Internet content providers immediately filed suit to prevent enforcement of COPA in 1998, and a U.S. District court granted a preliminary injunction stopping COPA from taking effect until a new review was conducted of the constitutional status of the regulation. Five years of litigation followed. In the end, on June 29, 2004, the Supreme Court upheld the injunction, returning the case to the original District Court for a potential trial.

In its 2004 decision, the Supreme Court noted:

> Content-based prohibitions, enforced by severe criminal penalties, have the constant potential to be a repressive force in the lives and thoughts of a free people. To guard against that threat the Constitution demands that content-based restrictions on speech be presumed invalid . . . and that the Government bear the burden of showing their constitutionality.[230]

In particular, both the Court of Appeals and the Supreme Court emphasized the plausibility of less restrictive measures, including filtering software that might achieve the same goals as COPA without infringing upon free speech.

Six years after the Congressional vote to enact COPA, the law was found to be unenforceable, and it is likely to be declared unconstitutional if the Justice Department pursues a full trial. Although there remains broad agreement about the goals of such laws as CDA and COPA—protecting minors from sexually explicit materials on the Internet—there is little consensus about the most effective, appropriate, and legal means of achieving this goal without violating the rights of others to free expression. Given the continuing growth of sexually explicit content online, the political and legal debates about the issues raised by CDA and COPA are likely to continue for many years.

Although the efforts to restrict online media content have met with successful legal challenges, the Federal Communications Commission has aggressively targeted content deemed "indecent" on broadcast television and radio. During CBS's 2004 Super Bowl halftime show, singer Justin Timberlake removed a portion of Janet Jackson's costume, revealing her bare breast for a second. The FCC acted quickly, fining Viacom, the corporate parent of CBS, more than $500,000 for this indecent display. Congress, acting on what appeared to be a popular issue with voters, moved quickly to increase the maximum fine for televised indecency. The popular radio "shock jock" Howard Stern was at the center of a much larger storm. After the FCC fined Clear Channel Radio $495,000 in 2004 for the content of Stern's broadcasts, Clear Channel dropped Stern's program from its six stations that broadcast the show.[231] A few months later, Viacom, the corporate parent of Stern's syndicator Infinity radio, agreed to pay a fine of $3.5 million to resolve claims that their stations broadcast obscene and indecent content, including Stern's program. In response to these and other fines, Stern announced that at the end of his contract he would move to satellite radio, which is not subject to the FCC's indecency rules.

The consequences of the FCC's newly aggressive approach to broadcast indecency may extend beyond the shock jock world. When ABC broadcast Stephen Spielberg's 1998 film *Saving Private Ryan* in November 2004, 66 ABC affiliates refused to air the film, citing the foul language and graphic violence in the Academy Award–winning film. The stations that elected not to broadcast the film cited concerns about the FCC's increased efforts to police the airwaves. Ray Cole, president of station owner Citadel Communications, noting that the FCC had recently changed its rules, said: "without an advance waiver from the FCC . . . we're not going to present the movie in prime time. Under strict interpretation of the indecency rules we do not see any way possible to air this movie."[232] It is noteworthy that many of the stations that chose not to air *Private Ryan* in 2004 did broadcast the film, unedited, on Veterans Day in 2001 and 2002.

Although the 2004 controversy over *Saving Private Ryan* was a new twist on indecency regulations, violence in media has long been the focus of efforts to restrict content. Concerns about violence on television, for example, date back to the early days of the medium, when it was introduced as a family-friendly technology. As with sexually explicit material, calls to restrict or prohibit violent images on television are generally presented as efforts to protect children.

During the early 1990s, efforts to rid popular culture—particularly children's entertainment—of graphic violence were often met by substantial public support. For example, concerns about violent content led the video gaming industry to adopt self-regulation to prevent government intervention. In 1994, the industry established what became known as the Entertainment Software Rating Board, to apply and enforce ratings, advertising guidelines, and online privacy principles adopted by computer and video game producers. These ratings were designed to help parents steer their children away from violent and otherwise mature video games.[233]

In 1993, the U.S. Congress took up the issue of violence on television, holding hearings about how best to reduce it. Responding to their sense of the public concern about the level of violence on television, members of Congress used the hearings to tell the television industry that it was time to change. Senator Howard Metzenbaum (D-Ohio), signaling the possibility of new regulations, warned network executives that Congress "would come down heavily on the television industry if you don't do that which is necessary."[234]

Several months after the hearings, new legislation to more strictly control and monitor television violence was introduced in Congress. One bill aimed to "ban the broadcast or cable transmission of violent programming during hours when children make up a substantial share of the audience."[235] Another would have required the FCC to develop regulations to reduce violence on fictional television programs. Those who did not comply would have been fined, and their broadcast license renewal would have been jeopardized.[236]

Responding to these new legislative proposals, the television industry took "voluntary" action, and new regulations restricting television content were never passed. Instead, the networks began broadcasting warnings prior to programs that contained violence. They also contracted with independent researchers for a multiyear study of the level and types of violence on television, pledging to reduce violent programming.

The Telecommunications Act of 1996 included provisions related to violence in the media. The act required the television industry to develop a program rating system indicating the age-appropriateness of the program content. It also mandated that television manufacturers install the so-called V-chip in new television sets, which enabled the electronic blocking of programs classified by the new rating system as violent.

The voluntary actions and new technological fixes were largely aimed at protecting children from materials considered inappropriate, a widely supported public goal. However, content restrictions are a problematic solution to an admittedly difficult situation for two reasons. First, it is virtually impossible for new rules to be drawn so narrowly that they restrict only children's access. Instead, adults are also restricted from viewing or accessing materials that are legal for them to see. This was one of the principal arguments supporting the injunction that prevented the implementation of COPA. Second, defining materials as "violent" or "harmful to children" is a notoriously difficult task, requiring judgments laden with contested moral assumptions. For example, is a Web site designed to assist gay teenagers struggling with their sexuality "harmful to children"? Those concerned about sexually explicit materials online would probably define such a site as harmful, even though it might contain exclusively educational materials. For these and other reasons, regulations to restrict media content almost always create larger problems than they solve.

Promoting Citizenship by Promoting Diversity

Perhaps the most enduring problem with regulations restricting content is that they divert our attention away from regulatory strategies aimed at *promoting citizenship*. Content restrictions are an effort to protect the public interest by preventing or limiting "negative" or "harmful" media content. Instead, we need to develop a media policy that encourages and even requires media content that contributes to a vibrant public sphere.

The media industry has worked hard to fend off regulation and generally has opposed both content restrictions and content requirements. The financial roots of such opposition are quite simple. The type of material to which proponents of content restrictions object is often among the most profitable for the industry; sex and violence sell. On the other hand, policies requiring a minimum commitment to a specific kind of programming—public affairs or education, for example—can crowd out more profitable media content. (It is noteworthy, however, that little of the discussion about these issues has focused on the dysfunctional aspects of unregulated markets and their broader implications for society.[237])

Even though the media industry is likely to oppose them, content requirements can be an effective strategy for making media responsive to public citizenship needs. The deliberative process through which such requirements could be defined would itself be a positive development. Public reflection about the ways that media can contribute to democratic life would be necessary. Dialogue about media's potential role as a citizen resource would be an important step toward enhancing public participation in media policy making and defining a more specific set of goals for what we expect, as citizens, from our media system.

One of the principal ways that media policy can enrich citizenship is by promoting diverse public expression in both entertainment and public affairs. Citizens should have ready access to viewpoints and experiences both similar to and different from their own. In some cases, media content can affirm convictions and beliefs commonly held in society. In this role, media can serve as a socializing force, promoting important common values and perspectives.

In other cases, media can serve as a forum for dissent and controversy. In this role, media provide an arena where different perspectives can be aired, including those outside the boundaries of the established consensus. By embracing diversity and dissent, a media policy based on content requirements can make a significant contribution to democratic public life. In short, media policy can serve the public interest by helping to build a media system ensuring the availability of a multiplicity of ideas from a variety of perspectives.

The 1998 Report of the Advisory Committee on Public Interest Obligations of Digital Television Broadcasters, generally known as the "Gore Commission," explored some of the ways that broadcasters might serve the public interest. However, the specific recommendations of the Gore Commission were rather tepid. The commission's final report did suggest the importance of identifying "minimum public interest requirements," but commission members did not reach consensus on specific, enforceable policy recommendations. In the end, the commission affirmed that broadcasters in the digital age should be required to serve the public interest, but it left the content of those public interest requirements rather vague. With several prominent broadcasters on the commission, including Co-chair Leslie Moonves, CEO of CBS Television, it is not surprising that the recommendations lacked specificity. In any case, the commission's final report was generally ignored by the news media and quickly sank into oblivion.[238]

We need to move beyond those broad generalizations about "the public interest, convenience, and necessity" that have given broadcasters enormous leeway in crafting their own definitions of their public interest obligations. We can do this only by developing a specific set of public interest requirements—not to restrict expression or dictate its specific content but to expand and deepen the contribution of media to public life. Such requirements must be enforceable, with clear consequences for noncompliance, including consideration when stations seek to renew their broadcast licenses. We suggest four such requirements.

1. Requirements for a Minimum Amount of Substantive Programming. Advocates of children's television have pursued a strategy based on requiring broadcasters to air a minimum amount of children's educational programming. In 1996, the FCC and broadcasters agreed on the "3-hour rule," by which stations committed to broadcasting at least 3 hours per week of legitimate, educational television.[239] This commitment should continue. In addition, this model could be extended to public affairs programming. Broadcasters should be required to air a minimum number of hours per week of substantive public affairs programming, focused on current issues of broad public concern. In addition to coverage of national political issues, stations should pay regular attention to issues of local concern and provide access so that various segments of the community can present their views on these issues. Currently, many stations broadcast public service announcements, brief ads about social issues, to satisfy a vague requirement to cover public affairs. This is clearly inadequate, as is most local news that focuses on "light," entertainment-oriented stories. More specific guidelines requiring a specific commitment to substantive programming reflecting the various perspectives and experiences of local communities would help institutionalize a more citizen-oriented policy.

2. Mandated Public Access Time Slots. On the cultural and entertainment side of media content, we should consider mandated public access time slots, during which local, independently produced programs would be aired on television. Such a concept will become increasingly attractive and feasible with the growing affordability of digital video cameras and video editing software. The coming years will bring an unprecedented explosion of creative ventures by independent and amateur filmmakers. Some of these will undoubtedly end up on commercial television as digital versions of *America's Funniest Home Videos* or exploitative "reality" programs. However, a public access requirement, overseen by a board of community representatives, could create a venue for a wide range of serious and entertaining independent material. The Internet is already experimenting with archiving independently produced video and animation.[240] Predictably, such Web sites have often focused on the commercial sale of video projects. Filmmakers are able to upload their creations to these sites and make them available for viewing to anyone who wants to see them. With the growth of broadband connections to the Internet, such efforts will expand dramatically. However, for the foreseeable future, television will continue to be unparalleled in its accessibility and its ability to reach a broad audience. We should insist that independent producers have some access to this platform.

3. Free Air Time for Politicians in Election Years. Another content requirement that might contribute considerably to an enhanced public sphere involves the electoral process. Broadcasters should be required to provide free air time to political candidates in election years. Because television is the dominant venue for political campaigns and the cost of campaign advertising has driven up the cost of running for office, the public interest would be served in three ways by requiring broadcasters to provide free air time. Access to television and radio in even 5-minute segments would allow candidates far more time than the 15- or 30-second campaign ad to define their agendas and make their cases. The short sound bite and dramatic image, which drive so much of our political world, could be challenged by more substantive presentations of ideas. In addition, free television time for candidates who meet some minimal threshold requirement of support would begin to open up the political process to those without access to big money. Citizens would be more likely to hear about alternatives to the two dominant political parties, perhaps loosening the stranglehold these parties have on political life. Finally, if the need to raise funds for advertising was dramatically reduced, the cost of running for office might decline as well, reducing the emphasis on fundraising.

4. Reinstate the Fairness Doctrine. The Federal Communications Commission should reinstate the Fairness Doctrine. Between 1949 and 1987, the Fairness Doctrine required broadcasters to devote a "reasonable" amount of time to the discussion of community issues and, more important, required "that such programs be designed so that the public has a reasonable opportunity to hear different opposing positions on the public issues of interest and importance in the community."[241] The doctrine did not require equal time for opposing views, but it did prevent broadcasters from continually airing only a single viewpoint. The doctrine was repealed in 1987 by the FCC, which argued that it was no longer needed. In that same year, Congress moved to have the doctrine made a federal law. Enjoying support from conservatives and liberals alike, the bill easily passed the House by a three to one margin and the Senate by a nearly two to one margin, only to be vetoed by President Ronald Reagan. It is an idea, however, that should be revived. As we have shown, the concentration of media ownership and the hypercommercialism of media have made the need for a Fairness Doctrine more necessary than ever.

These public interest requirements are a small part of a larger process of rewriting media policy so major instruments of public communication in our society do more than just entertain and sell us products. Also, because the expansive new digital spectrum will permit broadcasters to begin "multiplexing"—each broadcasting on several "channels" instead of just one—there will be plenty of room on the broadcast spectrum for public interest programming. Reaffirming that broadcasters are licensed to serve the public interest and need to do so in specific ways that enhance citizenship and enrich public life is an essential step toward a more democratic and accountable media. The very process of opening media policy up to public participation and debate will be, as Robert McChesney has shown,[242] an essential first step toward creating a more democratic media system. At the same time, we must also develop policies that encourage broader access to the media.

Access-Oriented Media Policy

Rapid technological changes are creating exciting new possibilities for the future of media. However, developments such as digital television multiplexing, high-speed broadband Internet access, and the convergence of the Internet and television are being driven primarily by market calculations and profit concerns. There is no doubt that commerce and entertainment will be the dominant uses of the newly evolving media system, but plenty of opportunity exists to develop more public interest–oriented uses as well—if only we have the political courage. The emerging multimedia system constitutes perhaps the central arena for public communication in contemporary society. As such, we need a proactive and visionary media policy that will steer new media technologies toward enhancing citizenship. With the new media environment still taking shape, the early 21st century is a critical juncture.

As ownership of the major media narrows, one of the dangers is that our public conversation will narrow as well. When the arenas of public discourse are owned and controlled by a select few, this handful of corporate players may supply large amounts of consumer-friendly entertainment in various formats. As we have seen, however, there is good reason for concern about whether such profit-seeking companies will have incentives to sustain the robust information and cultural environment that active citizens need. Indeed, strong evidence already exists that corporate media intend to emphasize commercial content at the expense of everything else. In this highly concentrated, but rapidly evolving, media industry, media policies focused on broadening access to channels for public communication can help keep the media system open to a variety of perspectives, not just those that serve the interests of the corporate sector. A media policy oriented toward citizens places the question of access at its center by including regulations that provide space for a multiplicity of perspectives.

Low-Power Radio

One modest development on the access front was the legalization of low-power FM (LPFM) radio stations. Following years of activism by "micro-radio" broadcasters, the FCC adopted new rules in 2000 to license low-power (or micro) radio stations on the FM band. These newly licensed low-power radio stations (100 watts or less) are required to be noncommercial, and owners of other media are not permitted to operate a low-power station. In its Report and Order *Creation of Low Power Radio Service*, the FCC argued that "the LPFM service authorized in this proceeding will provide opportunities for new voices to be heard and will ensure that we fulfill our statutory obligation to authorize facilities in a manner that best serves the public interest."[243] In short, LPFM would permit the licensing of new community radio stations, effectively opening the airwaves to new voices. This new licensing policy was a long time coming and was instituted over the objections of the commercial broadcasting industry.

This was only the beginning of the story. Immediately following the FCC 2000 ruling that created new LPFM licenses, the commercial broadcasting industry, in alliance with National Public Radio, sprang into action to prevent implementation of the LPFM policy. The National Association of Broadcasters (NAB) launched a major lobbying campaign to stop low-power radio, which broadcasters claimed would interfere with commercial radio signals—despite considerable scientific evidence to the contrary. To show the supposed dangers of the new policy, the NAB even flooded congressional offices with CDs that *simulated* the sounds of radio interference. The lobbying campaign, however, was a smokescreen obscuring the more fundamental economic threat posed by community radio. Broadcasters opposed low-power radio because it was a new competitor for market share and, perhaps more important, an incursion on the corporate domination of radio. In response to the NAB campaign, Congress included a provision in the 2001 Appropriations Act that dramatically limited the FCC's low-power radio plan and called on the FCC to conduct "an experimental program to test whether low-power FM radio stations will result in harmful interference to existing FM radio stations."[244]

After an independent report by the Mitre Corporation found that LPFM did not interfere with commercial radio signals, the FCC recommended that Congress lift the 2001 limits placed on low-power radio, opening up the possibility of the creation of many more low-power stations. Legislation introduced in 2004 by Senator John McCain in the U.S. Senate found that Congressional action limiting LPFM "prevented millions of Americans from having a locally operated, community based radio station in their neighborhood."[245] In addition, the 2004 legislation made it clear that the NAB's concerns about interference were unfounded. Referencing the Mitre report, the proposed legislation noted that "After 2 years and the expenditure of $2,193,343 in taxpayer dollars to conduct this study, the broadcasters' concerns were demonstrated to be unsubstantiated."[246] As of this writing, the McCain LPFM Bill was still awaiting a Congressional vote.

Before the new LPFM rules were established, many low-power stations operated throughout the 1990s without licenses. As this "pirate radio" movement grew, these stations represented a local alternative to the corporate media at a time when the consolidation of the radio industry was happening at breakneck speed. In issuing low-power licenses, the FCC instituted a simple and very locally oriented policy that demonstrably enhances public access to the airwaves. However, the FCC 100-watt limit is unnecessarily low, limiting reception to a radius of 3.5 miles at best. The FCC should improve the low-power radio concept by allowing more powerful—up to 1000 watt—stations as well. In focusing on citizens rather than consumers, low-power, non-commercial radio provides a model for use of the media to potentially enhance citizenship.

Television

Another avenue for increased access is broadcast television, in which digital technology has recently changed the playing field. Digital technology allows for five or six signals to be sent in the space that used to be occupied by one analog signal. This development raised the possibility of many new voices on the scarce public airwaves. Instead of opening the gates to new broadcasters, however, current broadcast companies were able to maintain control of all the new spectrum space. In a massive corporate giveaway in 1996, the FCC gave broadcasters, for free, licenses to broadcast on the newly accessible digital spectrum. As broadcasters received this giveaway, which by the FCC's own estimates was worth upwards of $70 billion, policy makers neither required nor asked for anything in return.

What will broadcast stations do with their new channels? It is likely that they will try to build a new, multiplex television world that contains a variety of new revenue streams, including e-commerce and home shopping programming, pay-per-view options, and plenty of room for advertiser-friendly programs directed at desirable market segments. The new television landscape is likely to be very consumer friendly, providing new shopping and entertainment options and, at a minimum, a vast expansion in the number of channels. Even so, it is not too late to require that digital broadcasters promote, in specific ways, the interests of citizenship as well.

One way to make the new digital broadcasting world citizen friendly is to take advantage of the expansion in channel capacity to increase access to the airwaves. Given the value of the licenses television stations received free of charge, it is entirely appropriate to consider strategies for requiring station owners to make one of their multiplexed channels a "public access" channel, available to organizations and individuals in the community. This would be an even better option than simply allocating a few hours of public access time each week. So far, public access channels have been limited to local cable systems, so they reach only a small audience. Including public access in broadcast television would mean a potentially much larger audience for such programming. This, in turn, could generate more interest in producing better quality programs. Such broadcast public access could include both public affairs programs and independently produced cultural content.

The Internet

Regulatory policy issues have achieved a new level of significance with the emergence of online media. With so much hype surrounding the growth of the Internet and with entrepreneurs driving new online ventures forward at breakneck speed, we need to think about how best to harness these new media technologies to enhance citizenship. There are three fundamental issues involved in Internet regulation: universal service, a level playing field for broadband, and the development of civic-oriented Internet content.

Universal Service. First we must work toward universal access to the Internet.[247] The idea of universal service has its origins in telephony, where public policy initiatives, using a variety of state and federal funding mechanisms, helped achieve wider access to affordable telephone service for rural and low-income households. The concept can be adapted to prevent a hardening of the "digital divide" between those who have access to the new Internet-based technologies and those who do not.

Adopting the rhetoric of public access, some commercial ventures tried offering Internet access free of charge in the late 1990s. Despite the language of public access that was part of the sales pitch, these free Internet ventures were built around a consumer framework based on a "broadcast model" of Internet access, in which advertisers rather than customers provided the revenue. To get "free" access, people had to subject themselves to a constant barrage of advertising that often framed their computer screens. Advertisers trying to reach Internet users, many of whom were quite adept at avoiding banner ads, saw these free access providers as a means of reaching a captive audience who could not turn the ads off. In some cases, free access was provided to schools, giving advertisers the extra benefit of reaching the lucrative youth market.

The other cost to many customers of free Internet service providers was the loss of their privacy. In exchange for free access, users agreed to allow providers to gather data on their online activities. This information was then used to enhance the providers' ad sales by giving evidence to advertisers of user interests and preferences. Such data could also be sorted and sold to other companies interested in targeting specific populations based on demographics and lifestyle. In these scenarios, Internet access did not require a monthly payment, but neither was it really free.

Such "free" Internet access providers did not have much success with the advertising-only model. By 2004, free Internet access had become little more than a promotional strategy, used to attract new customers for paid services. The free services are remarkably limited in time (just a few hours per month), speed, reliability, and support, offering the equivalent of a free online trial. With subscribers routinely offered opportunities to upgrade to a full service package for a monthly subscription fee, the free access model has changed. Instead of advertising supporting free Internet access, free access is now a form of advertising for the Internet service providers.

As an alternative to this consumer model, we should publicly fund universal access to the Internet. Although universal service to individual homes is unlikely any time soon, public policy initiatives can help make Internet service available to local schools, libraries, and community centers—especially those in low-income neighborhoods. This would open up the possibility of Internet access even to poor households without telephone service, a population overlooked by even the "free" commercial service providers (slightly more than one of every 20 households in the United States does not have a telephone). The Telecommunications Act of 1996 took a step in the right direction by expanding the universal service policy beyond telephones to include the Internet. Now funds can be provided for community institutions to connect to the Internet and other advanced communications networks. Such efforts need to be supported and expanded.

Even as telecommunications policy defines universal access to the Internet as a worthy goal, the means to achieving widespread public access is highly contested. Should local or state government subsidize the development of high-speed networks or even build their own public networks? A growing number of municipal governments consider widespread and affordable access as a core public good and seek to build their own municipal networks. In Kutztown, Pennsylvania, for example, the local government built a high-speed, fiber-optic network to which residents can subscribe for a monthly fee that is far below that charged by commercial providers. The Philadelphia city government announced plans in 2004 to build a wireless network that would be available in the entire city, citing the educational and civic value of a citywide wireless network.

The development of municipal Internet access is firmly rooted in a public interest understanding of online media, in which *access* to the Internet is the fundamental issue. Jeff Chester of the Center for Digital Democracy argues that "in today's world, access to broadband should be a right," emphasizing that local governments have a real stake in providing Internet access to citizens.[248] The telecommunications companies see municipal networks as unwanted competition, however, and have invoked the market perspective as they fight to prevent local governments from offering Internet access to residents. The telecommunications industry won an important victory in late 2004, when Pennsylvania governor Ed Rendell signed a bill that prevents local governments from offering telecommunications services to citizens unless the telecommunications company serving the area has declined to provide such services. News reports indicated that Verizon drafted the legislation; it was certainly the major beneficiary of the new Pennsylvania law. Although a negative public response to the legislation led Verizon to make a deal with Philadelphia to permit the development of their citywide network, this case highlights the tension between market goals and public interest goals. With Verizon and telecommunication industry lobbyists working hard to stop the proliferation of municipal networks, the public-private battle over the terms of Internet access may be only just beginning.

Leveling the Playing Field. We must ensure that broadband does not result in an unfair advantage for corporate media.[249] Most homes still access the Internet via dial-up over a standard telephone line. All that is changing rapidly, however, as new cable, phone, and satellite services allow for much faster access. With high-speed access, data-intensive media—such as high-quality video—become more practical. However, corporate media giants have tried to use their infrastructure ownership to give themselves unfair advantages. For example, in contrast to telephone lines that must be made available to competitors, cable companies are not currently required to make their networks available to competing Internet service providers. This undermines competition by effectively expanding the cable monopoly into a broadband Internet access monopoly as well. Regulations should be changed to require open access to cable lines to promote broadband competition.

Worse, the new broadband platform allows network operators to make distinctions based on content and the origins and destinations of material. This allows networks to potentially give preferential treatment to content they own and deliver material from competitors or nonprofit organizations at a slower transmission speed. In effect, the "information superhighway" could soon have a fast lane for commercial corporate material and a cluttered slow lane for everybody else. If such developments are allowed to occur, the Internet playing field will be dramatically tipped in favor of corporate producers in general and cable owners in particular. That is why one of the big questions for media policy in the 21st century will be ownership of, control of, and access to the wires that enter our homes, which will be the key to delivery of the evolving generation of digital media.

In addition, broadband service may come to resemble cable service in that it will be sold in "tiers." Just as basic cable service does not include premium movie channels and other specialized content, tiered broadband access could make some Internet sites available only to customers who pay more. Such a development should not be allowed to occur because it undermines the basic premise of universal access that is the core of the Internet's civic potential.

Developing Civic-Oriented Internet Content. We must support the development of civic-oriented Internet content. The early 1990s metaphor of the "information superhighway"—which suggested that the new media were fundamentally about public access to information—gave way to the dot.com world of e-commerce. There is no turning back on this consumer bonanza; the dot.com genie is out of the bottle, and a whole new sector of the economy is now based on a virtual world. We can, however, retain some of the underlying ethos of the information superhighway by creating and nourishing an online civic sector alongside the enormous commercial sector.

Public resources must be made available to nurture civic spaces on the Internet so at least one sector of the online media world is dedicated to strengthening democratic discourse. The major media companies have far more resources than do community groups to spend for the newest software, Web site design, regular content updates, and promotion. Media policy, therefore, needs to focus on developing innovative approaches for promoting civic culture on the Internet. Community organizations should be able to get free, noncommercial Internet space for their Web sites. They should also be eligible for technical assistance and financial support when their efforts are aimed at promoting civic culture.

Rather than focus on "virtual communities"—connections between people online—these new Internet civic efforts need to support the vitality of existing physical communities. Advocates of "civic networking" are developing policies that use the potential of new forms of online communication to strengthen citizen participation at the local level. For example, the nonprofit Center for Civic Networking is dedicated to using the Internet and other telecommunications infrastructure to enhance the public good.[250] These efforts include developing local government Web sites with user-friendly information about municipal statutes and social service agencies. Such sites also include links to a wide range of community organizations, electronic bulletin boards, and discussion groups that provide the opportunity for an ongoing conversation about issues, problems, and policies.

Finally, these Web sites provide information and links to resources on economic and community development. Other initiatives include using interactive multimedia and electronic mail to facilitate communication between citizens and local officials and to open up the local policy-making process by making public meetings, proposals, and documents more accessible to citizens. In short, the new media are potentially powerful tools that can enhance civic engagement. We should use public policy to support such innovative efforts.

Ensuring Diversity: The Problem of Money

As we have seen, one of the primary problems facing noncommercial media initiatives is the lack of funding to compete with commercial ventures. Noncommercial citizen initiatives can never displace better-funded alternatives, but there are things that can be done to help support noncommercial alternatives. Public policy initiatives can make access easier for noncommercial media, and they can provide direct support for citizen efforts to use media to enhance public life.

For example, reduced rates for mail delivery of periodicals have long been a useful subsidy to help maintain media diversity. If all publications had to pay first-class mail rates, many smaller magazines and papers would fold. By providing lower rates for such material, the government helps ensure the existence of a range of information. In 1995, however, the U.S. Postal Service suggested postal rate changes that would have limited such subsidies to only those periodicals that were presorted for automatic delivery. The lower rate could not have been used by periodicals going to fewer than 25 addresses in a single zip code as a result. The effect would have been to shift the postal subsidy to publications with higher circulations, lowering their postal rates by 14%. At the same time, it would have been more difficult than ever for smaller publications to survive because their postal rates would have risen by 17%. A compromise was eventually reached that kept the two-tiered system but reduced the gap between the two rates.[251] Although the current postal subsidy aids all print media, efforts should be developed to support noncommercial, independent media with rates that are even further reduced.

Newer media forms require more public support as well. Civic media efforts will not be able to survive in a commercial market environment. Instead, public funds to support television, radio, and Internet content need to be developed or expanded for noncommercial efforts aimed at promoting civic life. These funds should be available for both informational and cultural productions. Some funds are currently available, for example, through the National Endowment for the Arts, but as our media environment expands, more funds need to be targeted specifically at supporting civic media efforts. Such funds are essential to ensuring that civic programming and content is high quality and serves the purpose for which it was designed.

Antitrust and the Media Monopoly

To improve our chances for a vibrant media system, antitrust laws must be more actively used to stem the concentration of media ownership. With the large media conglomerates continuing to merge and grow, the number of major players in the media business continues to shrink. As we have seen, media critic Ben Bagdikian noted in 2004 that just 5 companies now dominate our media landscape, far fewer than the 50 companies that did so when Bagdikian published the first edition of his analysis in 1983.[252] With emerging technologies providing new opportunities and posing new challenges for the current media giants, the consolidation of the media industry seems far from over. Bagdikian has argued that with the growing concentration of media ownership, a new "private Ministry of Information" is emerging in the United States. With so few companies owning so much of our news and entertainment fare, the vitality of democratic discourse is in danger. That is why antitrust laws need to be used more actively.

It is true that an explosion in the volume of media outlets has accompanied the consolidation of the media industry. What we have is more media but fewer owners—or, in different terms, we have more products but fewer voices. As we have seen, the growing concentration of ownership in the media industry makes it far more difficult for new voices to compete for either public attention or investor support. In addition, the conglomerate structure of the media industry provides strong incentives for a continuing "sameness" in media content. The same products are simply repackaged for distribution in a variety of formats. Therefore, despite the increased volume in media, these commercial imperatives pose a threat to the vibrant nature of civic culture.

Concentrated ownership also raises the specter of an antidemocratic consolidation of power. Law professor Eben Moglen reminds us that "the connection between antitrust and the defense of democracy is intimate and long-standing, but largely ignored."[253] In other words, antitrust activity is fundamentally about protecting democracy by limiting the consolidation of private power. The original pieces of antitrust legislation—the Sherman Antitrust Act of 1890 and the Clayton Act of 1914—were created only after public outcry about the concentration of business power in oil, steel, railroads, and other basic industries. In today's information society, it is the media giants who loom large in our national cultural and political life. They reach into virtually every American home, are the primary arena where political activity occurs, and use these substantial resources to influence public policy. The unbridled growth in size, scope, and sheer cultural presence of the major media conglomerates is cause for new concern about the health of our democracy.

Already, a handful of media giants wield enormous power in setting the public agenda and defining the terms of legitimate discussion. This is one reason there is so little serious public debate about the relationship between the business of media and the health of democracy. As long as the major media industries provide the primary venues for media criticism, the public will not have the information it needs to make informed assessments about the role of media in contemporary society. Without such information, it is impossible to develop the political momentum to achieve effective media policies.

When understood in political terms, antitrust is much more than a method for protecting consumers; antitrust is a valuable instrument for enhancing democracy. Vigorous antitrust enforcement can be a powerful tool for halting and even reversing the consolidation of the media industry. A more proactive antitrust policy can be important in stimulating public discussion about the appropriate role of major corporate media and the development of effective media policy in the new digital age.

❖ PUBLIC POLICY AND PUBLIC BROADCASTING

More than 30 years after the 1967 Public Broadcasting Act created public broadcasting in the United States, the communications environment has changed dramatically. The era of 500 channels is rapidly approaching; the promise of an interactive multimedia future reverberates throughout policy-making, corporate, and media circles; and the major players—the television networks, cable companies, phone companies, software makers, and program suppliers—are positioning themselves for the convergence of old and new media.

In all of this, commercial forces—not the public interest—drive both the growth of new products and their applications. Still, commercial television has found ways to profit from programming that used to be exclusively associated with public television. Public television staples, such as children's educational programs, do-it-yourself shows, and nature programming, are now part of the cable universe.

Public broadcasting has also been changing. In recent years, public financing for the system has stagnated, and public broadcasting increasingly has turned to corporate underwriters and viewer donations to survive. Predictably, the more public broadcasting depended on advertisers and viewers in desirable demographics to survive, the more it began to resemble commercial broadcasting. In short, the expanding commercial media began doing some of what public broadcasting used to do, and public broadcasting began to resemble commercial media.

All of this raises the question of whether or not there is a role for public television in the new digital environment. Some critics suggest that the rise of cable has made public television obsolete. However, far from signaling the obsolescence of public television, we believe the limitations of the new media climate show how important it is to reassert some noncommercial presence on the airwaves. Even with vastly expanded television, advertising and profit considerations will continue to result in limited content dominated by commercial concerns.

Public broadcasting is uniquely positioned to contribute to democracy by providing an alternative to commercial broadcasting. An independent public broadcasting system can broaden the horizons of public discourse by serving as an electronic platform for perspectives, ideas, and cultural presentations that are largely unheard in commercial media. By providing citizens with access to a wide range of ideas, public broadcasting can help prepare citizens to become more active in other arenas of public life.

So far, public television has responded to the new multichannel environment by adopting a market approach. That is, public television has tried to compete in the new environment by becoming more commercially oriented. It has tried to survive by attracting larger—and presumably wealthier—audiences for its programming, which has been increasingly tailored to attract audiences. Moreover, it has survived by garnering more corporate dollars in the form of underwriting—a thinly disguised form of advertising. This strategy breaks from any concern about questions of democracy or the public sphere and, instead, tries to make the case for public television by demonstrating its commercial viability. The market model assumes that viewers are simply consumers—of both programming and products—and that television, in this case public television, should respond to them as such. Such an approach is misguided and shortsighted.

Instead of adopting a market approach, public television should refocus on those very questions about democracy and the public sphere that the commercial model eschews. By adopting a public model that assumes viewers are citizens, public television can reinvent itself as a system to meet fundamental citizenship needs. In this way, public television could ensure its future in the new media environment by making its own distinctive contribution much clearer. Ultimately, it is a renewed focus on citizenship and difference that can save public television from becoming a kinder and gentler version of commercial television.

The emerging, market-oriented approach in public broadcasting directs our attention away from fundamental questions about media and citizenship. Public television can be a valuable public resource by refocusing on its mission to broadcast programs that nourish citizenship and enhance public discourse. However, public broad-casting needs more than just a renewed commitment to a citizen-oriented mission: It must be more adequately funded and better protected from the political and economic pressures associated with its current funding structure.

One way to accomplish both goals—to provide enhanced, stable funding to public television that is free from congressional and under-writer pressures—is to fund a public broadcasting trust that would guarantee long-term, public funding to support public television. One potential source of funding for such a trust is the proceeds from the auction of the analog spectrum, which will be available once broad-casters shift over to digital-only signals (the shift is currently scheduled for 2009).

The leadership of public television has embraced the concept of a trust fund, and PBS president Pat Mitchell launched the Enhanced Funding Initiative in 2004 "with a goal of developing a report and pos-sibly a new policy proposal on how funding for public broadcasting overall can be increased to match current and future funding needs." At the top of the list of priorities for the Enhanced Funding Initiative is the analog spectrum auction idea, which, Mitchell noted, "has been a subject of discussion for some time and the window of opportunity on this option is closing, making it imperative that public broadcasting, as a whole community, consider this carefully, thoughtfully, strategi-cally."[254] With digital television on the horizon, including plans for PBS to partner with cable television giant Comcast to launch a new, com-mercial digital channel devoted to children's programming, the ques-tion of how best to fund public television to serve its public service mission remains a significant media policy question.

Rather than imitating their competitors by becoming more entertainment oriented, public broadcasting can engage citizens by developing programming that is both substantive and distinctive, by broadening the discourse beyond traditional voices, and by making local stations more accessible and democratic. Given the technological and economic forces restructuring the media environment, this is a pivotal moment for media policy in the United States. In the emerg-ing digital age, despite the temptations of commercialization, public broadcasting can be a valuable democratic resource if its leadership takes seriously its founding mission to broadcast programs that include fresh perspectives, expand dialogue, welcome controversy, and serve all segments of the public.

❖ JOURNALISM AS A PROFESSION

Journalism is widely considered to be a profession, which means that it has independent standards about good professional practice. As we have noted elsewhere in this book, the various codes of ethics adopted by journalism organizations speak of their public interest role. If the professional integrity of journalists is to be strengthened, the journalistic community needs to become more vocal about the ethical responsibilities that govern their profession. Just as the bottom-line orientation of HMOs must be tempered by the professional autonomy afforded doctors, so too must journalists insist on more independence to do their work within commercial media organizations.

One obvious area in need of attention is the trend toward eliminating the "wall" that separates the business side of news organizations from the content side. Professional journalism associations should actively resist this development. It is unrealistic to expect that individual journalists resisting the commercial pressures within the media today can have much impact. Instead, strengthened professional associations should insist on preserving the public interest function of media.

Second, journalists need to devote more space and time to covering the media's role in society. Obviously, we are not calling for new additions to the endless cross-promotion that already exists. Instead, there is a desperate need for news organizations to routinely give serious attention to issues and developments in the media world as they potentially affect society. There are valuable professional publications, such as the *Columbia Journalism Review,* and efforts, such as the Project for Excellence in Journalism, which provide models for thoughtful, critical, and balanced analyses of news media.[255] For example, in 2004, the Project for Excellence in Journalism released a report, *The State of the News Media,* which was the "first in what is to be an annual report on the state of the news media in America . . . to take stock each year of the state and health of American journalism."[256] However, such work is virtually unknown outside of journalism circles. Thoughtful and critical examinations of the role of media should be much more widely available via television, radio, and newspaper coverage. We should expect the media to scrutinize their own practices as well as they examine those of other institutions.

Finally, journalists need to seriously examine how their reporting intersects with public life and consider changing what they do to more effectively meet the needs of citizens. Several experiments in "public journalism" (also known as *civic journalism*) have shown the potential of such an approach.[257] Public journalism has emerged from a recognition of the symbiotic relationship between democracy and journalism. On the one hand, democracy needs the media to provide citizens with good, independent information to function well. On the other hand, journalism needs a healthy democracy in which citizens can pay attention to the news media. Rather than think of themselves as observers removed from civic life, public journalists see part of their role as contributing to the promotion of citizen engagement.

Although there have been some serious missteps and poorly conceived efforts in the name of public journalism, there have also been some creative efforts to produce journalism that treats people as citizens, that encourages civic participation, and that tries to contribute to productive, public deliberation. Some experiments in public journalism have focused on the issues that citizens have said most concerned them. Other efforts have shifted toward placing more emphasis on discussing possible solutions—and how citizens can get involved—rather than just focusing on problems. Still other experiments have initiated public deliberations about community issues—both in person and in the press. In constructing media that can reinvigorate public life, public journalism is a step in the right direction because public journalists are working to make news for a *public* that is more than just an *audience*.

❖ CITIZEN ACTIVISM AND ALTERNATIVE MEDIA

This chapter has tried to describe various ways that our media might be improved to contribute to a more vibrant public life. In doing so, however, we confront a chicken-and-egg dilemma. A responsive media system is necessary for active civic engagement, but active citizen engagement is necessary to create a responsive media system. Change in the media system will occur only if pressure is exerted from outside the system, because those with the most influence in today's media benefit from the current structure of the industry. Current policies that stress deregulation and foster the commercialization of public broadcasting are firmly entrenched and are generally beneficial to the large corporate players in the media industry. More generally, a market logic that substitutes profitability and competition for a broader definition of the public interest continues to reign supreme among policy makers and strategically minded media executives. Change, therefore, will occur only when citizens begin to pressure their elected officials and the media themselves.

Such efforts will inevitably generate resistance from an industry whose interests are threatened. The ongoing battle over low-power radio provides a good example of this dynamic. In the 1990s, radio activists faced a bleak situation. The commercial radio industry was increasingly concentrated, homogenized, and unresponsive to community needs. The FCC, too, was unresponsive to the call to license smaller community radio stations. As a result, some radio activists worked outside the system by developing "pirate" stations—unlicensed, low-power radio stations that operated illegally. Web sites and informal networks sprang up to support these activists. Such efforts dramatically illustrated the deep need for an alternative to the commercial radio giants.

The FCC became concerned about the proliferation of radio piracy and initiated both a crackdown on illegal broadcasters and a review of the low-power radio issue. After unprecedented citizen response to the idea, the FCC (as described earlier in this chapter) began licensing low-power FM radio. Citizen action had led to a policy change. As we have seen, the broadcasting industry fought the policy change, lobbying effectively on Capitol Hill to limit low-power radio. Activists, including the Media Access Project and the Prometheus Radio Project, continued to advocate for LPFM, building a movement to demand community radio as an alternative to the increasingly concentrated commercial radio industry. This long-standing activism seems to have paid off, as legislation moved through Congress in 2004 that seemed, as of this writing, likely to substantially expand low-power radio. According to the Prometheus Radio Project, "Approximately 400 Low Power FM (LPFM) radio stations currently serve communities across the United States. . . . If [the pending legislation] becomes law, thousands of stations will reach American communities, including at least one to four in most major cities."[258]

Citizen action, like that which led to the licensing of low-power radio, is also needed to balance the media industry's endless efforts at deregulation. In 2003, when the FCC proposed to again loosen ownership regulations (discussed in Chapter 3), citizens' groups mobilized quickly to oppose the effort. More than 2 million people contacted the FCC to protest the new rules, and the Media Access Project went to court to block their implementation. At the only public hearing on the matter, there was overwhelming public opposition to the proposed rules change.[259]

What was surprising in this activism was the makeup of the coalition that opposed the FCC's new rules. An unusually broad alliance spanning the political spectrum—including both the National Rifle Association and the National Organization for Women—worked together to coordinate their efforts. With widely divergent viewpoints, these groups were able to find common ground in their opposition to more consolidation of the media industry.

Although the FCC was largely unresponsive—despite Commissioner Michael Copps's concerns that "we know far too little to make an informed decision" about consolidation, as he told the crowd at the Richmond hearing[260]—members of Congress responded to the mobilization. The U.S. Senate passed a formal "resolution of disapproval" of the FCC's new rules, and both House and Senate committees approved provisions to roll back parts of the FCC's relaxed ownership restrictions. Finally, in June 2004, a U.S. Court of Appeals in Philadelphia found that the FCC "falls short of its obligation to justify its decisions to retain, repeal or modify its media ownership regulations with reasoned analysis"[261] and blocked implementation of the new rules.

Activists hailed this ruling as a historic victory in the fight to stop media ownership concentration. Although the court decision only returned the matter to the FCC for more comprehensive consideration of the consequences of the proposed rules changes, activist groups continued to mobilize to demand more public participation in the decision-making process. At the same time, media reform organizations worked with members of Congress to craft legislation to protect local and independent media and to identify clear guidelines to hold commercial media accountable for serving the public interest. The 2003-2004 mobilization to fend off further ownership concentration did not alter the existing media landscape, but it shone a light on the media policy-making process and helped to open up a broad public dialogue about media policy and the public interest.

Social change of any sort always faces opposition from those who benefit from the existing arrangements. Despite the alignment of massive opposition against it, the civil rights movement, to use an obvious example, used citizen pressure and strategic alliances with sympathetic supporters to initiate some significant social change. A clear-eyed assessment of the balance of power in the early 1950s as the movement began might have concluded that such change was impossible, given the powerful forces united against it, but the determination, solidarity, creativity, and vision of movement activists and ordinary citizens made the vision a reality. That promise of democratic participation has propelled many movements for social justice.

Faced with a highly concentrated media industry made up of high-profile, brand name companies, it is all too easy to conclude that the corporate forces aligned against change will make it impossible to reform the media system. Media activists face an increasingly powerful group of media conglomerates, which have friends in high places and a powerful resource—mass media visibility—to promote their political and economic interests. Those forces will prevail only if citizens fail to join in the effort for change. There is nothing inevitable about the direction of the media industry. Neither the political climate nor the specific set of media policies that currently exist are fixed. As they have done so many times in the past, citizens demanding a more just situation can influence the course of history. The broad public support for the federal government's effort to break Microsoft's monopoly power in the software industry is a sign that citizens are skeptical about the power of the major media companies. More generally, as media companies pursue new strategies for grabbing public attention, many citizens are becoming cynical about celebrity-oriented media culture. The question is whether that cynicism can be channeled toward positive efforts for change.

Ultimately, real change in the media landscape comes only from a sustained social movement focused on making the instruments of public communication more democratic. Already, many groups are organizing citizens to remake the media industry, although they are rarely visible in the major corporate media. For example, Free Press, launched in 2002, is a national organization "working to increase informed public participation in crucial media policy debates, and to generate policies that will produce a more competitive and public interest-oriented media system with a strong nonprofit and noncommercial sector."[262] As part of their work, Free Press works with other activist and educational organizations to support low-power radio, community wireless development, and, more generally, to stimulate public discussion of media policy and promote public interest media policies.

The public interest group Commercial Alert has organized a coalition that spans the political spectrum from Ralph Nader to Phyllis

Schlafly, to mobilize citizens to fight the increasing commercialization of American society.[263] One of their first targets was the classroom television news program *Channel One*, which boasts to potential advertisers that it offers a direct pipeline to the hard-to-reach youth audience in schools. The coalition's organizing has helped to generate debate on Capitol Hill, including congressional hearings in 1999, about the commercialization of schools. Commercial Alert also works with other advocacy groups to provide assistance to citizens and parents who oppose *Channel One* in their local school districts.

National media watchdog groups, such as Fairness & Accuracy In Reporting, and local and regional efforts, such as the Rocky Mountain Media Watch, also work in various ways to make the existing media industry more accountable to the public.[264] Such groups document and expose current media practices, launch campaigns on specific media issues, and provide citizens with vital information that all too often is left out of mainstream commercial media.

Any effort to restructure the media industry is certainly a long-term project. Media reformers face real obstacles. They do not yet agree on strategy, goals, or the role of media in contemporary society. Most media activists do implicitly agree that our mass media should be more than conduits for profit. In the coming years, that common insight will need to coalesce around a comprehensive alternative vision of a democratic media system. Events such as the National Conference for Media Reform—held in Madison, Wisconsin in 2003 and St. Louis in 2005—provide an opportunity to bring activists, scholars, media producers, and policy makers together to develop and clarify the strategies and goals of media reform.

Exercising Choice

Although significant restructuring of our media system is a long-term project, citizens are not powerless in the face of the continually growing media conglomerates. There are simple steps they can take now to improve their media diet.

First, media is not singular in grammatical terms, nor are our vast corporate media singular in their contents. There is a range of quality available in the commercial media, and citizens do have some room to maneuver in selecting which media they find helpful and which they want to avoid. Even though advertisers are often media's primary customers, citizens still have some power to influence media, because the industry often tries to present what they think certain audience segments want. One of the reasons there is more "quality" children's television available today is that the success of children's programs on public television demonstrated that there was a significant, and quite upscale, audience for such programs. If citizens demand more diverse or challenging media, it is possible that one of the media conglomerates, seeking to cash in on these demands, may be partially responsive.

Even more important, despite domination by media conglomerates, it is still possible to find independent, alternative forms of media for news, culture, and entertainment. There has long been a vibrant alternative media sector, consisting largely of publications, which provide ideas and perspectives that are not widely available in the major corporate media. Local free weekly newspapers and national journals of opinion; campus papers and youth 'zines; and issue-oriented publications about race, sexuality, foreign policy, and the state of the corporate media all provide an alternative window on the world, with different stories and new interpretations of current issues and events. In addition, community and college radio provide a venue for independent music. Pacifica Radio—a listener-supported, community-based radio network of noncommercial stations with such programming as the daily news show *Democracy Now*—provides access to voices that are rarely heard in the major news media.[265]

Most of the independent media do not try to compete directly with the major corporate media; they have comparatively small audiences and little or no advertising. They routinely struggle with their finances and often rely on foundation grants and individual donations to cover their expenses. In short, the alternative media sector is rarely, if ever, driven by profit goals. Instead, alternative media are much closer to the public interest model of media: They exist to circulate ideas and engage citizens.

Often, people accustomed to slick, corporate content do not take alternative or independent media seriously. Ironically, however, the corporate media industry sees great value in independent media. In many respects, college radio remains "alternative," playing "indie" music that cannot be heard on the commercial stations or bought from the big labels. At the same time, college radio serves as a version of the "minor leagues" in the music industry, from which the next "big leaguers" arise. College radio serves as a kind of development ground for the major music labels, who pay careful attention to what's hot on college radio, attend college music gatherings, and see college radio as a perfect place to recruit future staff.

The Internet has become home to a wealth of independent media, such as the independent media organizations networked at the Independent Media Center, which have become pioneers of a global online alternative media sector.[266] The Internet dramatically reduces the cost of distributing content because there are no printing or mailing expenses involved. As a result, more and more alternative media—including newspapers and magazines, radio, book publishers, and independent filmmakers—are going online. With the Internet, they can expand the range of materials they provide, include archives of previous volumes or programs, and provide information on how to obtain their offline media. With so much of the alternative media struggling to make ends meet, the Internet may give a needed boost to a sector of media that has heretofore resisted the temptations of the market.

For those who are already connected to alternative media, the Internet provides an important resource. It will become increasingly fast and inexpensive to connect online to alternative media sites, which continue to grow in both number and sophistication. Also, because alternative media routinely provide links to other alternative media sites, citizens are likely to find it easier to learn about and connect with the broad range of alternative media heretofore hampered by the costs and logistics of distribution.

The Internet is not a panacea for alternative media, however. As the number of Internet sites grows exponentially, it is likely that most alternative sites will be invisible to most citizens and rarely visited by those who are not familiar with the offline version. Certainly, the world of online media will have a robust alternative sector, but the Internet will not level the playing field. Alternative media will not be directly competing with the major media conglomerates, which have brand name recognition and large promotional budgets. That is why transforming mainstream media continues to be an important goal. Meanwhile, most alternative media are likely to remain independent and somewhat marginal, but their existence continues to make a significant contribution to the public sphere.

We will continue to rely on corporate media for much of our information and entertainment; therefore, it is important that we hone our "media literacy" skills. Media literacy is education that teaches critical analysis skills so people can better understand the socially constructed nature of the media they watch, read, and listen to.[267] Media literacy programs teach people how media are constructed, what the conventions of various media are, and how media may influence them. In effect, they help people arm themselves against the influence of mass media by helping them understand how the media work. It is often said that media-literate people do not necessarily know all the answers, but they do know what questions to ask—such as, Who created this message and why? How and why did they choose what to include? What and who were left out?

Different forms of media literacy can be taught to people of all ages. For example, simple analyses of the conventions in commercials can help young children better understand the manipulative distortions often embedded in ads aimed at them. Older children and teens can be taught about production conventions in various media and the sociological significance of various types of media messages. Older teens and adults might be taught about the media industry and the influence of commercial pressures on media content. In countries such as Canada, Australia, and England—where American media products have historically dominated—a course in media literacy is required to graduate from the U.S. equivalent of high school. The decentralized nature of the U.S. school system makes it virtually impossible to nationally mandate such a class, but every school should incorporate media literacy into its curriculum.

Much as literacy—the ability to read and write—is an essential skill for citizens in industrial societies, media literacy is becoming a vital skill for citizens of our information society. Media literacy should not be a replacement for efforts to actually reform the media industry. However, it can help arm citizens against undue influence by the media. Citizens who are better informed about the nature of the mass media are more likely to demand better quality from the media. Also, teaching media literacy often involves having students produce their own media content, so it may encourage the development of independent media.

It is not surprising that some corporate media players are trying to divert the media literacy movement for their own purposes. Already, *Channel One*—the school-based commercial television news broadcast—is becoming a significant participant in media literacy; it argues that it seeks to help students develop critical reading skills.[268] This is a very different message from what *Channel One* tells its potential advertisers. Media literacy advocates need to critically appraise such corporate efforts to coopt their work. Only time will tell whether media literacy programs are able to maintain an independent focus on educating citizens rather than becoming yet another means of attracting consumers.

❖   THE LIMITS OF MEDIA, THE IMPORTANCE OF MEDIA

We believe that the media have an important role in a democratic society. In this book, we have argued that the corporate commercialism so rampant in today's media has dramatically undermined the potential contribution of the media to our public life. We conclude by noting that an exclusive emphasis on the media misses a larger dynamic involving other social institutions in our society. In particular, the decline of other mediating institutions has operated concurrently with the rise of media's influence.

Mediating institutions are those organizations that stand between citizens and the powerful elements of society, particularly government and corporations. Church groups, labor unions, consumer organizations, social movement groups, and even political parties all have important roles in a democracy. They serve as places where citizens can gather to deliberate, articulate their views, advocate for their interests, and work for the greater good of society. The commercialization of social life—in which media have played a central part—has transformed citizens' identities into those of consumers. Consuming corporate products, especially mass media products, now takes up an increasing part of people's daily lives. Community meetings and projects are too often replaced by prime-time television and surfing the Internet. Corporate media has sapped life from civil society.

The revitalization of civic life, however, will not occur solely—or even primarily—from the restructuring of media. It will occur only through the broader renewal of a vibrant civic culture. This renewal must include a revitalization of educational institutions, public interest groups, labor organizations, the faith community, and other elements of civic life. Citizens active in such organizations constitute the force for change in the media system.

The media industry cannot be blamed for all of society's ills; neither should it be seen as the primary solution to those problems. However, the transformation of corporate media and the strengthening of independent media are significant parts of a broader project to revitalize civic engagement and public life.

Appendix

Select Online Resources for Studying the Media Industry, Media Policy, and Media Education

The business of media changes rapidly. Fortunately, the Internet offers a wide variety of Web sites with up-to-date industry information and policy discussions. It also offers a large number of educational and advocacy resources. The following is a selected list of such sites, many of which have links to more sites. The descriptions were adapted from each organization's Web site in January 2005.

Media Policy

American Library Association: Office for Information Technology Policy

http://www.ala.org/ala/washoff/oitp/oitpofficeinformation.htm

The Office for Information Technology Policy promotes information technology policies that support and encourage efforts of libraries to ensure access to electronic information resources as a means of upholding the public's right to a free and open information society. It works to ensure a library voice in information policy debates and to promote full and equitable intellectual participation by the public.

The Benton Foundation

http://www.benton.org/

The Benton Foundation seeks to articulate a public interest vision for the digital age and to demonstrate the value of communications for solving social problems.

Center for Democracy and Technology

http://www.cdt.org/

The Center for Democracy and Technology promotes democratic values and constitutional liberties in the digital age. With expertise in law, technology, and policy, center staff members seek practical solutions to enhance free expression and privacy in global communications technologies. The center is dedicated to building consensus among all parties interested in the future of the Internet and other new communications media.

Center on Democratic Communications of the National Lawyers Guild

http://www.nlgcdc.org/

The Center on Democratic Communications of the National Lawyers Guild works to protect the right of all people to communicate; that is, the right of all people to a system of media and communications based on principles of democracy and cultural and informational self-determination, not dominated by commercial concerns. Since 1988, the center has worked with groups challenging the FCC's ban on low-power radio, participated heavily in the FCC's "rulemaking" while they were considering legalization, and now emphasizes help to community groups in applying for and getting the new low-power FM licenses.

Consumer Federation of America

http://www.consumerfed.org/backpage/media_policy/

Since 1968, the Consumer Federation of America has provided consumers with a well-reasoned and articulate voice in decisions that affect their lives. Day in and day out, the federation's professional staff gathers facts, analyzes issues, and disseminates information to the public, policy makers, and the rest of the consumer movement. Understanding the complexities of media issues has become increasingly important in this age of media mergers and deregulation. The information on their Web site should help you learn more about issues such as media ownership, cable, broadband, media regulation, and other subjects of interest.

Consumer Project on Technology

http://www.cptech.org/

The Consumer Project on Technology was started by Ralph Nader in 1995. Currently, the project focuses on intellectual property rights and health care, electronic commerce (very broadly defined), and competition policy

Federal Communications Commission

http://www.fcc.gov/

Most of the material available on the FCC Web site is generated by the FCC's major regulatory bureaus and offices. Each bureau and office has its own suite of pages, or home page, within the FCC Web site. In addition to a wealth of information on bureau-specific issues, these home pages contain the primary links to FCC releases, such as orders, news releases, public notices, and Notices of Proposed Rule Makings.

The Future of Music Coalition

http://www.futureofmusic.org/

The Future of Music Coalition is a not-for-profit collaboration between members of the music, technology, public policy, and intellectual property law communities. The coalition seeks to educate the media, policy makers, and the public about music technology issues, as well as bringing together diverse voices in an effort to come up with creative solutions to some of the challenges noted on their Web site.

Intellectual Property and Technology Forum at Boston College Law School

http://infoeagle.bc.edu/bc_org/avp/law/st_org/iptf/

This forum is a legal publication dedicated to providing readers with rigorous, innovative scholarship; timely reporting; and ongoing discussion from the legal community concerning technology law and intellectual property.

Internet Society

http://www.isoc.org/

The Internet Society is a professional membership society, with more than 150 organizations and 16,000 individual members in more than 180 countries. It provides leadership in addressing issues that confront the future of the Internet and is the organization home for the groups responsible for Internet infrastructure standards, including the Internet Engineering Task Force and the Internet Architecture Board.

Media Access Project

http://www.mediaaccess.org/

The Media Access Project is a 30-year-old, nonprofit, public interest law firm that promotes the public's First Amendment right to hear and be heard on the electronic media of today and tomorrow.

National Telecommunications and Information Administration

http://www.ntia.doc.gov/

The National Telecommunications and Information Administration, an agency of the U.S. Department of Commerce, is the executive branch's principal voice on domestic and international telecommunications and information technology issues. The administration works to spur innovation, encourage competition, help create jobs, and provide consumers with more choices and better quality telecommunications products and services at lower prices.

Media Industry

Advertising Age Online

http://adage.com/

Online version of the industry publication *Advertising Age,* updated daily.

Broadcasting & Cable Online

http://www.broadcastingcable.com/

Online version of the industry publication *Broadcasting & Cable,* with a daily briefing on developments in the media industry.

Columbia Journalism Review's Who Owns What

> http://www.cjr.org/tools/owners/
> The review's online guide to what the major media companies own.

Current Online

> http://www.current.org/
> The Web service about public broadcasting, with selected content from *Current,* the biweekly newspaper covering public TV and radio in the United States.

Poynter Online: Romenesko

> http://www.poynter.org/column.asp?id=45
> Media industry news, commentary, and memos compiled by Jim Romenesko, updated daily. Hosted by the Poynter Institute.

Los Angeles Times: Entertainment Business

> http://www.latimes.com/business/custom/cotown/
> News on the entertainment business from the *Los Angeles Times,* updated daily.

MediaWeek Online

> http://www.mediaweek.com/mediaweek/index.jsp
> Online version of the industry publication *MediaWeek,* updated daily.

Nielsen Media Research

> http://www.nielsenmediaresearch.com/
> Online home of the television ratings company.

The Online NewsHour: Mediawatch

> http://www.pbs.org/newshour/media/
> The Media Unit of the *NewsHour with Jim Lehrer* was established in August of 1998 to provide regular reporting and analysis of the information industries. Mediawatch follows and reports on developments, trends, and controversies as they arise in the worlds of television, cable, newspapers, magazines, the Internet, and publishing.

Veronis Suhler Stevenson

http://www.veronissuhler.com/index.cfm

Veronis Suhler Stevenson's home page includes a range of up-to-date materials on various segments of the media industry, assembled primarily for potential investors.

Media Education and Media Advocacy

Adbusters

http://www.adbusters.org/

Operated by The Media Foundation, a global network of artists, activists, writers, pranksters, students, educators, and entrepreneurs who want to advance the new social activist movement of the information age. Their aim is to topple existing power structures and forge a major shift in the way we will live in the 21st century. Adbusters Media Foundation publishes *Adbusters* magazine, operates this Web site, and offers its creative services through PowerShift, their advocacy advertising agency.

Alliance for Community Media

http://www.alliancecm.org/

The Alliance for Community Media is committed to ensuring everyone's access to electronic media. The alliance advances this goal through public education, a progressive legislative and regulatory agenda, coalition building, and grassroots organizing.

Alliance for Public Technology

http://www.apt.org/

The Alliance for Public Technology is a nonprofit membership organization based in Washington, DC and concerned with fostering access by all people to affordable and useful information and communication services and technologies.

Center for Digital Democracy

http://www.democraticmedia.org/

The Center for Digital Democracy is committed to preserving the openness and diversity of the Internet in the broadband era and to realizing the full potential of digital communications through the development and encouragement of noncommercial, public interest programming.

The Center for International Media Action

http://www.mediaactioncenter.org/index.html

The Center for International Media Action is a nonprofit organization created to strengthen connections among grassroots organizers, public-interest advocates, activists, and researchers focused on media policy and social justice. The center seeks to increase the efficacy of organizing and activism around media issues by providing tools and services to help groups share knowledge, build relationships, and use existing resources.

Center for Media and Democracy

http://www.prwatch.org/cmd/index.html

The Center for Media and Democracy is a nonprofit organization that works to strengthen democracy by promoting media that are "of, by and for the people"—genuinely informative and broadly participatory— and by removing the barriers and distortions of the modern information environment that stem from government- or corporate-dominated, hierarchical media.

Citizens for Independent Public Broadcasting

http://www.cipbonline.org/

Citizens for Independent Public Broadcasting is a national membership organization dedicated to putting the *public* back into *public broadcasting* so that we can all join in the debate about our nation's future.

Commercial Alert

http://www.commercialalert.org/

Commercial Alert's mission is to keep the commercial culture within its proper sphere and prevent it from exploiting children and subverting the higher values of family, community, environmental integrity, and democracy.

Community Technology Centers' Network

http://www.ctcnet.org/

The Community Technology Centers' Network was founded on the recognition that in an increasingly technologically dominated society, people who are economically disadvantaged will be left further behind if they are not provided with access to and training on information tools. The network envisions a society in which all people are equitably empowered with these tools, and it is committed to achieving this end.

Computer Professionals for Social Responsibility

http://www.cpsr.org/

Computer Professionals for Social Responsibility is a public-interest alliance of people concerned about the impact of information and communications technology on society. They work to influence decisions regarding the development and use of computers, because those decisions have far-reaching consequences and reflect our basic values and priorities.

Creative Commons

http://creativecommons.org/

Creative Commons is a nonprofit organization that offers a flexible range of protections and freedoms for authors and artists. They have built upon the "all rights reserved" of traditional copyright to create a voluntary "some rights reserved" copyright. They work to offer creators a best-of-both-worlds way to protect their works and still encourage certain uses of them.

Electronic Frontier Foundation

http://www.eff.org/

The Electronic Frontier Foundation is a donor-supported membership organization working to protect our fundamental rights regardless of technology; to educate the press, policy makers, and the general public about civil liberties issues related to technology; and to act as a defender of those liberties.

Fairness & Accuracy In Reporting

http://www.fair.org/

FAIR, the national media watch group, has been offering well-documented criticism of media bias and censorship since 1986. FAIR works to invigorate the First Amendment by advocating for greater diversity in the press and by scrutinizing media practices that marginalize public interest, minority, and dissenting viewpoints.

Free Press

http://www.freepress.net/

Free Press is a national, nonpartisan organization working to increase informed public participation in crucial media policy debates and to generate policies that will produce a more competitive and public interest–oriented media system, with a strong nonprofit and non-commercial sector.

Independent Media Center

http://www.indymedia.org/

The Independent Media Center is a network of collectively run media outlets for the creation of radical, accurate, and passionate tellings of the truth. The Independent Media Center was established by various independent and alternative media organizations and activists in 1999 for the purpose of providing grassroots coverage of the World Trade Organization protests in Seattle. The center acted as a clearinghouse of information for journalists and provided up-to-the-minute reports, photos, and audio and video footage through its Web site.

MediaChannel.org

http://www.mediachannel.org/

MediaChannel.org is a nonprofit, public interest Web site dedicated to global media issues. MediaChannel offers news, reports, and commentary from their international network of media-issues organizations and publications, as well as original features from contributors and staff. Resources include thematic special reports, action toolkits, forums for discussion, an indexed directory of hundreds of affiliated groups, and a search engine constituting the single largest online media-issues database.

Media Democracy Legal Project

http://medialegalproject.org/

The Media Democracy Legal Project is engaged in building the popular political movement necessary for the creation of diverse, democratic broadcast communication. It is preparing to file a ground-breaking case that constitutionally challenges the present broadcasting monopoly.

Media Education Foundation

http://www.mediaed.org/
The Media Education Foundation produces and distributes video documentaries to encourage critical thinking and debate about the relationship between media ownership, commercial media content, and the democratic demand for free flows of information, diverse representations of ideas and people, and informed citizen participation.

National Institute on Media and the Family: MediaWise

http://www.mediafamily.org/
MediaWise provides information about the impact of media on children and gives people who care about children the resources they need to make informed choices. MediaWise is an initiative of the National Institute on Media and the Family, a nonprofit organization.

NetAction

http://www.netaction.org/
NetAction is a California-based nonprofit organization dedicated to promoting use of the Internet for effective grassroots citizen action campaigns and to educating the public, policy makers, and the media about technology policy issues.

Paper Tiger Television

http://www.papertiger.org/
Paper Tiger Television is an open, nonprofit, volunteer video collective. Through the production and distribution of our public access series, media literacy–video production workshops, community screenings, and grassroots advocacy, Paper Tiger works to challenge and expose the corporate control of mainstream media.

Project Censored

http://www.projectcensored.org/
The mission of Project Censored is to educate people about the role of independent journalism in a democratic society and to tell "the news that didn't make the news" and why. Project Censored is a media research group out of Sonoma State University that tracks the news published in independent journals and newsletters. From these, Project Censored compiles an annual list of 25 news stories of social

significance that have been overlooked, underreported, or self-censored by the country's major national news media.

Prometheus Radio Project

http://www.prometheusradio.org/

The Prometheus Radio Project is a nonprofit organization created by radio activists to facilitate the growth of the Free Radio Movement and present an organized demand for the democratization of the airwaves.

Radio4All

http://www.radio4all.org/

This site is a clearinghouse for the movement to reclaim the airwaves, with links to a wide range of microradio resources, including many local radio projects.

Notes

1. Descriptions of the deal are from various media accounts, including "AOL and Time Warner" (2000). See also Hansell (2000).
2. In discussing the value of older media deals in this book, we usually report both the current value at the time of the deal and the constant dollar value (in parentheses), adjusted for inflation, based on the value of the 2004 dollar. Constant dollar adjustments are based on the Bureau of Labor Statistics' Consumer Price Index (see http://www.bls.gov/cpi/home.htm). Constant dollar values should be considered approximate.
3. Several recent journalistic accounts explore the personalities behind, and problems associated with, the AOL Time Warner merger. See, for example, Klein (2004), Swisher and Dickey (2003), and Munk (2004).
4. See Flew and Gilmour (2003), who note that "The general consensus is that the failings of the AOL-Time Warner merger prove the limits of synergising content and delivery platforms across traditional broadcast and online media" (p. 18).
5. See Lieberman (2004), who notes: "America Online's ill-fated acquisition of Time Warner in 2001 probably did more than any other single event to prompt investors and analysts to reassess their assumptions about media."
6. Quoted in "Excerpts From Comcast Letter" (2004).
7. General Electric (2004).
8. Habermas (1989/1962).
9. See, for example, Calhoun (1992), Dahlgren and Sparks (1991), Dahlgren (1995), Hallin (1994), and Kellner (1990).
10. Murdock (1992).
11. Kuttner (1997).
12. Quoted in Sunstein (1997), p. 167.
13. Albarran (1996), p. 27.
14. Society of Professional Journalists (1996).
15. American Society of Newspaper Editors (2002).
16. Radio-Television News Directors Association (2000).
17. Details of the Communications Act of 1934 are provided in Kahn (1978).
18. Ang (1991).
19. *Ibid.*

20. The quotes and descriptions of the Disney deal are from Farhi (1995), Roberts (1995), and Kurtz (1995).
21. This discussion is based on material from the "Who Owns What" section of the *Columbia Journalism Review* Web site (http://www.cjr.org/tools/owners/), Herman and McChesney (1997), and Naureckas (1995).
22. Newspaper circulation data: U.S. Bureau of the Census (1965) and Newspaper Association of America (2004).
23. Greco (1996), Milliot (2004).
24. U.S. Bureau of the Census (1981), "Digital Cable TV" (2004).
25. U.S. Bureau of the Census (1995), McCarthy (2004).
26. Motion Picture Association Worldwide Market Research (2004).
27. U.S. Bureau of the Census (2004, 2005).
28. *Ibid*.
29. Ziff Davis Media Game Group (2004). See also Tanaka (2004).
30. Data are from various editions of Census Bureau's *Statistical Abstracts*. Conversion to constant dollars is based on the U.S. Department of Labor's CPI Inflation Calculator.
31. Ives (2004).
32. Baker (2004).
33. For a more detailed discussion of sociological approaches to studying media, see Croteau and Hoynes (2003).
34. For example, see Postman (1985).
35. Baldasty (1992).
36. Schudson (1978).
37. For useful descriptions and analyses of Hearst's newspaper empire, see McGerr (1986), Nasaw (2000), and Swanberg (1961).
38. See Douglas (1987) and Engelman (1996).
39. For a careful historical analysis of the early debate about the organization of broadcasting in the United States, see McChesney (1994).
40. Address by Newton N. Minow to the National Association of Broadcasters, Washington, DC, May 9, 1961 (in Kahn, 1978).
41. Baughman (1992).
42. Schatz (1997).
43. The Fairness Doctrine reads, in part, "This requires that licensees devote a reasonable percentage of their broadcasting time to the discussion of public issues of interest in the community served by their stations and that such programs be designed so that the public has a reasonable opportunity to hear different opposing positions on the public issues of interest and importance in the community" (13 FCC 1246, June 1, 1949, in Kahn, 1978).
44. For a helpful discussion of regulatory policy and children's television, see Hendershot (1998).
45. For a thorough discussion of the background to and significance of the Telecommunications Act, see Aufderheide (1999).
46. See "100 Leading Media Companies" (1984, 2004).

47. Details of the Viacom-CBS deal were obtained from company press releases and media accounts, including the following: Farhi (1999), Hofmeister (1999), Lowry (1999), Mifflin (1999), de Moraes (1999), Sarasohn (1999), Schwartz and Farhi (1999).
48. Federal Communications Commission (1995).
49. Mandese (2004).
50. Belson (2004).
51. Thompson (1999).
52. See, for example, the latest list of popular sites at http://www.comscore .com or http://www.nielsen-netratings.com, each of which uses different methodology to measure Web site traffic.
53. Time Inc. (1989).
54. Pope (1999).
55. See McConnell (2003) and Turner (2004).
56. "A Flawed Communications Bill" (1995).
57. Albarran (2003).
58. Carter (1999).
59. Schwartz (1999).
60. Quoted in Beckerman (2003).
61. Federal Communications Commission (2000b).
62. See the changes and related material at the FCC Web site: http://www.fcc .gov/ownership.
63. "Too Much Communication" (2003).
64. See testimony at http://www.fcc.gov/ownership/richmond022703.html.
65. Layton (2004).
66. Hearst Corporation (2005).
67. Tanaka (2004).
68. Vargas (2004).
69. Schiesel (2001).
70. Turner (2004).
71. MTV descriptive information is from the Web sites of Viacom (http://www .viacom.com) and MTV (http://www.mtv.com) and from Viacom annual reports.
72. Albarran (2003). For an earlier version of this study, see Albarran and Dimmick (1996).
73. Bagdikian (2004).
74. Aufderheide (1999), p. 90.
75. Mandese and Fadner (2004).
76. Gruley (1999).
77. When adjusted for inflation, some older films have earned more than *Titanic*. Movie revenue numbers are notoriously difficult to pinpoint, and different methodologies can result in different rankings. See, for example, the listings at http://www.the-movie-times.com, http://www.imdb.com, or http://www.boxofficemojo.com.

78. Data for *Titanic* sales were gathered from various media and industry accounts, including "Ship Sets Sail" (1998) and Hirschberg (2004).

79. The now-defunct Web site http://www.titanicproducts.com was the source for items that are not otherwise referenced in this section.

80. "Sony Signatures Creates" (1998).

81. Hammond (1998).

82. "Titanic Sales Onto QVC" (1998).

83. From the J. Peterman Web site, http://www.jpeterman.com, and Elliott (1998).

84. Seal (1998).

85. Barrett (1998).

86. Germain (2004).

87. Miller (1997).

88. The quote from Jeff Bezos, Amazon.com CEO, and other information in this paragraph are from Swisher (1998).

89. Bark (1995).

90. Orwall and Lippman (1999).

91. Auletta (1998a).

92. Beatty (1998).

93. Walt Disney Internet Group (2003).

94. Orwall and Lippman (1999).

95. Pope and Swisher (1999).

96. Beatty (1998).

97. Berger (2004).

98. Romano (2004).

99. Advertisement for FOX (*Wall Street Journal*, December 3, 1998, p. A11).

100. Coe (1996).

101. Nielsen ratings reported online at http://www.nielsenmedia.com.

102. Auletta (1998b).

103. Carr (2004).

104. Lenzner (1989).

105. Levin (1994).

106. Hell (2004).

107. News Corporation (2004).

108. News Corp Web site, http://www.NewsCorp.com, and Gapper (1997).

109. Bagdikian (1997), p. xi.

110. Ahrens (2003).

111. Reilly (1998, 1999).

112. Auletta (1997b).

113. McAllister (1996), p. 136.

114. U.S. v. Microsoft Corporation (1999), para. 33. See http://www.usdoj .gov/atr/cases/f3800/msjudgex.htm for the full "Findings of Fact" from the case.

115. U.S. v. Microsoft Corporation (1999), para. 412.
116. U.S. v. Microsoft Corporation (2000).
117. Farhi (1993).
118. Lippman (1998).
119. See "Six Makers of CD's" (1996), Labaton (2000), and Deutsch (2002).
120. McQuail (1992), p. 2. See chapter 3 for a review of the "public interest" concept.
121. Beacham (1994).
122. Miller (1997).
123. "Media Mergers" (1996).
124. "Big Media Experts" (1999/2000).
125. Project3Media (2004).
126. Quoted in Picasso (n.d.).
127. Project for Excellence in Journalism (2004).
128. Risser (1998).
129. Lee (2003).
130. Tristani (1998).
131. Bagdikian (1997), p. 160.
132. Johnson (1997).
133. Carmody (1996).
134. Lowry (1999).
135. *Ibid.*
136. Quoted in Rogers (1996).
137. Rogers (1996).
138. "Bottom Line Pressures" (2004).
139. Hickey (1998).
140. Project for Excellence in Journalism (2004).
141. Kent (1998).
142. "Q&A: Dan Rather" (1998).
143. Schiffrin (1999).
144. Project for Excellence in Journalism (2004).
145. For some classic treatments of the sociology of news production, see Epstein (1973), Fishman (1980), Gans (1979), and Tuchman (1978).
146. Underwood (1993).
147. See Shepard (1997), Rappleye (1998), and Osborne (1998).
148. Rappleye (1998).
149. Shaw (1999). Subsequent quotes are from this story as well.
150. Coyle (1998).
151. Underwood (1998).
152. "Buying History" (1996).
153. Cooper (1999), pp. 21-22.
154. McFadden (2002) and http://www.kirotv.com.
155. Cooper (1999), p. 17.

156. Shepard (1999).
157. Effron (1999).
158. Hansell (1999).
159. Rosman (1999).
160. Anders (1999).
161. Buskin (1999).
162. See Croteau and Hoynes (1994) and Croteau, Hoynes, and Carragee (1996).
163. Quoted in Ellis (2003).
164. Alter (1995).
165. Quoted in Rosenwein (1999/2000), p. 93.
166. "Self-Censorship" (2000).
167. Bergman (2000), p. 50.
168. See, for example, Grossman (1996). After the scandal was revealed and the incident was resolved, the story was dramatized in a Hollywood film, *The Insider.* For the ABC incident, see Weinberg (1995).
169. Bergman (2000), p. 50.
170. Rutenberg (2004).
171. Alger (1998), p. 183.
172. Auletta (1997a).
173. "We Paid $3 Billion" (1998), p. 1.
174. "Hightower Gets" (1995).
175. Corn (1998).
176. Alger (1998), p. 109.
177. Layton (2003/2004).
178. Quoted in Rosenwein (1999/2000), p. 94.
179. Snider and Page (1997), quoted in Alger (1998), p. 110.
180. Stevens (1998/1999).
181. Putnam (1991).
182. Cohen and Solomon (1995), p. 235.
183. Auletta (1997a), p. 226.
184. Cohen and Solomon (1995), p. 78.
185. Quoted in Baker (1997), p. 30.
186. "Self-Censorship" (2000).
187. Soley (1997).
188. *Ibid.*
189. "You Can't Say" (1998).
190. Bagdikian (1997), p. xii.
191. Rosenwein (1999/2000), p. 95.
192. See, for example, Bryant and Zillmann (2002).
193. For a more comprehensive analysis of *Channel One,* see De Vaney (1994) and Hoynes (1998).
194. See "The New" (1998); Shattuck (1999), p. 60; "Captive Kids" (1995); and "Reading, Writing and Revenue" (2004).

195. White (1999).
196. Berselli (1998).
197. "What's Up, Doc?" (1999), McCurdy (2002).
198. Schor (2004).
199. Pecora (1998), p. 153.
200. *Ibid.*, p. 154.
201. Cowles Business Media (1996).
202. Turow (1997), p. 2.
203. Delaney (1999).
204. Cranberg (1997), p. 52.
205. Newspaper Association of America, "1995 Circulation Facts, Figures, and Logic," summarized in Cranberg (1997).
206. Kaplan (1998).
207. Morlino (2004), Federal Communications Commission (2001).
208. Williams and Jindrich (2003).
209. Dunbar (2004).
210. Center for Responsive Politics (n.d.a).
211. Safire (1996).
212. Levinson (1995), p. 27.
213. Boyer (1986).
214. Johnson (1968).
215. Silverstein (1998), p. 30.
216. Baker (1998). See also Sherrill (1995), "Who's Afraid of" (1995), Abramsky (1995), and Silverstein (1998).
217. Forbes (2000).
218. Heilbrunn (1999).
219. *Ibid.*
220. Robb (2004).
221. Loeb (1999), Bedard (2004).
222. For critiques of the political effects of media, see, for example, Cook (1998), Croteau and Hoynes (1994), Edelman (1988), Entman (1989), Fallows (1997), Graber (2001), Kellner (1990), and McChesney (1999).
223. Drinkard and Memmott (2005).
224. Kurtz (2005).
225. Government Accountability Office (2005).
226. Kovach and Rosenstiel (1999).
227. Moeller (1999), p. 9.
228. Telecommunications Act of 1996. The full text of the act is available online at www.fcc.gov/telecom.html. For an abridged version, see Aufderheide (1999).
229. McChesney (1999).
230. Ashcroft v. American Civil Liberties Union et al. (2004).
231. "Clear Channel Nixes" (2004).

232. de Moraes (2004).
233. For more on the Entertainment Software Rating Board, see their Web site at http://www.esrb.org.
234. Rosenberg (1993).
235. Hollings (1993).
236. See Edwards (1993).
237. See Hamilton (2000) for a discussion of the violence on television as a result of market failure.
238. Advisory Committee on Public Interest Obligations of Digital Television Broadcasters (1998).
239. See Federal Communications Commission (1996).
240. See, for example, Wild Brain at http://www.wildbrain.com/.
241. See 13 FCC 1246 (1949) in Kahn (1978), p. 230.
242. McChesney (2004).
243. Federal Communications Commission (2000a), p. 2.
244. Section 632 of the 2001 Appropriations Act.
245. McCain LPFM Bill: a bill (S. 2505) sponsored by Senator John McCain with the title "To implement the recommendations of the Federal Communications Commission report to the Congress regarding low power FM service." Introduced June 4, 2004, and as of this writing, still pending in the U.S. Senate.
246. *Ibid.*
247. For an introduction to universal service, see the Center for Digital Democracy online at http://www.democraticmedia.org/issues/openaccess/index.html.
248. Chester (2004).
249. See the Center for Digital Democracy's broadband primer online at http://www.democraticmedia.org/primer.html.
250. See Managing Information with Rural America (n.d.) and Doheny-Farina (1996).
251. Cook (1998), p. 184.
252. Bagdikian (2004). The first edition of *The Media Monopoly* was published in 1983.
253. Moglen (1998).
254. Mitchell (2004).
255. The *Columbia Journalism Review* is online at http://www.cjr.org/. The Project for Excellence in Journalism is online at http://www.journalism.org/.
256. Project for Excellence in Journalism (2004).
257. See Rosen (1999) and Glaser (1999).
258. Prometheus Radio Project (2004).
259. Free Press (n.d.b).
260. Quoted in Shields (2003).

261. Prometheus Radio Project v. Federal Communications Commission (2004). The quotation is from p. 121 of the decision.

262. Free Press (n.d.a).

263. See Commercial Alert online at http://www.commercialalert.org/blog/.

264. FAIR is online at http://www.fair.org/index.php. Both authors have worked with FAIR. Rocky Mountain Media Watch is online at http://www .bigmedia.org/.

265. If a Pacifica radio station is not available in your community, hear some of their programs online at http://www.pacifica.org/.

266. For further information on independent media organizations and the Independent Media Center, see http://www.indymedia.org/en/index .shtml.

267. For resources on media literacy, see, for example, the Center for Media Literacy (http://www.medialit.org/) and the University of Oregon's Media Literacy Online Project (http://interact.uoregon.edu/MediaLit/ HomePage).

268. See Manning (1999).

References

Abramsky, Sasha. "Citizen Murdoch," *Extra!* (November/December, 1995): 16-17.

Advisory Committee on Public Interest Obligations of Digital Television Broadcasters. "Charting the Digital Broadcasting Future" (final report, December 18, 1998), Washington, DC.

"A Flawed Communications Bill," *New York Times* (June 20, 1995): A14.

Ahrens, Frank. "Media Giants Getting Together," *Washington Post* (November 6, 2003): E1.

Albarran, Alan. *Media Economics* (Ames: Iowa State University Press, 1996).

Albarran, Alan. "US Media Concentration: The Growth of Megamedia." Pp. 63-74 in A. Arrese, ed. *Empresa Informativa y Mercados de la Communicacion* (Pamplona, Spain: EUNSA, 2003).

Albarran, Alan, and John Dimmick. "Concentration and Economies of Multiformity in the Communications Industries," *Journal of Media Economics*, vol. 9, no. 4 (1996): 41-50.

Alger, Dean. *Megamedia* (Lanham, MD: Rowman & Littlefield, 1998).

Alter, Jonathan. "A Call for Chinese Walls," *Newsweek* (August 14, 1995): 31.

American Society of Newspaper Editors. *Statement of principles* (2002). Retrieved March 3, 2005, from http://www.asne.org/kiosk/archive/principl.htm

Anders, George. "The Clout of the Online Critic," *Wall Street Journal* (June 28, 1999): B1.

Ang, Ien. *Desperately Seeking the Audience* (New York: Routledge, 1991).

"AOL and Time Warner to merge in $166 billion stock deal." *New York Times* (January 10, 2000). Retrieved January 10, 2000, from http://www.ny times .com

Ashcroft v. American Civil Liberties Union et al., S. Ct. No. 03-218 (2004). Retrieved March 16, 2005, from http://supreme.lp.findlaw.com/supreme_court/briefs/03-218/03-218.mer.pet.html

Aufderheide, Patricia. *Communications Policy and the Public Interest* (New York: Guilford Press, 1999).

Auletta, Ken. "American Keiretsu," *New Yorker* (October 20, 1997a): 225-227.

Auletta, Ken. "The Impossible Business," *New Yorker* (October 6, 1997b): 51-63.

Auletta, Ken. "The Last Sure Thing," *New Yorker* (November 9, 1998a): 40-47.

Auletta, Ken. "Synergy City," *American Journalism Review* (May, 1998b): 18-35.

Bagdikian, Ben. *The Media Monopoly,* 5th ed. (Boston: Beacon Press, 1997).

Bagdikian, Ben. *The New Media Monopoly* (Boston: Beacon Press, 2004).

Baker, Russ. "The Squeeze," *Columbia Journalism Review* (September/October, 1997): 30-35.

Baker, Russ. "Murdoch's Mean Machine," *Columbia Journalism Review* (May/June, 1998): 51-56.

Baker, Stephen. "The Online Ad Surge," *Business Week* (November 22, 2004): 76.

Baldasty, Gerald. *The Commercialization of News in the Nineteenth Century* (Madison: University of Wisconsin Press, 1992).

Bark, Ed. "M-I-C-K-E-Y's got A-B-C T-V," *Richmond Times-Dispatch* (August 13, 1995): J1.

Barrett, Patrick. "Replica Rivals in Titanic," *Marketing* (April 9, 1998): 1.

Baughman, James L. *The Republic of Mass Culture* (Baltimore, MD: Johns Hopkins University Press, 1992).

Beacham, Frank. "Superhighway for Sale," *Extra!* (July/August, 1994): 24-25.

Beatty, Sally. "NBC Puts Its Firepower Behind Snap!," *Wall Street Journal* (September 15, 1998): B8.

Beckerman, Gal. "Tripping Up Big Media," *Columbia Journalism Review* (November/December, 2003).

Bedard, Paul. "Team Bush Lends a Hand to a Brand-New TV Show," *US News & World Report* (April 12, 2004): 2.

Belson, Ken. "Cable's Rivals Lure Customers With Packages," *New York Times* (November 22, 2004): C1.

Berger, Joseph. "Wave of Foreign TV Becomes an 'Emotional Outlet' for Immigrants," *New York Times* (February 23, 2004): B1.

Bergman, Lowell. "Network Television News: With Fear and Favor," *Columbia Journalism Review* (May/June, 2000): 50-51.

Berselli, Beth. "Free-Mail?," *Wall Street Journal* (August 20, 1998): G1, G3.

"Big Media Experts," *Brill's Content* (December, 1999/January, 2000): 97.

"Bottom Line Pressures Now Hurting Coverage, Say Journalists" *Pew Research Center for People and the Press* (May 23, 2004). Retrieved March 12, 2005, from http://people-press.org/reports/display.php3?ReportID=214

Boyer, Peter. "NBC Head Proposes Staff Political Contributions," *New York Times* (December 9, 1986): A1.

Bryant, Jennings, and Dolf Zillmann, eds. *Media Effects,* 2nd ed. (Hillsdale, NJ: Lawrence Erlbaum, 2002).

Buskin, John. "Online Persuaders," *Wall Street Journal* (July 12, 1999): R12, R26.

"Buying History," *Extra!* (July/August, 1996): 5.

Calhoun, Craig, ed. *Habermas and the Public Sphere* (Cambridge: MIT Press, 1992).

"Captive Kids: A Report on Commercial Pressures on Kids at School" *Consumers Union* (1995). Retrieved March 11, 2005, from http://www.consumersunion.org/other/captivekids/index.htm

Carmody, John. "The TV Column," *Washington Post* (November 27, 1996): B6.

Carr, David. "Putting 40,000 Readers, One by One, on a Cover," *New York Times* (April 5, 2004): C8.

Carter, Bill. "FCC Will Permit Owning Stations in Big TV Markets," *New York Times* (August 6, 1999): A1.

Center for Digital Democracy. "Broadband Primer" (n.d.). Retrieved March 11, 2005, from http://www.democraticmedia.org/primer.html

Center for Digital Democracy. "Open Access" (n.d.). Retrieved March 11, 2005, from http://www.democraticmedia.org/issues/openaccess/index.html

Center for Responsive Politics. "Influence, Inc.: TV/Movies/Music" *opensecrets .org* (n.d.a). Retrieved March 11, 2005, from http://www.opensecrets .org/pubs/lobby98/topind16.asp

Center for Responsive Politics. "2000 Presidential Race: Top Contributors" *opensecrets.org* (n.d.b). Retrieved March 11, 2003, from http://www.open secrets.org/2000elect/contrib/AllCands.htm

Chester, Jeff. "Rendell's Early Xmas Gift to Verizon: Larger Net Monopoly. Pennsylvania Governor Pays Back Verizon's Campaign Gifts. Statement from Jeff Chester" *Center for Digital Democracy* (December 1, 2004). Retrieved March 11, 2005, from http://www.democraticmedia.org/news/Rendell .html

"Clear Channel Nixes Howard Stern" *CNNMoney* (April 8, 2004). Retrieved March 11, 2003, from http://money.cnn.com/2004/04/08/news/fortune500/ stern_fines/

Coe, Steve. "CBS Kills 'Murder,' Re-Ups Saturday," *Broadcasting & Cable*, vol. 126, no. 14 (April 1, 1996): 32.

Cohen, Jeff, and Norman Solomon. *Through the Media Looking Glass* (Monroe, ME: Common Courage Press, 1995).

Cook, Timothy. *Governing with the News* (Chicago: University of Chicago, 1998).

Cooper, Gloria. "Darts & Laurels," *Columbia Journalism Review* (July/August, 1999): 21-22.

Cooper, Gloria. "Darts & Laurels," *Columbia Journalism Review* (September/ October, 1999): 17.

Corn, David. "Saturday Night Censored," *The Nation* (July 13, 1998): 6-7.

Cowles Business Media. "A Glut of TV Choices" (1996). Retrieved June 28, 1999, from http://www.demographics.com/publications/fc/96_nn/9604_nn/ 9604nn05.htm

Coyle, Joseph. "Now, the Editor as Marketer," *Columbia Journalism Review* (July/August, 1998): 37-41.

Cranberg, Gilbert. "Trimming the Fringe," *Columbia Journalism Review* (March/April, 1997): 52-54.

Croteau, David, and William Hoynes. *By Invitation Only: How the Media Limit Political Debate* (Monroe, ME: Common Courage Press, 1994).

Croteau, David, and William Hoynes. *Media/Society*, 3rd edition. (Thousand Oaks, CA: Pine Forge Press, 2003).

Croteau, David, William Hoynes, and Kevin Carragee. "The Political Diversity of Public Television: Polysemy, the Public Sphere, and the Conservative Critique of PBS," *Journalism and Mass Communication Monographs*, vol. 157 (June 1996): 1-55.

Dahlgren, Peter. *Television and the Public Sphere* (London: Sage, 1995).

Dahlgren, Peter, and Colin Sparks, eds. *Communications and Citizenship* (London: Routledge, 1991).

Delaney, Kevin J. "Microsoft's Encarta Has Different Facts for Different Folks," *Wall Street Journal* (June 25, 1999): A1.

de Moraes, Lisa. "Can Fledgling UPN Fly to New Viacom Nest?," *Washington Post* (September 8, 1999): C1.

de Moraes, Lisa. "'Saving Private Ryan': A New Casualty of the Indecency War," *Washington Post* (November 11, 2004): C1.

De Vaney, Ann, ed. *Watching Channel One* (Albany: SUNY Press, 1994).

Deutsch, Claudia. "Suit Settled Over Pricing of Music CDs at 3 Chains," *New York Times* (October 1, 2002): C1.

"Digital Cable TV to Grow by 2009," *DCD Business Report*, vol. 10, no. 19 (September 13, 2004).

Doheny-Farina, Stephen. *The Wired Neighborhood* (New Haven: Yale University Press, 1996).

Douglas, Susan J. *Inventing American Broadcasting, 1899-1922* (Baltimore, MD: Johns Hopkins University Press, 1987).

Drinkard, Jim, and Mark Memmott. "HHS Says it Paid Columnist for Help," *USA Today* (January 28, 2005): A1.

Dunbar, John. "Anatomy of a Lobbying Blitz," *Center for Public Integrity* (October 8, 2004). Retrieved March 11, 2005, from http://www.publicintegrity .org/ telecom/report.aspx?aid=395

Duncan, Apryl. "Product Placement Makes a Virtual Leap" *About.Com* (2005). Retrieved March 11, 2005, from http://advertising.about.com/od/ promotions/a/prodplacegames_2.htm

Edelman, Murray. *Constructing the Political Spectacle* (Chicago: University of Chicago Press, 1988).

Edwards, Ellen. "Congress Takes Aim at TV Violence," *Washington Post* (August 5, 1993): C1.

Effron, Eric. "The Big Blur," *Brill's Content* (July/August, 1999): 56-57.

Elliott, Stuart. "The Success of 'Titanic' Has Marketers Scrambling to Create Product Tie-Ins," *New York Times* (February 18, 1998): D7.

Ellis, Rick. "The Surrender of MSNBC," *Common Dreams News Center* (February 26, 2003). Retrieved March 11, 2005, from http://www.commondreams .org/views03/0226–11.htm

Engelman, Ralph. *Public Radio and Television in America* (Thousand Oaks, CA: Sage, 1996).

Entman, Robert. *Democracy without Citizens* (New York: Oxford University Press, 1989).

Epstein, Edward Jay. *News from Nowhere* (New York: Vintage, 1973).

"Excerpts From Comcast Letter Informing Disney of Bid," *New York Times* (February 12, 2004): C6.

Fallows, James. *Breaking the News* (New York: Vintage, 1997).

Farhi, Paul. "TCI Memo Called for Price Hikes: Blame Re-Regulation, Managers Were Told," *Washington Post* (November 16, 1993): C1.

Farhi, Paul. "Disney to Buy CapCities/ABC for $19 Billion," *Washington Post* (August 1, 1995): A1, A16.

Farhi, Paul. "Viacom to Buy CBS, Uniting Multimedia Heavyweights," *Washington Post* (September 8, 1999): A1.

Federal Communications Commission. *The Fairness Doctrine* [13 FCC 1246] (June 1, 1949).

Federal Communications Commission. *Comments Sought on November 1995 Expiration of Fin-Syn Rules* [New Report No. DC95-54] (April 5, 1995). Retrieved October 12, 1999, from http://www. fcc.gov

Federal Communications Commission. *Policies and Rules Concerning Children's Television Programming* [FCC 96-335] (August 8, 1996).

Federal Communications Commission. *Creation of Low Power Radio Service* [MMDocket No. 99-25] (January 20, 2000a).

Federal Communications Commission. *FCC Approves Transfer of CBS to Viacom: Gives Combined Company Time to Comply with Ownership Rules* [Press release] (May 3, 2000b). Retrieved May 8, 2000, from http://www.fcc.gov

Federal Communications Commission. *Chairman Powell Names Marsha Macbride as FCC Chief of Staff; Also Announces Transition and Personal Staff* [Press release] (January 25, 2001). Retrieved March 11, 2005, from http://www.fcc.gov/Bureaus/Miscellaneous/News_Releases/2001/nrmc0101.html

Federal Communications Commission. *Telecommunications Act of 1996* (March 29, 2004). Retrieved March 11, 2005, from http://www.fcc.gov/telecom.html

Fishman, Mark. *Manufacturing the News* (Austin: University of Texas Press, 1980).

Flew, Terry, and Callum Gilmour. "A Tale of Two Synergies: An Institutional Analysis of the Expansionary Strategies of News Corporation and AOL-Time Warner." Paper presented at the Australia and New Zealand Communications Association Conference "Managing Communication for Diversity" (July 9-11, 2003).

Forbes, Daniel. "Prime-Time Propaganda," *Salon* (January 13, 2000). Retrieved March 11, 2005, from http://www.salon.com/news/feature/2000/01/13/drugs/index.html

Free Press. "About Free Press" *Freepress.net* (n.d.a). Retrieved March 11, 2005, from http://www.freepress.net/about/

Free Press. "Media Ownership Rules: About the FCC June 2 Vote" *Freepress.net* (n.d.b). Retrieved March 11, 2005, from http://www.freepress.net/rules/page.php?n=fcc

Gans, Herbert. *Deciding What's News* (New York: Vintage, 1979).

Gapper, John. "News Corporation Raises Coverage," *Financial Times* [United States edition] (September 15, 1997): 23.

General Electric. "NBC and Vivendi Universal Entertainment Unite to Create NBC Universal" [Press release] (May 12, 2004).

Germain, David. "Production Costs Surge for Top Hollywood Studio Films," Associated Press (March 23, 2004).

Glaser, Theodore L., ed. *The Idea of Public Journalism* (New York: Guilford Press, 1999).

Government Accountability Office. *Office of National Drug Control Policy: Video News Release* [B-303495] (January 4, 2005).

Graber, Doris. *Mass Media and American Politics*, 6th ed. (Washington, DC: Congressional Quarterly Press, 2001).

Greco, Albert N. *The Book Publishing Industry* (Boston: Allyn & Bacon, 1996).

Grossman, Lawrence. "Lessons of the '60 Minutes' Cave-In," *Columbia Journalism Review* (January/February, 1996): 39-51.

Gruley, Bryan. "Why Laissez Faire Is the Washington Line on Telecom Mergers," *Wall Street Journal* (May 10, 1999): A1, A8.

Habermas, Jurgen. *The Structural Transformation of the Public Sphere* (Cambridge: MIT Press, 1989). Thomas Burger and Frederick Lawrence, Trans. Original work published 1962.

Hallin, Daniel. *We Keep America on Top of the World* (London: Routledge, 1994).

Hamilton, James T. *Channeling Violence* (Princeton: Princeton University Press, 1998).

Hammond, Teena. "A Titanic Color Tie-In for Max Factor," *WWD*, vol. 175, no. 117 (June 12, 1998): 31.

Hansell, Saul. "Alta Vista Invites Advertisers to Pay for Top Ranking," *New York Times* (April 15, 1999): C2.

Hansell, Saul. "America Online Agrees to Buy Time Warner for $165 Billion: Media Deal Is Richest Merger," *New York Times* (January 11, 2000).

Hearst Corporation [Home page]. (2005). Retrieved March 8, 2005, from http://www.hearstcorp.com

Heilbrunn, Leslie. "The Pentagon Goes Hollywood," *Brill's Content* (March, 1999): 72-76.

Hell, Irene. "The Interview: Richard Parsons," *Independent on Sunday* [London] (December 5, 2004).

Hendershot, Heather. *Saturday Morning Censors: Television Regulation Before the V-Chip* (Durham: Duke University Press, 1998).

Herman, Edward, and Robert McChesney. *The Global Media* (London: Cassell Academic, 1997).

Hickey, Neil. "Money Lust," *Columbia Journalism Review* (July/August, 1998): 28-36.

"Hightower Gets the Mickey Mouse Treatment," *Extra! Update* (December, 1995).

Hirschberg, Lynn. "What Is an American Movie Now?" *The New York Times Magazine* (November 14, 2004): 89.

Hofmeister, Sallie. "Viacom, CBS to Merge in Record $37-Billion Deal," *Los Angeles Times* (September 8, 1999). Retrieved September 9, 1999, from http://www.latimes.com

Hollings, Ernest F. "TV Violence: Survival vs. Censorship," *New York Times* (November 23, 1993): A21.

Hoynes, William. "News for a Teen Market: The Lessons of *Channel One*," *Journal of Curriculum and Supervision*, vol. 13, no. 4 (1998): 339-356.

Walt Disney Internet Group. "Investor Relations" (2003). Retrieved March 9, 2005, from http://corporate.disney.go.com/investors/index.html

Ives, Nat. "Rules for Counting Online Ad Viewers," *New York Times* (November 16, 2004): 6.

Johnson, Nicholas. "The Media Barons and the Public Interest," *Atlantic Monthly* (June 1968): 43-51.

Johnson, Steve. "How Low Can TV News Go?," *Columbia Journalism Review* (July/August, 1997): 24-29.

Kahn, Frank J., ed. *Documents of American Broadcasting*, 3rd ed. (Englewood Cliffs, NJ: Prentice Hall, 1978).

Kaplan, Sheila. "Payments to the Powerful," *Columbia Journalism Review* (September/October, 1998): 54-56.

Kellner, Douglas. *Television and the Crisis of Democracy* (Boulder, CO: Westview Press, 1990).

Kent, Arthur. "Bringing Down the Barriers," *The Nation* (June 8, 1998): 29.

Klein, Alec. *Stealing Time : Steve Case, Jerry Levin, and the Collapse of AOL Time Warner* (New York: Simon and Schuster, 2004).

Kovach, Bill, and Tom Rosenstiel. *Warp Speed* (New York: Century Foundation Press, 1999).

Kurtz, Howard. "Administration Paid Commentator." *Washington Post* (January 8, 2005): A1.

Kurtz, Howard. "Mousetrap? Disney Stuns ABC News," *Washington Post* (August 1, 1995): E1, E4.

Kuttner, Robert. *Everything for Sale* (New York: Alfred A. Knopf, 1997).

Labaton, Stephen. "5 Music Companies Settle Federal Case on CD Price-Fixing," *New York Times* (May 11, 2000): A1.

Layton, Charles. "News Blackout," *American Journalism Review* (December/January, 2004): 18-31.

Lee, Jennifer. "On Minot, ND Radio, A Single Corporate Voice," *New York Times* (March 31, 2003): C7.

Lenzner, Robert. "Super Merger," *Boston Globe* (March 12, 1989): A1, A9.

Levin, Gerald. "The Business of Entertainment: The Big Picture." Speech presented at the Wertheim Schroder-Variety Conference (April 12, 1994). Retrieved August 29, 2000, from http://www.timewarner.com/corp/about/timewarner/corporate/speeches/wertheim041294.html

Levinson, Marc. "Mickey's Wake-Up Call," *Newsweek* (August 14, 1995): 27.

Lieberman, David. "Aging Media Giants' Glamour Fades." *USA Today* (September 14, 2004): B1.

Lippman, John. "NBC's Standoff With Hollywood Studios Jeopardizes Next Fall's Program Lineup," *Wall Street Journal* (October 19, 1998): B10.

Loeb, Vernon. "The CIA's Operation Hollywood," *Washington Post* (October 14, 1999): C1.

Loftus, Tom. "We interrupt this fantasy . . ." *MSNBC* (August 25, 2004). Retrieved January 6, 2005, from http://www.msnbc.msn.com/id/5722377/

Lowry, Brian. "Network seeking to redefine 'reality'," *Richmond Times-Dispatch* (December 18, 1999): B11.

Lowry, Brian. "What Effect? Only Prime Time Will Tell," *Los Angeles Times* (September 8, 1999). Retrieved September 9, 1999, from http://www.latimes.com

Managing Information With Rural America. "Project Scrapbook. Projects: The Center for Civil Networking & Lopez Community Land Trust" (n.d.). Retrieved March 11, 2005, from http://mira.wkkf.org/grantees/ctcnet/ccn.htm

Mandese, Joe. "Universe Collapses: Well, TV's, Anyway," *MediaPost* (July 1, 2004). Retrieved October 6, 2004, from http://www.mediapost.com/dtls_dsp_news.cfm?cb=073051P&newsID=257842

Mandese, Joe, and Ross Fadner. "Casting Milestones: The Internet Is Now More Wired Than Cable," *MediaPost's MediaDailyNews* (February 24, 2004). Retrieved January 5, 2005, from http://www.mediapost.com/PrintFriend.cfm?articleId=239319

Manning, Steven. "*Channel One* Enters the Media Literacy Movement," *Rethinking Schools*, vol. 14, no. 2 (1999): 15.

McAllister, Matthew P. *The Commercialization of American Culture* (Thousand Oaks, CA: Sage, 1996).

McCain LPFM Bill, S. 2505 (2004; pending)

McCarthy, Michael. "Music sales bounce back—at least a bit," *USA Today* (October 1, 2004): B4.

McChesney, Robert. *The Problem of the Media* (New York: Monthly Review Press, 2004).

McChesney, Robert. *Rich Media, Poor Democracy* (Urbana: University of Illinois Press, 1999).

McChesney, Robert. *Telecommunications, Mass Media, and Democracy* (New York: Oxford University Press, 1994).

McConnell, Bill. "Over Our Dead Bodies: Nets Blast Proposal for 25% Prime Time Set-Aside for Indies," *Broadcasting and Cable* (January 6, 2003): 1-2.

McCurdy, Deirdre. "Bigger Role for Product Placement," *The Gazette* [Montreal] (November 21, 2002): B4.

McFadden, Kay. "KIRO Web site shows the perils of mixing news and ads," *Seattle Times* (June 7, 2002): E1.

McGerr, Michael E. *The Decline of Popular Politics* (New York: Oxford University Press, 1986).

McQuail, Denis. *Media Performance* (London: Sage, 1992).

"Media Mergers" [Roundtable discussion] *Media Studies Center* (July 9, 1996). Retrieved August 7, 1998, from http://www.mediastudies.org/ny merger .html

Mifflin, Lawrie. "Viacom Set to Acquire CBS in Biggest Media Merger Ever," *New York Times* (September 8, 1999). Retrieved September 9, 1999, from http://www.nytimes. com

Miller, Mark Crispin. "The Crushing Power of Big Publishing," *The Nation* (March 17, 1997): 11-18.

Miller, Mark Crispin. "Who Controls the Music?" *The Nation* (August 25, 1997): 11-16.

Milliot, Jim. "Bowker: Titles Up 19% in 2003," *Publishers Weekly* (May 31, 2004): 7.

Minow, Newton N. Address to the National Association of Broadcasters, Washington, DC, May 9, 1961. In Frank J. Kahn, ed., *Documents of American Broadcasting*, 3rd ed. (Englewood Cliffs, NJ: Prentice Hall, 1978).

Mitchell, Pat. [Speech at the Cultural Policy Center, University of Chicago] (December 2, 2004). Retrieved March 11, 2005, from http://www.pbs.org/ aboutpbs/news/20041202_mitchellchicagospeech.html

Moeller, Susan D. *Compassion Fatigue* (New York: Routledge, 1999).

Moglen, Eben. "Antitrust and American Democracy," *The Nation* (November 30, 1998): 11-13.

Morlino, Robert. "Broadcast Lobbying Tops $222 Million" *Center for Public Integrity* (October 28, 2004). Retrieved December 15, 2004, from http://www .publicintegrity.org/telecom/report.aspx?aid=406

Motion Picture Association Worldwide Market Research. "U.S. Entertainment Industry: 2003 MPA Market Statistics" (2004). Available from the Motion Picture Association at http://www.mpaa.org/useconomicreview/

Munk, Nina. *Fools Rush In: Steve Case, Jerry Levin, and the Unmaking of AOL Time Warner* (New York: Harper Business, 2004).

Murdock, Graham. "Citizens, Consumers, and Public Culture." Pp 17-41 in M. Skovmand and K. C. Schröder, eds., *Media Cultures: Reappraising Transnational Media* (London/New York: Routledge, 1992).

Project3Media. "Music for the People, by the People" [Interview with Ian MacKaye]. (November 23, 2004) Retrieved March 9, 2005, from http:// www.project3media.com/main/articles/articles.php

Nasaw, David. *The Chief: The Life of William Randolph Hearst* (New York: Houghton Mifflin, 2000).

Naureckas, Jim. "Media Monopoly: Long History, Short Memories," *Extra!* (November/December, 1995): 8-9.

News Corporation. *News Corporation Annual Report: 2003* (2003). Retrieved March 11, 2005, from http://www.newscorp.com/Report2003/2003_annual_report.pdf

Newspaper Association of America. "2004 Facts About Newspapers" (2004). Retrieved March 12, 2005, from http://www.naa.org/info/facts04/

Nielsen Media Research [Home page]. (2005). Retrieved March 12, 2005, from http://www.nielsenmedia.com

"100 Leading Media Companies." *Advertising Age* (August 23, 2004): S4.

"100 Leading Media Companies." *Advertising Age* (June 28, 1984).

Orwall, Bruce, and John Lippman. "Return of the Franchise," *Wall Street Journal* (May 14, 1999): B1, B6.

Osborne, D. M. "The Devil Might Be an Angel," *Brill's Content* (November, 1998): 97-101.

Pecora, Norma Odom. *The Business of Children's Entertainment* (New York: Guilford Press, 1998).

Picasso. "The Little Folksinger That Could," *Literary Kicks* (n.d.). Retrieved March 9, 2005, from http://www.litkicks.com/BeatPages/page.jsp?what=AniDiFranco

Pope, Kyle. "Disney to Merge Television Studio With ABC Network," *Wall Street Journal* (July 9, 1999): B4.

Pope, Kyle, and Kara Swisher. "An NBC Deal Will Rev Up Web Strategy," *Wall Street Journal* (May 11, 1999): B1, B4.

Postman, Neil. *Amusing Ourselves to Death* (New York: Penguin, 1985).

Project for Excellence in Journalism. "The State of the News Media 2004" *Journalism.com* (2004). Retrieved March 10, 2005, from http://www.stateofthenewsmedia.org/

Prometheus Radio Project. "Senate Commerce Committee Passes Historic Bill to Expand Low Power FM Community Radio!" [Press release] (July 22, 2004). Retrieved December 17, 2004, from http://www.prometheusradio.org/release_win_s2505.shtml

Prometheus Radio Project v. Federal Communications Commission. 121 (3rd Cir. 2004). Retrieved March 15, 2005, from http://www.uscourts.gov/staymotion/033388p.pdf

Putnam, Todd. "The GE Boycott: A Story NBC Wouldn't Buy," *Extra!* (January, 1991): 4-5.

"Q&A: Dan Rather on Fear, Money, and the News." *Brill's Content* (October, 1998): 117.

Radio-Television News Directors Association. "Code of Ethics and Professional Conduct" (2000). Retrieved March 3, 2005, from http://www.rtnda.org/ethics/coe.shtml

Rappleye, Charles. "Cracking the Church-State Wall," *Columbia Journalism Review* (January/February, 1998): 20-23.

"Reading, Writing and Revenue," Associated Press (January 15, 2004).

Reilly, Patrick. "Barnes & Noble Draws Fire Over Plan to Buy Ingram Book for $600 Million," *Wall Street Journal* (November 9, 1998): B11.

Reilly, Patrick. "Barnes & Noble Closes Book on Attempt to Buy Ingram, Amid FTC Objections," *Wall Street Journal* (June 3, 1999): B18.

Risser, James. "Endangered Species," *American Journalism Review* (June, 1998): 20.

Robb, David. *Operation Hollywood* (New York: Prometheus, 2004).

Roberts, Johnnie L. "The Men Behind the Megadeals," *Newsweek* (August 14, 1995): 22-27.

Rogers, Madeline. "Moguls Past and Present," *Media Studies Journal* (Spring/ Summer, 1996). Retrieved August 29, 2000, from http://www.mediastudies .org/mediamergers/rogers.html

Romano, Allison. "Adios, Anglo," *Broadcasting and Cable* (March 8, 2004): 22.

Rosen, Jay. *What Are Journalists For?* (New Haven, CT: Yale University Press, 1999).

Rosenberg, Howard. "Execs Vow Change While Programming Violence," *Los Angeles Times* (May 24, 1993): F12.

Rosenwein, Rifka. "Why Media Mergers Matter," *Brill's Content* (December, 1999/January, 2000): 92-95.

Rosman, Katherine. "Booking Plugs on Amazon.com," *Brill's Content* (April, 1999): 42.

Rutenberg, Jim. "Disney Is Blocking Distribution of Film that Criticizes Bush," *New York Times* (May 5, 2004): 1.

Safire, William. "Stop the Giveaway," *New York Times* (January 4, 1996): A21.

Sarasohn, Judy. "Special Interests: A Silence That May Not Be Golden," *Washington Post* (September 9, 1999): A19.

Schatz, Thomas. "The Return of the Hollywood Studio System." Pp. 73-106 in P. Aufderheide, E. Barnouw, R. M. Cohen, T. Frank, D. Lieberman, M. C. Miller, et al., eds. *Conglomerates and the Media* (New York: New Press, 1997).

Schiesel, Seth. "Media Giants: Overview: The Corporate Strategy; Where the Message Is the Medium." *New York Times* (July 2, 2001). Retrieved March 16, 2005, from http://query.nytimes.com/gst/abstract.html?res=FB0C14 F6385D0C718CDDAE0894D9404482&incamp=archive:search

Schiffrin, Andre. "Random Acts of Consolidation," *The Nation* (July 5, 1999): 10.

Schor, Juliet. *Born to Buy* (New York: Scribner, 2004).

Schudson, Michael. *Discovering the News* (New York: Basic Books, 1978).

Schwartz, John. "FCC Opens Up Big TV Markets," *Washington Post* (August 6, 1999): E3.

Schwartz, John, and Paul Farhi. "Mel Karmazin's Signal Achievement," *Washington Post* (September 8, 1999): E1.

Seal, Kathy. "Cruise Sales Hit Titanic," *Hotel and Motel Management*, vol. 213, no. 8 (May 4, 1998): 4.

"Self-Censorship: How Often and Why. Journalists Avoiding the News." *Pew Research Center for the People and the Press* (April 30, 2000). Retrieved March 10, 2005, from http://people-press.org/reports/display.php3?ReportID=39

Shattuck, Jessica. "Home(page) Schooling," *Wired* (March, 1999): 60.

Shaw, David. "A Business Deal Done—A Controversy Born for the Record," *Los Angeles Times* (December 20, 1999): V1.

Shepard, Alicia. "Blowing Up the Wall," *American Journalism Review* (December, 1997): 19-27.

Shepard, Judith. "The Death of the Free Obit," *American Journalism Review* (April, 1999): 43-47.

Sherrill, Robert. "Buying His Way to a Media Empire," *The Nation* (May 29, 1995): 749-754.

Shields, Todd. "Good Copps, Bad Copps," *Mediaweek* (March 17, 2003). Retrieved December 17, 2004, from http://www.mediaweek.com/mediaweek/headlines/article_display.jsp?vnu_content_id=1839274

"Ship Sets Sail September 1," *Video Business*, vol. 18, no. 241 (1998).

Silverstein, Ken. "His Biggest Takeover: How Murdoch Bought Washington," *The Nation* (June 8, 1998):18-32.

"Six Makers of CD's Accused of Price-Fixing," *New York Times* (July 10, 1996): D8.

Snider, J. H., and Benjamin I. Page. "The Political Power of TV Broadcasters: Covert Bias and Anticipated Reactions." Paper presented at the Annual Meeting of the American Political Science Association, Washington, DC (August 28-31, 1997).

Society of Professional Journalists. "Code of Ethics" (1996). Retrieved March 3, 2005, from http://spj.org/ethics_code.asp

Soley, Lawrence. "The Power of the Press Has a Price," *Extra!* (July/August, 1997): 11-13.

"Sony Signatures Creates Sweet Partnership." *Business Wire* (June 9, 1998).

Stevens, Elizabeth Lesly. "Mouse-ke-fear," *Brill's Content* (December, 1998/January, 1999): 95-103.

Sunstein, Cass R. *Free Markets and Social Justice* (New York: Oxford University Press, 1997).

Swanberg, W. A. *Citizen Hearst* (New York: Scribner, 1961).

Swisher, Kara. "Mating Game: Worried Web Players Rush to Pair Up," *Wall Street Journal* (October 8, 1998): B4.

Swisher, Kara, and Lisa Dickey. *There Must Be a Pony in Here Somewhere: The AOL Time Warner Debacle and the Quest for a Digital Future* (New York: Crown Business, 2003).

Tanaka, Wendy. "Video-Game Industry Becoming Increasingly Mainstream, Profitable," *Philadelphia Inquirer* (March 14, 2004): E1.

Telecommunications Act of 1996, P.L. 104-104, Stat. 56 [S. 652] (1996). Retrieved March 16, 2005, from http://www.fcc.gov/Reports/1934new.pdf

"The New (and Improved!) School," *Mother Jones* (September/October, 1998): 26-27.

Thompson, Maryann Jones. "Got a Million Bucks? Get a Web Site," *Industry Standard* (June 7, 1999). Retrieved August 29, 2000, from http://www.thestandard.com/research/metrics/display/0,2799,9845,00.html

Time, Inc. *1988 Annual Report*.

"Titanic Sales onto QVC" *PR Newswire* (July 8, 1998).

"Too Much Communication for FCC." *CNNMoney* (May 30, 2003). Retrieved January 7, 2005, from http://money.cnn.com/2003/05/30/news/companies/fcc_calls/index.htm

Tristani, Gloria. "'Keeping the Local in Local Radio': Remarks of FCC Commissioner Gloria Tristani Before the Texas Broadcasters Association" (September 3, 1998). Retrieved March 12, 2005, from http://www.fcc.gov/Speeches/Tristani/spgt811.html

Tuchman, Gaye. *Making News* (New York: Free Press, 1978).

Turner, Ted. "My Beef with Big Media," *Washington Monthly* (July/August, 2004). Retrieved January 7, 2005, from http://www.washingtonmonthly.com/features/2004/0407.turner.html

Turow, Joseph. *Breaking Up America: Advertising and the New Media World* (Chicago: University of Chicago Press, 1997).

2001 Appropriations Act, § 632 P.L. 106-553, 114 Stat. 2762A-111 (2001). Retrieved March 16, 2005, from http://www.nist.gov/hearings/publaw/pl106th.htm

Underwood, Doug. "It's Not Just in L.A," *Columbia Journalism Review* (January/February, 1998): 24-26.

Underwood, Doug. *When MBAs Rule the Newsroom* (New York: Columbia University Press, 1993).

U.S. Bureau of the Census. *Statistical Abstract of the United States* (Washington, DC: U.S. Government Printing Office, 1965).

U.S. Bureau of the Census. *Statistical Abstract of the United States* (Washington, DC: U.S. Government Printing Office, 1981).

U.S. Bureau of the Census. *Statistical Abstract of the United States* (Washington, DC: U.S. Government Printing Office, 1995).

U.S. Bureau of the Census. *Statistical Abstract of the United States* (Washington, DC: U.S. Government Printing Office, 2004-2005). Retrieved March 15, 2005, from http://www.census.gov/prod/www/statistical-abstract-04.html

United States of America v. Microsoft Corporation, C.A. 98-1232 (1999), "Court's Findings of Fact." Retrieved March 11, 2005, from http://www.usdoj.gov/atr/cases/f3800/msjudgex.htm

United States of America vs. Microsoft Corporation, C.A. 98-1232 (2000), "Memorandum and Order; Final Judgment." Retrieved March 12, 2005, from http://usvms.gpo.gov/

Vargas, Jose Antonio. "Musicians Are Making Tracks to Video Games," *Washington Post* (December 9, 2004): A1.

Viacom. *Securities and Exchange Commission Report* (Form 10-K) (March 15, 2004).

Weinberg, Steve. "Smoking Guns: ABC, Philip Morris and the Infamous Apology," *Columbia Journalism Review* (November/December, 1995): 29-37.

"We Paid $3 Billion for These TV Stations. We Will Decide What the News Is," *Extra! Update* (June, 1998): 1.

"What's Up, Doc? Bugs, Others Appear on GM Vans," *Richmond Times-Dispatch* (August 6, 1999): B6.

White, Erin. "'Station Domination' Takes Over Transit," *Wall Street Journal* (July 12, 1999): A23.

"Who's Afraid of Rupert Murdoch?" *Frontline* (air date November 7, 1995).

Williams, Bob, and Morgan Jindrich. "On the Road Again—and Again," *Center for Public Integrity* (May 22, 2003). Retrieved January 7, 2005, from http:// www.openairwaves.org/telecom/report.aspx?aid=15

Wong, May. "Advertisements get more play in video games." Associated Press (October 17, 2004).

"You Can't Say That on TV." *Extra!* (January/February, 1998): 5.

Ziff Davis Media Game Group. "Digital Gaming in America 2004" (August 10, 2004). Retrieved March 15, 2005, from http://www.ziffdavis.com

Index

About the Authors

David Croteau is the author of *Politics and the Class Divide: Working Class People and the Middle Class Left*. For a decade he taught courses on media, social movements, and economic inequality at Virginia Commonwealth University, where he was Associate Professor in the Department of Sociology.

William Hoynes is Professor of Sociology and Director of the Media Studies Program at Vassar College, where he teaches courses on media, culture, and social theory. He is the author of *Public Television for Sale: Media, the Market, and the Public Sphere*.

Croteau and **Hoynes** are the coauthors of *By Invitation Only: How the Media Limit Political Debate* and *Media/Society: Industries, Images, and Audiences*. Along with Charlotte Ryan, they are the editors of *Rhyming Hope* and *History: Activists, Academics, and Social Movement Scholarship*.